"David Ayers offers a [...] [...]e
sexual revolution. It i [...] [...]a-
sons for hope. In a C[...] [...] of its own
history of sexual and marital instruction, this book covers territory old and
new. The discerning evangelical will profit from reading Ayers, whose real-
ism and biblical faith drives him to ask and answer questions—and then to
offer informed advice—in ways that only a sociologist can."

—**MARK REGNERUS,** professor of sociology,
University of Texas-Austin;
author of *The Future of Christian Marriage*

"Ayers's *After the Revolution: Sex and the Single Evangelical* is one of those
resources I'd like to require for every ministry student, every parent, every
pastor, and every youth worker. This wonderfully readable book—described
by the author as 'rooted in the Scriptures, an appreciation for the need to
live out plain, faithful, normal Christianity, the experience and teaching of
successful practices from Christian and social science sources, and an understanding of the causes of sexual promiscuity'—is an essential resource. No
shouting, no angry finger-pointing, no apocalyptic sensationalism, no head-
in-the-sand wishful thinking; just an understandable account of the biblical
vision for sexuality, where, why, and how we are falling short of that vision—
especially with young people and singles—and what we can do as parents,
youth workers, and pastors to respond to this reality with grace and truth."

—**DUFFY ROBBINS,** professor of Christian ministry,
Grove City College, Grove City, PA

"The very paths that the current course of this world say will result in sexual fulfillment actually undermine and undo our human flourishing. Through a balanced, multi-disciplinary approach that skillfully merges biblical theology with sociology and anthropology, David Ayers offers a thorough, up-to-date description of what is on the current cultural landscape regarding sexuality. But rather than presenting only a description of current beliefs and behaviors, he centers readers on what should be by laying out timely prescriptive measures for recovering biblically-faithful sexuality for singleness that glorifies God and advances our human flourishing. Pastors, youth workers, parents, and students will find *After the Revolution: Sex and the Single Evangelical* to be a helpful tool in our efforts to live and lead into God's grand and glorious design for his good gift of sexuality."

—**WALT MUELLER,** Center for Parent/Youth Understanding

"David Ayers has stated explicitly what we evangelicals have known for some time but have been reluctant to speak about. For too long evangelicals have been incrementally imitating the world's sex-crazed culture that separates sex from marriage. We need to return, says Ayers, to 'abstinence outside marriage and monogamous faithfulness in marriage.' Time to face facts! Ayers has assembled the data relying on rigorous sociological research and the results are quite disturbing and incontrovertible. For evangelicals, there needs to be widespread soul searching on our knees. It's not the particular sin in itself; it's also the consequences of sexual sin that Ayers brings to our consciousness. This is a book for individual Christians who need to be informed or reminded of the need to jettison the licentious values of this age. It's a beacon for parents looking to provide clear direction for their children and a measuring rod for pastors who need to take the measure of their flock."

—**ROBERT G. HALL,** retired minister, Bronx Household of Faith

"After a generation of rejected norms implemented through the sexual revolution, succeeded by a generation of sexual disorder increasingly encouraged by our cultural institutions, the church finds itself and its sexual ethic almost indistinguishable from the surrounding culture. There are, however, signs of hope as the evangelical church in the twenty-first century is today positioned to recover its biblical convictions regarding sexuality and return to normative Christian sexual practices. Dr. Ayers's research is a welcome and much needed resource to help support such a recovery. His scholarship as a sociologist and his wisdom as a seasoned disciple of the Lord Jesus Christ allows Dr. Ayers to not only clearly describe the problems, but to offer solutions. His book is a tremendous gift to the church that informs, corrects, and encourages Christian singles to live within the blessings of biblically defined sexuality, while offering a distinct alternative to our culture's sexual confusion."

—**NATHANAEL DEVLIN,** senior pastor,
Beverly Heights Presbyterian Church

"David Ayers has provided us with an important reminder that sociology is still the only academic discipline that can help us to understand the kind of transformations in character and worldview that have occurred to lead us to our current sexual obsessions. Using sociological data and social theory to illustrate our dilemma—but presented in a conversational, friendly style as he might use when speaking with his own students—Professor Ayers kindly warns us about the spiritual and natural consequences of sin that we can find throughout the Bible. But more importantly, he reminds us that grace is always available to us—even when we sin—as a way to lead us back to God through goodness, repentance, and faith in his redemptive sacrifice for us."

—**ANNE HENDERSHOTT,** professor of sociology and director
of the Veritas Center for Ethics in Public Life at Franciscan University

"This is a very important and timely book by David Ayers, who knows this subject and the data like few others and has presented it in a readable and even engrossing way. Readers will be hooked from the outset by an introduction that is compelling, personal, honest, and, best of all, redemptive. The book will alarm and anger—not just evangelicals, but Protestants generally and also Catholics and believers of all stripes. That's the righteous reaction to disturbing data that do not lie. Ayers is blunt and does not cower from controversy or sensitive sexual subjects. And yet, to alarm and anger is not Ayers's ultimate goal. His goal is to awaken and point us to truth—truth in love about biblical-natural sexuality, marriage, and the family. This is about God's design for sexuality and for holiness. It's about what God's children must know and aspire to. Ayers is to be commended for his courage and commitment to those truths."

—**PAUL KENGOR,** senior director,
The Institute for Faith & Freedom at Grove City College

"Just like David Ayers's full-length book on marital and sexual ethics, this publication is a must-read. His observations are sobering. I cried several times as I processed the cumulative weight of his research. His counsel is countercultural, yet his research proves its wisdom. His writing is full of Christ-centered grace and wisdom, and I deeply appreciate his unique perspective. He is a wonderful mix of professional sociologist, committed Christian, experienced pastor, and nurturing parent. What a gift to the church! I wish this content could be somehow downloaded and stored in my own heart and in the heart of everyone I lead."

—**JOE TYRPAK,** pastor, Tri-County Bible Church;
coauthor of the *Gospel Meditations* series (Church Works Media);
producer of *The Life of David Brainerd: A Documentary*

AFTER THE REVOLUTION

Sex and the Single Evangelical

AFTER THE REVOLUTION

Sex and the Single Evangelical

DAVID J. AYERS

LEXHAM PRESS

After the Revolution: Sex and the Single Evangelical

Copyright 2022 David J. Ayers

Lexham Press, 1313 Commercial St., Bellingham, WA 98225
LexhamPress.com

Print ISBN 9781683595779
Digital ISBN 9781683595786
Library of Congress Control Number 2021948182

Lexham Editorial: Elliot Ritzema, Allisyn Ma, Kelsey Matthews, Mandi Newell
Cover Design: Micah Ellis, Brittany Schrock
Typesetting: ProjectLuz.com

To Pastor Jack Roberts
of the Bronx Household of Faith,
and Director of Hope Christian Center

For over thirty years,
you have been a living model to me
of Christian integrity rooted in love for Christ
and a deep commitment to the word of God.
And the dearest of friends.

CONTENTS

Foreword by Carl R. Trueman   xiii

Introduction   1

1. God's Design for Sex and Marriage   7

2. From an Ethic of Covenant to an Ethic of Consent   34

3. From Covenant to Consent in the Pews (Part 1):   71
   What American Evangelicals Believe About Sex
   Outside Marriage

4. From Covenant to Consent in the Pews (Part 2):   102
   How Sex among Unmarried Evangelicals
   Compares to Other Religious Groups

5. From Covenant to Consent in the Pews (Part 3):   126
   How Demographic Factors and Religious
   Disciplines Affect the Sex Lives of Unmarried
   Evangelicals

6. The Theological and Philosophical Roots of   139
   Sexual Liberalism among Evangelical Singles

7. Social Influences on Sexual Activity among   179
   Evangelical Singles

8. The Consequences of Sex Divorced from Marriage   210

9. A Framework and Principles for Churches to   246
   Promote Sexual Purity

Methodology Appendix   283

Acknowledgments   289

Endnotes   291

Subject and Major Names Index   329

FOREWORD

Sigmund Freud may have been wrong about many things, but concerning sexual behavior he was indisputably correct: sexual codes—the rules and customs by which societies control the sexual activities of their members—lie right at the heart of culture. Among many other things, they define the relationships of men and women, the nature of the family, and the difference between childhood and adulthood. As such, these codes indicate that the most private and intimate of human activities has a profound and pervasive effect on the nature and structure of society at large.

The implications of this view are significant: changes in a society's sexual codes are not the equivalent of, say, changes in the income tax rate or the speed limits allowed on interstate highways. Those are marginal shifts that have no real impact on how a society operates or understands itself. Changes in sexual codes, by contrast, go to the very heart of a society's self-understanding and fundamental principles of organization. That is what makes the developments we are witnessing in the West today—abortion, easy divorce, the mainstreaming of pornography, the impact of LGBTQ activism on legislation—so disturbing. Our culture is engaging in an experiment that is changing society's very essence, an experiment that has never been attempted so comprehensively or rapidly before. And perhaps most worrying of all, nobody knows where it will end or if it will produce any form of sustainable society.

For Christians, this is old news. We have watched the unfolding of the sexual revolution for decades. Indeed, nobody born after 1960 has any memory of a West in which traditional sexual mores were not under constant revision by the captains of our culture—the politicians, Hollywood, academia, and the law schools. In a sense, while the stakes are now higher perhaps than they have been for generations (can the emerging societies in the West survive these changes in sexual mores?), the church faces the same challenge it has always faced: being a small inbreaking of the kingdom of heaven here on earth. So, is there cause for special concern today?

Certainly, the church has always faced a hostile counter to her culture in the attitudes of the surrounding world: Nero was no friend to the Christians, nor were the many enemies of the faith who have held high office and shaped the world's policies in the centuries since. So what? The world's cultures are always ephemeral and passing; only the church will ultimately transcend history and find a place in the eschaton. So why worry about the sexual revolution?

The answer is simple: the sexual revolution is not simply "out there" in the world; it is alive and kicking in the church. And as it has shattered lives in the wider world, so it is shattering lives within the church. Talk to any pastor and he will tell you that use of pornography among men (and increasingly women) is one of the major pastoral problems the church faces today. And then there is the extent to which the sexual assumptions of the world—the legitimacy of sex before marriage, of homosexuality, of a sexual ethic that sees morality purely in terms of consent—have come to shape the imaginations and then the behavior of the rising generation. As the men of Sodom (the Gentiles out there!) in Genesis 19 find their counterparts in the men of Gibeah (the men of God in here!) in Judges 19, so we need to be aware that the morality of the church's culture is far from immune to that of the world.

That is where this book by David Ayers is so important—for pastors, for elders, for parents, indeed for any Christian who wants to be informed about the nature and extent of the transformation of the Christian sexual imagination by the world around it. David writes both as a sociologist and a Christian. This work contains careful reflection on the biblical teaching on marriage, hard data on how the morality of the world is having practical impact within the church, how the broader cultural context within which we must all live is shaping the moral intuitions and behavior of Christians, and, perhaps most helpfully, some thoughts on how we might move forward.

The book is a depressing read but an important one. If Freud is correct, then the culture of the church, as much as that of the wider world, needs to pay attention to sexual morality if it is (humanly speaking) to survive. How might we do this? Well, some months ago I attended a lecture by Father Robert Spitzer, SJ, on defending Catholic moral teaching today. His answer: show people the statistics that indicate the damage the world's sexual practices are doing. The best arguments for Christian morality are (sadly) the ruined lives of those who ignore it. This book does for Protestants what Father Spitzer seeks to do for Catholics: it arms pastors and laypeople alike to face what is the most pressing issue of our day.

Carl R. Trueman
Grove City College
January 2022

INTRODUCTION

When I was a young professor I taught at a small fundamentalist college. Students had to sign a statement of faith that was quite explicit regarding salvation and the inerrancy of Scripture, as well as a behavioral pledge that prohibited drinking alcohol, dancing, playing cards, or using tobacco. However, while visiting a pro-life pregnancy center near campus with a group of students, the director pulled me aside for a private chat. She gravely informed me that a lot of our students were sexually active, and quite a few of the women were getting pregnant. Some had even gotten abortions after visiting the center to consider pro-life alternatives. I was shocked, and we talked about ways to increase awareness. It was a lot for a young evangelical sociologist—still in graduate school and his early thirties—to absorb.

In the Social Research Methods class I taught at the time, I had the whole class work together on one research project involving a student survey. Being young and foolish, I decided to focus the research on sexual practices. I went in assuming we would find some students sexually active, but not most.

In those days, computerized statistical analysis involved putting data into a software program and requesting output tables. The results were sent to a remote printer and manually collected. Being the only one who knew how to program the statistical requests, I had students stationed in the printer room to collect and sort the tables. At one point, a student had not reported back in a long time, so I walked to the printer room to see if everything was all right. I found her in front of the stack of green and white printouts. She turned to me, tears streaming down her face, and said, "These are really bad." She even asked if we could forget the survey—if we could dump and delete everything.

If the survey was to be believed, the majority of our students were virgins when they arrived as freshmen but not when they left as seniors. Moreover, even with the respondents' anonymity carefully protected, I knew that on items like this—especially in a fundamentalist religious environment—the reality was probably worse than a survey would show. At least some students would not be comfortable admitting to having premarital sexual intercourse, even anonymously.

There is no evidence that our college was unusual in the evangelical world in the degree of sexual sin in our midst at that time. Nor have things gotten better since. The problem has dramatically escalated.

I wrote this introduction as ugly news unfolded in national headlines about Hillsong Church in New York City. First, their celebrity pastor was removed after being caught in adultery. Then, it was discovered that this was one of many affairs he had over several years. Then, a deep pattern of sexual abuse and unfaithfulness involving church staff and volunteers emerged. And all this came on the heels of the ugly revelations about sexual abuse by Ravi Zacharias (a major Christian apologist), the downfall of Jerry Falwell Jr. (the former president of Liberty University), and the news of sexual purity guru Joshua Harris's divorce and defection from Christianity.

We can chalk this all up to the defects of stardom and mega-churches, but the statistics tell a different story: evangelical churches as a whole are not marked by sexual faithfulness. Not even close. We have a serious hypocrisy problem on sexual issues. These revelations about national ministries and figures are like the visible part of an iceberg that indicates the presence of a much larger, much more dangerous reality beneath the surface.

This is not just "out there" in parts of evangelicalism that are far from me. Sexual compromise exists among evangelicals in my town, in my church, and too often in me. What do I let myself get away with? How serious am I in pursuing sexual holiness, not only in my deeds but in my thoughts and affections? Are there times when I turn a blind eye to things destroying people I love out of fear of rejection or loss of status? As a parent, have I always done the best things for my children in preparing them well for the sexualized culture in which they live? Am I more concerned about celebrities promoting transgenderism and homosexuality than I am about rampant sex outside marriage and cohabitation in my own world? Writing a book like this is hard because it is not just others I am subjecting to difficult analysis, but myself as well.

Yet hopefully, that also applies to the encouragement, hope, and balance I am trying to bring to this discussion. There is bad news—and you will see a lot of it in this book—but that makes the good news shine all the brighter and the biblical solutions God offers all that much more necessary as well as inviting. God descended into this world to save it; he did not leave us hopeless. He did not despise us for our conditions but loved us despite them and determined to redeem us in and from our sin. He not only gave us solutions, plans, ideas, and truths—he has given us *himself*, totally, without reservation, forever.

I offer this book as one of many resources I believe can help us to understand and address our major problem with sexual holiness, particularly sex among unmarried heterosexual evangelicals. My aim is to add to other helpful resources with the goal of becoming a sexually faithful church, for our good, God's glory, and the advancement of God's kingdom. I rely on hard data, sound social-science research, good social history and cultural analysis, and solid works of Christian doctrine, theology, and anthropology. More than anything, though, I rely on the Bible—the inerrant word of God.

I do not apologize if I alarm and even at times stir up anger by communicating hard truths. But I do want to exercise charity, maintain balance, avoid censorious judgment and mean-spirited finger-pointing, provide solutions, and give hope. I have tried to avoid communicating difficult truths in sinful ways. My goal is to be "speaking the truth in love," so that together we can "grow up in every way into him who is the head, into Christ" (Ephesians 4:15).

I begin in chapter 1 by laying out a biblical understanding of sex rooted in the Christian understanding of the design and purposes of marriage. In chapter 2, I sketch out the modern worldviews that have substantially supplanted the biblical perspective, seduced our culture, and infiltrated the church. Following that, I spend chapters 3 through 5 using hard data and research to describe the beliefs and practices of evangelicals regarding sex between unmarried persons, including cohabitation and pornography, compared to other religious groups, and looking at important variations among evangelicals based on aspects of faith commitment. The data in these chapters will seem heavy at points, but I believe it is critical to provide it. After that, I consider the reasons for the widespread rejection of a biblical sexual ethic in belief and action among evangelicals, looking first at philosophical and theological errors that encourage it in chapter 6, and then at various social and interpersonal causes for it in chapter 7. Then I look at the awful consequences of sexual unfaithfulness, not only for those who engage in illicit sexual activity but for others, in chapter 8. Finally, in chapter 9 I set forth a vision for a sexually faithful church and give some practical solutions and recommendations, all of which flow naturally out of the preceding chapters.

I realize that readers often want to get to solutions right away. We do that too often, however, without fully understanding the depth and scope of our problems, their sources, and their real-world consequences. So, when I lay out positive strategies in the final chapter of this book, I hope that this will flow naturally from, and be rooted in, all that preceded it.

There is a bright and redemptive ending to the story that I opened this introduction with. Much later, after I had moved to another state, I received a letter from the student who had been crying in the printer room. It turns out that, at the time, she had just discovered she was pregnant. She had initially planned on having an abortion but changed her mind, partly in response to talks I had with her and other students about abortion and partly because of that same dedicated pro-life pregnancy center that started all this. She wrote, "As I write this, I am holding my daughter in my lap. She is alive because of you. I thought you'd want to know that."

It is hard to confront reality without turning away from it or softening it. Yet we believers have a gospel that does not ignore the requirements of the moral law. We must talk about truth and love, about sin and redemption. Even with my missteps, that became vibrantly real to me as I read the letter. God used two blunders—mine and that wonderful young lady's—ultimately for good, through his perfect power and kindness. "And we know that for those who love God all things work together for good, for those who are called according to his purpose" (Rom 8:28).

Recently, I was a guest speaker at a southern church, talking to parents and teens about God's design for sex, the current state of the church, and ways to do better in pursuing sexual holiness. A parent asked how I got started focusing on and researching this issue. I shared this story with them because that was a pivotal moment for me. It confirmed my growing awareness that I was being called by God to use my sociological training and skills—along with the Bible, Christian doctrine, cultural criticism, and social history—to honestly document our current condition and to help the church in whatever ways I could to do better in the areas of sex, marriage, and the family, for the glory of God and the good of his people.

I offer this with the prayer that God will use this book to help people recover what has been lost and move forward from there. With or without this book, in the decades ahead, may we see a church that honors true chastity and pursues holiness much more than we see today, shining all the brighter as a witness to the gospel in our increasingly sexualized, lost culture. I am flawed. So is this book. But *Deus est bonus; Deus est fidelis.*

GOD'S DESIGN FOR SEX
AND MARRIAGE

Q. 71. What is required in the seventh commandment?

A. The seventh commandment requireth the preservation of our own and our neighbor's chastity, in heart, speech, and behavior.

Westminster Shorter Catechism

When you sleep with your Catharine and embrace her, you should think: "This child of man, this wonderful creature of God has been given to me by my Christ. May He be praised and glorified." On the evening of the day on which, according to my calculations, you will receive this, I shall make love to my Catharine as you make love to yours, and thus we will be united in love.

Martin Luther, "Letter to Georg Spalatin"

O f course we're living together. Don't worry, pastor, we are planning on getting married." "Yes, I know the Bible's rules about sex outside of marriage, but what's the big deal? It's not like I'm hurting anyone, and besides, I can't get married for a while, and I have these needs." "Sure, God teaches we aren't supposed to do that—usually. But my situation is different." "Where does it say that engaged couples can't have sex? Show me the verse." "I can't understand why you told my kid that she's sinning. What are you trying to do—drive her away from the church?"

Evangelical pastors and youth workers are increasingly hearing these kinds of things when they try to instruct and admonish professing believers on biblical chastity.[1] As a Christian college professor teaching marriage and family courses, I often hear remonstrations like these from my students. More and more evangelicals acknowledge what the Bible teaches in these areas yet dismiss it generally or individually. Others use convoluted reasoning to explain away the "rules." Parents trying to hold the line on these issues find themselves increasingly fighting an uphill battle against not only the outside world but against their children's evangelical peers and even other adults in their churches. Why is it that so many who claim to believe the Scriptures and love the Lord no longer find biblical teaching on sex to be compelling?

Evangelicals who talk like this often view themselves as sophisticated and well-informed on sexual matters compared to narrow and out-of-date traditionalists who are hopelessly hung up and behind the times. However, comments like these actually reveal that those who make them do not understand or appreciate the biblical teachings about sexuality nearly as well as they think they do. Their vision for sex is cramped and inferior next to what God truly teaches us about this wonderful gift he has given to humankind.

God's perfect plan and foundation for human society combines qualities that our limited minds often consider opposites.

His plan is uncomplicated but complex; plain but lovely; earthy but spiritual; regulating but liberating; guileless but mysterious; simple but difficult; humble but lofty; limiting but liberating; common but sacred. It is the enjoyment of sexual intimacy and—God willing—the procreation and rearing of children. It is doing so *only* within the exclusive, lifelong, covenantal union of a man and a woman united as one flesh through the divinely ordained institution of holy matrimony. It is marriage united to sex and children.

That God's moral law binds sex to lifelong, exclusive marital bonds between one man and one woman has never been contested by any wing of orthodox Christianity. This clear ethic cuts through all the sexual what-ifs that have been tossed out to try to obfuscate the obvious and rationalize our way out of submission to God's commands. In recent history, we have seen accelerating waves of assaults on many long-established, timeless Christian truths. These are coming not only from atheists or those claiming to be members of rival faiths but from professing Christians. Typically, they claim to be taking "fresh looks" at key portions of Scripture whose plain meaning conflicts with modern Western culture. While theological liberalism has long questioned the accounts of miraculous events in Scripture, this has more recently expanded to refuting basic moral claims. Nowhere is this more evident than in Christian doctrines related to sexuality and sexual identity.

There have always been those who claim to be Christians but reject Christian sexual mores, but they have typically been those who have given up any serious commitment to uphold *any* biblical teaching that clashes with modern sensibilities, prejudices, or practices. In recent times, though, there are many who profess the lordship of Jesus Christ and submission to biblical revelation who are abandoning the teaching that sexual intimacy is only legitimate and truly good between a man and a woman who are married to each other. This ranges from carving out exceptions to wholesale abandonment.

The sexual practices of professing Christians increasingly reflect their growing compromise or relinquishment of the biblical sexual ethic. Sex outside marriage—up to and including cohabitation and multiple partners over time—is now widely practiced by many who regard themselves as conservative Protestants. Among Protestants, those who embrace and seek to live by the plain teachings of the Bible on sex are increasingly rare.

When I was a new believer, freshly converted from the hippie lifestyle during the Jesus Movement in the mid-1970s, a nice woman moved in with the man next door. She was a Bible-believing, even fundamentalist, Christian. She posted lots of Scripture verses and other religious messages in the kitchen. It appears they eventually married. Still, as a young believer, I found their sexual cohabitation shocking. How could she reconcile this behavior with the clear teachings of the Bible? This kind of thing no longer surprises me.

Where do we begin if we want to turn the professing church back toward fidelity to the biblical sexual ethic? It will take more than mere sermonizing. But we do need to start with solid teaching on sexual relationships, with instruction that avoids both the modern error of carnal license and the more ancient mistake of being hostile to even marital erotic love. Both misguided teachings harm people and dishonor God.

Teaching about sex should not be primarily learning and enforcing rules derived from biblical proof texts. Yes, there are commandments about sex and they ought to be taken seriously, but those requirements exist within a larger order created and maintained by God and ultimately point to truth about him and the reality that he called into existence. They are ultimately about achieving our highest purpose as human beings, which is to glorify and enjoy God.[2]

In this chapter, I will introduce the understanding of marriage—and, with it, sex and the human body—that flows out of creation itself. In particular, I want to show how this helps us see what it means for two to become one flesh and how this represents both the Trinity and the relationship between Christ and the church. I will also consider how the creation account established a unique and powerful understanding of the physical body, which has profound implications for sex. After laying this foundation, I will explore teaching in the Bible about sexual immorality in general, and sex outside marriage in particular, looking first at the Old and then the New Testaments. Following this, I will consider "celibacy" and "chastity" as they have been presented in the Bible and understood by the Protestant Reformers. Finally, I will point to the hope and redemption that all of us who have failed to obey God sexually are offered freely in our Savior, the Lord Jesus Christ.

Now, let us start where God starts—in the book of Genesis.

Genesis 1–2: Our Foundation for Understanding the Place, Meaning, and Purpose of Sex

The book of Genesis gives us an account of the creation of humans and society, and with it of marriage, sex, and procreation. In it, we see the place, meaning, and purpose God gave to sex when he formed humankind along with the natural order. These are clearly embedded in the place, meaning, and purpose that God gave to the institution of marriage. This includes the ultimate source in God himself and in his plan for humanity that accounts for marriage's design. The Christian sexual ethic is inseparable from the Christian marital ethic, which is derived from the nature of God and his glorious plan to redeem, purify, and marry his bride, the church.

The heart of this teaching is embedded in Genesis 1:27–28 and 2:7–8, 18–24. Here we learn that humankind was created as male and female, in the image of God: "So God created man in his own image, in the image of God he created him; male and female he created them" (1:27). We see in these passages that marriage is a procreative union ("Be fruitful and multiply and fill the earth," 1:28) of man and woman as one flesh ("Therefore a man shall leave his father and his mother and hold fast to his wife, and they shall become one flesh," 2:24). We also learn here that the marital relationship is not just about sex or procreation, but it is designed to provide men and women with mutual help and companionship (2:18) as they serve and obey the Lord (1:26, 28; 2:15–17) and enjoy his abundant provisions together (1:29; 2:9, 16).

One Flesh

THE UNION OF TWO AS ONE FLESH, SEALED AND EXPRESSED BY SEXUAL INTERCOURSE

The Puritan divine Thomas Adams stated that "as God by creation made two of one, so again by marriage he made one of two."[3] "Wedding Song" by Noel Paul Stookey, who was a member of the 1960s folk group Peter, Paul and Mary, puts it this way:

A man shall leave his mother, and a woman leave her
home. They shall travel on to where the two shall be
as one. As it was in the beginning, is now until the end,

woman draws her life from man and gives it back again. And there is love.[4]

The explosive reality at the heart of this is the one-flesh nature of marriage. No other human relationship can be described in these terms. Jesus Christ rested his teaching about marriage and divorce squarely on it, citing these Genesis passages directly (Matthew 19:4–6; Mark 10:6–8). He even pointed to this beginning to shed light on why divorce concessions were embedded in the Mosaic law—it was due to people's "hardness of heart" (Matthew 19:8). The apostle Paul pointed to the one-flesh teaching in these passages to teach the Ephesians about the exclusive and sacrificial level of love and respect they should have toward their partners (Ephesians 5:22–33).

In addition to the public ceremony and covenantal vows we associate with the wedding ceremony, we have always understood that the one-flesh relationship is uniquely revealed, physically, in vaginal sexual intercourse. This reality is in many respects a mystery that is hard to adequately describe. A pastor friend said to me once, "The one-flesh union has a transcendent quality that is expressed physically."[5] In an extensive discourse on Genesis 2:24, René Gehring notes that the connection between sex and the one-flesh marital bond is widely accepted among biblical scholars.[6] Sherif Girgis and his coauthors point out that the nature of marriage as a "comprehensive union" requires that the husband and wife experience this "bodily union."[7]

It is significant that in the Old Testament the Hebrew word *yada* is not only used for sex (Genesis 4:1, 17, 25; 19:5; Num 31:17) but for many variations of the basic concept "to know."[8] As Greg Smalley has written, "Sex as knowing ... implies discovery, actively pursuing knowledge about your spouse." It means seeing into and revealing oneself to another at a deep level of emotional intimacy and vulnerability. Smalley writes, "God's idea of *yada* is for you to know your spouse completely, for you to be deeply known by your spouse and for both of you to enjoy each other sexually."[9] This was meant by God to be for husband and wife alone. No one but my spouse has the right to know me in this way, nor do I have the right to know anyone but my spouse in this way.

In fact, sexual intercourse is viewed as the consummation of a marriage.[10] Provisions in the Mosaic law demonstrate that the new husband and wife were expected to engage in this marital act following their public vows (Deut 22:13–21). The Puritans (as most people did in their day) did not believe a marriage existed until the couple had sexual intercourse following the public vows.[11]

When Martin Luther married former nun Katharina von Bora, he took this quite seriously. In fact, their sexual consummation was literally witnessed by his good friend Justus Jonas, following local custom.[12] I do not recommend this; I doubt there are any today who face the unique challenges of an ex-priest and an ex-nun proving they had truly married against the background of vehement opposition from the medieval Catholic Church. Still, Luther's decision shows just how centrally he viewed sex in sealing true marriage.

Certainly, the one-flesh reality of marriage cannot be reduced to the sexual relationship alone. It encompasses the totality of the marital bond. It cuts across every dimension of the relationship of husband and wife. However, the sealing of the marital bond in sexual intercourse is vital and powerful in not only its symbolism but in its reality. For example, Paul forbids married people from unnecessarily abstaining from sexual intercourse for lengthy periods of time (1 Corinthians 7:5).

The very nature and place of sexual intercourse in the one-flesh union of marriage makes clear that it is exclusively for the marital bond and not to be engaged in outside of that relationship. In virtually all orthodox expressions of Protestantism, sexual fulfillment is seen as one of marriage's fundamental purposes. In the Anglican matrimonial service's declarations of the purposes of marriage, it states, "It was ordained for *a remedy against sin,* and *to avoid fornication; that such persons as have not the gift of continence might marry,* and keep themselves unde-filed members of Christ's body."[13] Paul states categorically that marriage is the only place in which sexual expression is permit-ted (1 Corinthians 7:9), as does the writer of Hebrews (13:4).

Lest we miss the point regarding the inherent one-flesh nature of sexual intercourse, Paul makes it clear, citing Genesis 2:24: "Or do you not know that he who is joined to a prostitute becomes one body with her? For, as it is written, 'The two will become one flesh'" (1 Corinthians 6:16). As John Calvin sug-gests regarding this passage, sex outside of marriage corrupts something that God has designed for marriage, and doing so brings a curse rather than a blessing.[14]

Sex is delightful, beautiful, and wholesome in its proper place. It is a good gift of God, as is our desire for sex. But out of its place it becomes perverted, a mockery of this lovely blessing and the God who gifted it to the human race. To truly appre-ciate a fine painting, we place it in a frame and setting that is appropriate to it and enables its inherent qualities and message to be experienced fully. If we take the same painting, put it in an ugly frame, and hang it up in a filthy animal stall, we make it appear ludicrous. Sexual immorality does this to sex—mocking sexual intercourse and making it incomprehensible, destroying the true meaning of sex by divorcing its form from its content.

THE TRINITY IS REPRESENTED IN THE
ONE-FLESH BOND OF MARRIAGE

In Genesis 1:26–28, marriage as a procreative union is tied closely to the creation of humankind as male and female in the image of God. This is a God who exists in three persons, and we see in verse 26 he uses plural pronouns of himself regarding this creative act ("Let us make man in our image, after our likeness") along with singular pronouns in verse 27 ("So God created man in his own image, in the image of God he created him, male and female he created them"). Marriage has historically been recognized by the church as pointing us to the life-begetting, perfect communion of the Trinity.[15] Sex within marriage, when it is enjoyed in reciprocal love, does so as well. As David White writes, it "provides a reflection of the delight experienced in the three-in-one relationship within the Trinity."[16] It mirrors the enjoyment that Father, Son, and Holy Spirit have in one another (see Luke 3:22).[17]

CHRIST AND THE CHURCH ARE REPRESENTED
IN THE ONE-FLESH BOND OF MARRIAGE

The Genesis account tells us even more about the one-flesh union of marriage—the answer to a great mystery about its creation and essential nature. Paul addressed this wonderful reality in Ephesians 5:17, 21–33. He is consistent in appealing to this as he sets forth the mutual responsibilities of husband and wife. Notice how he encourages men to "love their wives as their own bodies" because any husband "who loves his wife loves himself" (5:28). After all, he goes on, "no one ever hated his own flesh, but nourishes and cherishes it" (5:29). As he drives home these practical points, he draws on the theme that God's design for marriage points us back to the nature of Christ and his relationship with his church. This leads to a crescendo emanating from Genesis 2:24: " 'Therefore a man shall leave his father and mother and hold fast to his wife, and the two shall become one flesh.' This mystery is profound, and I am saying that it refers to Christ and the church" (Ephesians 5:31–32).

As S. M. Baugh points out, Paul is saying here that "the original created institution of union of husband and wife was itself modeled on Christ's union with the church as his 'body.' "[18] The classic Anglican matrimonial service reminds congregants of this fact, saying that marriage symbolizes "the mystical union that is betwixt Christ and his church."[19] Marriage anticipates the wedding of Christ to the church at the end of history, when she has been fully purified and clothed in radiant garments, as shown in the beautiful visions recorded in Revelation 19:7–9 and 21:2, 9–11.

Sexual intercourse is integral to the one-flesh bond of marriage, which was modeled after Jesus Christ and his relationship to his people, woven into the natural order by God at creation. Our relationship with Jesus is not sexual, but marital sex points to the gospel by which he reconciles and draws us to himself. As we are united to God and each other in salvation, and each knows delight in that union, so too the husband and wife come together in sexual union and take pleasure in that, especially when they engage in it "heartily, as for the Lord" (Col 3:23).[20]

It is obvious from this that sexual intercourse is not only lovely; it is sacred. As made clear in the passage in 1 Corinthians 6:16 cited above, sex outside its proper place—the relationship of a husband and wife—defiles what God has declared to be holy. Sexual immorality takes this unique human act invested by God with great purpose, consequence, and power, and renders its meaning incomprehensible. Sex outside of marriage is in many ways analogous to treating the bread and wine in the Lord's Supper carelessly, as if they were common elements to satisfy our hunger and thirst, which is a grave insult against the Lord (1 Corinthians 11:27). What God has anointed as a symbol of himself must be treated with reverence.

Moreover, Paul did not invent this teaching about the connection of marriage with the relationship of Christ and his people. We have extensive prophetic statements in the Old Testament picturing God as a loving and caring husband nurturing his people Israel as his bride or betrothed, as we see in Isaiah 54:5a, "For your Maker is your husband, the LORD of hosts is his name." The Old Testament also depicts the distinction between proper marital love and sexual immorality. In these passages, God is often described as an aggrieved husband confronting Israel's idolatry, which is pictured as sexual unfaithfulness, prostitution, and promiscuity (see Jeremiah 3:1–14, 20; 13:27; Ezekiel 16; Hosea 2; see also Exodus 34:15). This teaching is echoed by James when he refers to Christians who love the world more than God as adulterous (James 4:4).

What does all of this teach us about sexual activity outside of marriage? As Francis Schaeffer observed in a discussion on adultery and sexual sin, "God never allows us to tone down on the condemnation of sexual sin. Sexual sin shatters the illustration of the relationship of God and his people, of Christ and his church."[21] Teachings showing God as the betrothed husband often anticipate the eschatological reality of marrying his pure bride. Paul makes this clear in his warning to the Corinthians against being seduced by a false gospel (2 Corinthians 11:2): "For I feel a divine jealousy for you, since I betrothed you to one husband, to present you as a pure virgin to Christ." In Hosea 1, God draws a picture of Israel's idolatry in the prophet's marriage to a woman who had become sexually defiled (1:2–3). These illustrations clearly show God's rejection of all sexual immorality, not just adultery.

Sex and Our Created Bodies

The creation account in Genesis reminds us that males and females are created in the image of God: "God formed the man of dust from the ground and breathed into his nostrils the breath of life, and the man became a living creature" (2:7). Later, as we have already read, God formed Eve from Adam's side (2:21–22). The man then refers to her as "bone of my bones and flesh of my flesh" (2:23). The sexual union is a joining of physical bodies, of flesh to flesh, and from this comes the birth of physical children.

The Christian view of the body begins with these stunning physical encounters and realities. There is nothing ethereal about it. Christianity has nothing in common with religions or philosophies that ignore or denigrate the physical world, including the body. It is a religion with real feet planted on solid earth, lived out by people with flesh and blood. An indispensable element in the Christian hope for eternal life is the resurrection of the body, as we affirm in the Apostles' Creed: "I believe in ... the resurrection of the body, and the life everlasting." Paul discusses this in great detail in 1 Corinthians 15:35–55. We even see graves opening and the bodies of departed saints going forth upon Christ's resurrection (Matthew 27:52–53).

Why is this relevant to how Christians ought to comprehend sex outside marriage and many other sins committed with the body? Our theology of the body has been sadly neglected and with that an important part of how we think about sex. As Peter Jones wisely observes, citing Paul's admonition that we offer our "bodies as a living sacrifice, holy and acceptable to

God" (Romans 12:1), "physical things are indispensable to the Creator's present and future intention." Jones is not going too far when he points out that "from one perspective the gospel is the revelation about what God does with flesh-and-blood bodies."[22]

Here C. S. Lewis reflects on Christianity's view of the body, tying it specifically to Christian teachings on chastity:

> I know some muddle-headed Christians have talked as if Christianity thought that sex, or the body, or pleasure, were bad in themselves. But they were wrong. Christianity is almost the only one of the great religions which thoroughly approves of the body—which believes that matter is good, that God Himself once took on a human body, that some kind of body is going to be given to us even in Heaven and is going to be an essential part of our happiness, our beauty, and our energy.[23]

When we submit our bodies to the Lord, it is an act of worship, a way we glorify God and also enjoy him. When we defile our bodies, we do the opposite. In 1 Corinthians 6:13b–20, Paul draws on the truths about the sanctity and redemption of our bodies and the one-flesh relationship we have with Christ to illustrate the kind of degradation that sexual immorality wreaks. He reminds us that "the body is not meant for sexual immorality, but for the Lord, and the Lord for the body" (6:13b). It is joined to Christ (6:15a, 17). Therefore, he goes on, we must "flee from sexual immorality" (6:18a). When we defile ourselves sexually, we sin against our own bodies (6:18b), which are now temples of the Holy Spirit who lives within us (6:19a). We who have been bought by Christ's blood recognize that our bodies are not our own, and that we therefore ought to "glorify God" in the ways that we use them (6:19b–20).

Our bodies are formed after those of Adam and Eve, whose bodies were crafted directly by God. God integrated this body to our full and true selves. Sexual pleasure cannot be limited to something that we only use our bodies to achieve. It profoundly involves and affects the whole person.[24] Our bodies are temples of the Holy Spirit and reflect the image of God. Christians are called by God to use and bear their bodies with dignity and to treat the bodies of others with the same regard. This pleases and glorifies the Lord, enriching both ourselves and our brothers and sisters as we grow together in holiness. As Paul said in 1 Thessalonians 4:3–7:

> For this is the will of God, your sanctification: that you abstain from sexual immorality; that each of you know how to control his own body in holiness and honor, not in the passion of lust like the Gentiles who do not know God; that no one transgress and wrong his brother in this matter, because the Lord is an avenger in all these things, as we told you beforehand and solemnly warned you. For God has not called us for impurity, but in holiness.

More Biblical Teachings against Fornication

"Fornication" means "consensual sexual intercourse between two persons not married to each other."[25] It is differentiated from adultery, which is when at least one of the partners is married to someone else. The Greek word *porneia* is often translated as "sexual immorality." At times, as in 1 Thessalonians 4:3, it refers to all sexual activity outside of marriage, including adultery and fornication, and activities such as bestiality, prostitution, homosexuality, and the like. In other contexts, it is differentiated from adultery and thus more specific, sometimes meaning "fornication."[26] Adultery is certainly a graver offense than fornication.

Old Testament teaching on heterosexual activity prior to marriage is less strict than we find in the New Testament. Hebrew women were expected to be virgins at marriage (Deut 22:13–21). Single males did not have to be. However, if they had sex with a virgin to whom they were not married, they had to marry her or pay a bride-price (Exodus 22:16–17). Men faced no legal punishment for visiting prostitutes, though doing so was not viewed as morally honorable (see Genesis 38:15–26). Men could have more than one wife, as well as concubines. However, this was an allowance for a human practice that had become established, and God strictly controlled it (Exodus 21:10). Although God did use polygamy for positive ends—as he does many sinful things, such as Joseph's kidnapping (Genesis 50:20)—it was never encouraged. It appears to have been allowed for the same reason Jesus told the Pharisees that the Mosaic law provided for easier divorce—the hardness of their hearts (Matthew 19:3–9). Polygamy was certainly voided in the New Testament, where every Christian male was called to be a "one-woman man" (cf. 1 Tim 3:2; Titus 1:6).[27]

The New Testament repeatedly condemns fornication, directly and within larger statements denouncing sexual immorality. Jesus warns us away from the physical act, but also against sexual lust we may treasure in our heart or indulge in with our eyes and minds (Matthew 5:27–28). He regards sexual immorality as evil and teaches that such thoughts and deeds defile us (Matthew 15:19–20; Mark 7:20–23). In the book of Revelation, Christ tells John that the unrepentant "sexually immoral" will be cast into the lake of fire (21:8, see also

22:15). Strong words warning against fornication, as with other sexual sins, are given to us by Jude (1:7), the writer of Hebrews (12:16; 13:4) and often by Paul (1 Corinthians 5:1, 9–11; 6:9–10, 13, 15–20; 7:2; 10:8; 1 Thessalonians 4:3–5; Ephesians 5:3–5; Galatians 5:19–21; Colossians 3:5). It was clearly something the apostles taught to the gentiles (Acts 15:20, 29). This was not surprising given the widespread tolerance of sexual immorality among the pagans of the Roman Empire.

Far from the idea that sex outside marriage represents freedom, it becomes a form of slavery—like all sin to which we give ourselves. As Jesus said, "Everyone who practices sin is a slave to sin" (John 8:34). It does not make us more alive. In fact, if we do not turn away from it, like all other sin, it leads to death (James 1:15). Despite the world applauding those who engage in sexual immorality as being more honest with themselves, the Scriptures repeatedly tell us that to embrace sin is to love falsehood (Romans 1:25; 1 John 2:3–4). Those who choose to live a life of sexual immorality lie to—and about—both themselves and God.

Beyond this, like adultery, engaging in sex outside of marriage involves two people, each encouraging and enabling the other to sin. This increases and spreads the guilt. Fornication is not consistent with loving our neighbor as ourselves (Matthew 22:39; Mark 12:31; Luke 10:27), or truly loving one another (John 13:34–35). The catechism question and answer at the beginning of this chapter reflects this truth: honoring God's plan that we engage in sex only within marriage involves concern for the purity of others and not just ourselves. As the Puritan divine Richard Baxter said regarding fornication, using the earthy and direct language of his day, "It is the greater sin because it is not committed alone; but the devil taketh them by couples. Lust inflameth lust: and the fuel set together makes the greatest flame. Thou art guilty of the sin of thy wretched companion, as well as of thine own."[28] Loving our intended partner in the best, highest, most godly way involves protecting them from fornication, not engaging in it with them. If God's plan is for both of you to marry, the right time will come to enjoy each other sexually. If not, by abstaining sexually, each of you has blessed and honored both yourselves and your future spouses.

Those who claim to follow Christ and to hold up the Bible as the authoritative word of God have no excuse for defending sex outside of marriage, or viewing it as just a trifling, insignificant transgression. The witness against it is powerful, clear, and repeatedly given. It is one of the clearest, starkest teachings in all of Scripture.

Celibacy and Chastity

God calls every person to either celibacy or chastity. Chastity, as Christians understand it, is sexual purity—abstinence before marriage and faithfulness to one's spouse during it. Although the word is sometimes used to indicate "abstention from all sexual intercourse," the way that most Christians, Protestant and Catholic alike, understand it is "abstention from unlawful sexual intercourse."[29] Celibacy is a call to live as a single person, refraining from marriage and sex for the sake of one's Christian calling. As indicated above, sometimes the term "chastity" is used for this, but it is confusing and unnecessary to do so.

Too often, Protestants have marginalized singles and failed to honor celibacy as they should. To the contrary, we ought to positively recognize, support, value, and encourage those among us who are called to a life of celibacy.

However, as R. C. Sproul noted, "Because the biblical sex ethic is stated so strictly and the penalties are so severe, many people have come to the erroneous conclusion that God regards sex as intrinsically evil."[30] In this view, only celibacy can be fully pure. This was true for the medieval Roman Catholic Church, following early church fathers such as Ambrose, Augustine, Jerome, Origen, and Tertullian. For them, sex was only justified by procreation and could never be enjoyed without some degree of sinful lust. Some even went to extremes to claim that Adam and Eve never had sexual intercourse prior to the fall and that, had they never sinned, they would have procreated by other means. Married people who refrained from sex entirely were often praised as especially virtuous and self-controlled.[31]

Thankfully, the Protestant Reformers rejected this teaching and viewed marital sex positively. It is for this reason that, as we have seen, Protestants understand sexual fulfillment as a distinct purpose of marriage, rather than viewing sex as only fulfilling a central marital purpose when it is connected to the possibility of procreation, which Roman Catholics teach.[32] The Puritans went well beyond this. They celebrated and encouraged married couples delighting and regularly engaging in their sex lives, and exhorted them to never treat it—regardless of the age, skill, or physical appearance of the spouses—as a mere duty.[33] At the same time, they argued that marital sex was about much more than mere physical pleasure, involving "their minds, emotions and souls as well as their bodies."[34] Lust and using another person merely for one's own gratification is wrong, even when it takes place within marriage.

Sproul notes that in Paul's widely cited commendation of celibacy in 1 Corinthians 7, his "comparison between marriage and celibacy is not a contrast between good and bad but between good and better."[35] The apostle Peter was married (Matthew 8:14–15; Mark 1:29–31; Luke 4:38–39), as were "the other apostles and the brothers of the Lord" (1 Corinthians 9:5). Jesus and Paul both explicitly stated that while celibacy is good, not all have this gift (Matthew 19:11–12; 1 Corinthians 7:7). Paul connected his recommendation of celibacy for unmarried Corinthians to particular times and callings in which the challenges of Christian service are not compatible with the obligations of marriage and family life (1 Corinthians 7:26, 28, 32–35). He even carefully points out that he is sharing his opinion, not a "command from the Lord" (1 Corinthians 7:25, also v. 6). In fact, as I have noted, he warns married persons *not* to neglect their sex lives and to only abstain from sex for agreed-upon periods of dedicated prayer (1 Corinthians 7:3–5).

The Scriptures teach us that celibacy is a wonderful calling that God has given some people. Those called to it are equipped spiritually for it by the Lord. Fellow believers ought to affirm them in this calling and ensure they are fully integrated into the life of the church. Viewing Christian celibacy as a way of being set apart in special ways for service and devotion to God, which Catholics have always recognized, has a great deal of merit (1 Corinthians 7:32–35). For those believers who are strongly same-sex attracted and unable to overcome this enough to rightly marry, this support may be especially crucial.

Yet observation and common sense teach us that most Christians are called to marriage. It is also a high and holy calling that the Lord uses to build up his church. In a pure world, God himself united Adam and Eve in marriage, and it did not detract from the purity of creation or the human race; in fact, it completed them. As A. A. Hodge noted, "God created man male and female, and so constituted them, physically and morally, that they are mutually adapted to each other and mutually helpful to each other under the law of marriage."[36] Sex is integral to marriage. It is healthy and lovely within a marriage marked by mutual love and respect. Neither celibacy nor sex within marriage is to be denigrated. God rejects sex outside of marriage, not erotic love between husbands and wives or abstinence among singles.

Hope for Transgressors

We have seen what the Bible has to say about the proper place of God's gift of sex. How should we respond to those who have violated God's mandates in this regard? Extreme responses to this question have caused serious problems.

In the summer of 2019, Joshua Harris, well-known leader of the anti-dating and sexual purity movement and author of *I Kissed Dating Goodbye: A New Attitude Toward Relationships and Romance, Boy Meets Girl: Say Hello to Courtship,* and *Sex Is Not Wrong (Lust Is): Sexual Purity in a Lust-Saturated World,*[37] renounced Christianity, divorced his wife, left his family, and began championing LGBTQ causes. This was not the first time a well-known person connected to the sexual purity movement spectacularly fell, as the sad biography of actress and music star Miley Cyrus attests.[38]

Harris's defection was preceded by his repudiation of his teaching on courtship, dating, and sexual purity, as attested to in his film *I Survived I Kissed Dating Goodbye.*[39] Both this film and then his later, highly publicized renunciation of his faith and his marriage led to a great deal of critical reflection upon his earlier teachings and much of what has been taught in the sexual purity movement. Committed Christians should reject those reactions that throw the baby out with the bathwater, especially when they call for giving up on teaching biblical chastity. For example, as one writer opined about toning down encouraging abstinence until marriage, "Many younger Christians think they can better adhere to modern society while sacrificing no teachings of God or Jesus."[40] However, as we have seen, the "teachings of God or Jesus" on the sinfulness of sex outside marriage are abundantly clear. So are the reminders that, as James put it, "friendship with the world," which he literally referred to as a type of adultery, is "enmity with God" (4:4; see also 1 John 2:15).

What Joshua Harris and many of his allies originally tried to do was admirable. First and foremost, he was trying to get single believers to take chastity, including abstinence until marriage, seriously. He encouraged them to avoid practices and thought patterns that excused and even led to fornication. This included the modern trend of serial, recreational dating. Even secular social scientists point out that the latter is tied to premarital promiscuity and is *not* a solid foundation for marriage.[41]

However, the sexual purity movement that Harris and others championed veered, in some critical ways, from a balanced scriptural framework. Many of those criticizing the sexual purity movement have correctly highlighted the poor theology that some—not all—churches and individuals involved in it propagated. The most important and valid concerns by far were the flawed views of some sexual purity teaching about the nature of our Christian hope and defective views about grace, sanctification, and repentance.[42]

First, proper and ultimate concerns with glorifying and enjoying God and learning to appreciate and live within his creational design were replaced with promises of amazing marital sex and great marriages. As one writer put it, paraphrasing an interview with evangelical author Jeremy Roloff, this movement too often "misled teens into believing that abstaining from sex will lead to personal fulfillment and marital bliss. Ultimately … it's a selfish theology that misses God's good and perfect vision for sex."[43] In doing this, as Katelyn Beaty notes, it became a kind of "sexual prosperity gospel."[44] As the prosperity gospel guarantees health and wealth to those who are faithful, sexual purity teaching has too often done the same: promising marital nirvana and awesome sexual pleasures to those who abstain from premarital sex. Either way, material blessings replace glorifying and enjoying God by submitting to, trusting, and knowing him as the central aim of sexual obedience. Here, it helps to recall C. S. Lewis's famous statement: "If you aim for heaven, you get earth along with it. If you aim for earth, you get neither."[45]

The second and probably most destructive diminishment of the gospel in this movement was tied to the illegitimate use of shame and guilt, which tended to bring hopelessness into the lives of those who sexually fell, even if they honestly repented. David French, the evangelical and conservative political commentator, had been a youth pastor in a church that fully implemented sexual purity movement ideas. He had a front row seat to the reception and uses of Harris's early teachings. The purity culture as he experienced it, said French,

> reversed the gospel message, teaching Christian kids that they risked being defined by their sins, not by Christ. It worked like this—sexual sin stained young persons, even if Christ forgave them. They would walk into marriage diminished in some crucial ways. The white dress, fundamentally, was a lie. ... They were no longer "pure." They could never be "pure" again.[46]

This shaming often employed a double standard—strongly placing the onus on women to maintain sexual purity rather than holding both sexes equally responsible. Images like the rose, the crushing of which is an old symbol of the loss of a woman's virginity, were used to make such lessons hit home.[47]

Sanctification is a process that involves failure, repentance, and perseverance, not perfection. Following Christ in any area, including the sexual arena, means that we balance two important things. On the one hand, we should use all the grace of the Holy Spirit and provisions we are given in our families, churches, peer support, and so on to resist sin. We should be on guard against our tendency to presume upon God's grace, to cheapen it, treating his mercy as if it is a doormat upon which to wipe our feet—"I will sin today and ask for Christ's forgiveness tomorrow." As many of us have learned by bitter experience, and King David attested to, such presumptuous sinning is a fast track to becoming deeply enslaved to sin (Psalm 19:13).

On the other hand, we must recognize our weaknesses, failures, and constant need for the forgiveness of God and his strength to pursue holiness. When we fall, we must cry out in sincerity to Christ and, by his grace, rise and walk. In his first epistle, John speaks of this marvelous balance of pursuing holiness while relying on God's mercy: "My little children, I am writing these things to you so that you may not sin. But if anyone does sin, we have an advocate with the Father, Jesus Christ the righteous. He is the propitiation for our sins, and not for ours only but also for the sins of the whole world" (1 John 2:1–2). Speaking of the coming Messiah, the prophet Isaiah said, "A bruised reed he will not break, and a faintly burning wick he will not quench" (42:3). Jesus quoted this regarding himself (Matthew 12:20). He does not seek to destroy what is damaged but to redeem it. His warnings against sexual sin are urgent, but his kindness toward those who turn to him for mercy are stunning. They may be ashamed of their sin, but he is not ashamed of them. We see this in Jesus's interactions with the Samaritan woman at the well (John 4:1–26), the woman caught in adultery (John 8:3–11), and the great sinner who washed Jesus's feet with her tears and wiped them with her hair

(Luke 7:37–50). Their sins were never minimized but neither was Jesus's love for them.

Those who have, by the grace of God, abstained from sexual sin should be grateful, meek, and humble in relating to those who have succumbed, remembering their own weaknesses. Without censorious judgment or shrugging off such transgressions, they ought to encourage repentance and rejoice if, and when, it takes place. Those who sincerely turn to Christ from *any* sin must be embraced not as "damaged goods" but without reservation, as full brothers and sisters in the faith, just as Paul encouraged us in Galatians 6:1–3: "Brothers, if anyone is caught in any transgression, you who are spiritual should restore him in a spirit of gentleness. Keep watch on yourself, lest you too be tempted. Bear one another's burdens, and so fulfill the law of Christ. For if anyone thinks he is something, when he is nothing, he deceives himself."

In Scripture, as strong as the condemnations and warnings against fornication are, the promises of total cleansing for those who turn to Christ are more powerful still. The very picture of the relationship of Christ and his church revealed in the sacred, and sexual, bond of marriage beautifully points to this. The cleansing and embracing of a formerly adulterous and prostituted people by God, their aggrieved husband, is a constant theme of the Old Testament. The church is not anticipated and loved by Christ as his splendid bride because she has maintained a perfect purity of works. It is *his* purity, love, and constancy—not hers—that is our confident hope. The church is *made* a "spotless virgin" (2 Corinthians 11:2) through the washing of his blood, the credit of his perfect righteousness applied to her, and the ongoing sanctifying work of the Holy Spirit. It will not be that she has never sinned but that those sins have been removed "as far as the east is from the west" (Psalm 103:12). The promise for all who repent, for *every* sin, are generous beyond comprehension: "Though your sins are as scarlet, they shall be as white as snow, though they are red like crimson, they shall become like wool" (Isaiah 1:18). That— not our own good deeds or a perfect future predicated upon them—is our only hope. But what a hope it is!

Conclusion

The Scriptures and historic Christian doctrine teach us that all sexual activity outside of the monogamous marriage of man and woman is sinful. Submitting to these commandments glorifies God and enhances our enjoyment of and trust in him, while also protecting our social order and personal well-being. The requirements of biblical sexuality are embedded in a creational order of great power, beauty, and significance. Too often, in seeking to promote chastity, we have pushed "rules" that seem arbitrary when disconnected from the larger tapestry of revelation.

We have also erred by viewing sex, even between lawful spouses, as inherently polluted. That is absurd. Sexual relationships between those united as one flesh enjoying God and expressing their love for one another, as well as celebrating his good gift of procreation, are sacred, spiritual, and lovely.

Another way we have defrauded believers is by encouraging abstinence before marriage in ways that have treated those who have "messed up" as if they are permanently stained. Too often we have consigned them to second-class status in the kingdom of God and to diminished marriages. This hard attitude toward singles who have had sex has been a grave insult against the perfect grace, complete forgiveness, and awesome goodness of God toward repentant sinners.

As we are about to see in the next chapter, in these difficult days we are contending with powerful ideas about sex that are in stark opposition to biblical revelation. These ways of thinking about sex are rooted in larger views of God, nature, and humankind that are eclipsing historic Christian morality while marginalizing and even demonizing those who continue to embrace it. They are seductive, promising appealing goods beyond mere sexual pleasure, such as personal liberation, authenticity, becoming truly connected with oneself, others, and nature, and even a more relatable and tolerant God. These beliefs are infiltrating our churches, subverting not just biblical teachings about sex but Christian theology more generally. Those attempting to hold on to orthodox sexual morality are increasingly a shrinking and embattled subculture, facing resistance from without and within the professing church. No person, family, congregation, or denomination is immune. For those pursuing and defending biblical sexual faithfulness the way ahead is not going to be easy. It is likely that things are going to get worse before they get better, and those who believe that quick fixes or miracle cures are coming our way will be sadly disappointed.

Therefore, as we seek to advance sound Christian sexual teaching and practice in this exceptionally challenging landscape, may we ever hold the balance of passion for holiness and perseverance through failure, trusting solely in the perfect righteousness of Christ as Paul taught us to do in Philippians 3:13–14: "Brothers, I do not consider that I have made it my own. But one thing I do: forgetting what lies behind and straining forward to what lies ahead, I press on toward the goal for the prize of the upward call of God in Christ Jesus."

FROM AN ETHIC OF COVENANT
TO AN ETHIC OF CONSENT

We are confused ... for one simple reason: we have no clear conception of the meaning of sex.

Dennis P. Hollinger, *The Meaning of Sex*

The heresy of heresies was common sense. ... How do we know that two and two make four? Or that the force of gravity works? Or that the past is unchangeable? If both the past and the external world exist only in the mind, and if the mind itself is controllable—what then?

George Orwell, *1984*

Most thoughtful evangelicals are aware of the contemporary view that holds that the biblical and sexual ethic, and those who embrace it, is bigoted, repressive, and destructive. This huge cultural shift happened in a short period of time and shocks many of us who are old enough to have experienced these changes directly. With respect to our sexual and marital ethic, the experience of evangelicals who hold to biblical teachings on marriage and sex are more like early believers living among pagans in the Roman Empire than to Christians of sixty or seventy years ago. We see this but often do not understand the underlying, rival reality that informs this expanding rejection of, and even hostility to, biblical sexual ethics.

To understand dominant contemporary views about sexual morality, we must start with assumptions about reality, the nature and sources of moral authority, the fundamental direction and purpose of life, and the like. All of this inescapably involves theological underpinnings, whether this is acknowledged or not, whether people believe themselves to be religious—or to even have a worldview—or not. This is the key to grasping the divide between a biblical sexual ethic and what a huge and still growing majority of people in our age use to make sexual judgments and decisions.

This is why I started this book with an understanding of the ultimate nature of God and the created order, rather than proof-texted rules. Dennis Hollinger's claim about sexual ethics is not an overstatement: "Ethical character, judgments, and actions come ultimately from worldview commitments."[1] Unless we get the former right, our moral rules will hang in midair. They will eventually be abandoned because they do not have a firm foundation in something more comprehensive and fundamental.

In this chapter we will look, first, at fundamental shifts in the United States and Western civilization generally. These have had a huge impact on the way we think about truth, reality, and moral authority along with the purpose and meaning of sex and marriage, as we have moved dramatically away from the old Judeo-Christian consensus. I will introduce three classic sociological thinkers: Philip Rieff, Pitirim Sorokin, and David Riesman. I will also look at Kristin Luker's research on the basic worldviews of pro-choice versus pro-life activists. Then I will pull these together to see how these developments have led to the establishment of an "anti-culture" in which the old moral authorities and the verities they upheld are being swept away.

From there, I will contrast the old ethic of "covenant" that has historically guided our thinking about sex and marriage with the new, dominant ethic of mutual "consent." Finally, I will look at the concrete evidence and fruits of this that show how much the ground under our feet has shifted, using key statistics about sex between unmarried adults, cohabitation, and pornography.

Those of us who are attempting to understand and correct unbiblical ideas and practices related to fornication among evangelicals must have an accurate grasp of modern worldviews and ethics, as well as what practices have become normal and taken for granted in our culture. Unless we do, it is hard to fully comprehend and combat the pressures that increasingly seduce evangelicals.

Sociological Insights on Worldview Transformations

Why should we begin with sociology and not something else, like philosophy or history? This is a reasonable question, especially for those who are unfamiliar with some of the big thinkers and public intellectuals of my academic discipline, as opposed to the everyday polls and other studies people often see discussed in the newspapers or on social media.

The answer is that sociology is a synthesizing social science that, from its inception in the nineteenth century, has devoted some of its greatest energies and biggest talents to understanding and predicting the trajectory of the modern world through one cataclysmic upheaval after another. By "synthesizing," I mean that it brings together history, culture studies, linguistics, psychology and social psychology, demographics, philosophy, the study of law, politics, and even anthropology and economics. It uses a range of sources of information, including many of the statistics we will be examining in this book, but also interviews, historical documents, literature, content analysis of media, and a lot more. Sociologists read generously from the works of specialists in other disciplines whose interests converge on their topic. This has been the approach of sociologists such as Max Weber, Émile Durkheim, William Whyte, Daniel Bell, James Coleman, Robert Merton, Rodney Stark, and the key thinkers I want to talk about here.

Sociologists have produced major studies of transformations in character and worldview. They have also done some of the most important work on issues related to sexuality, marriage, and family, connecting shifts in these areas to other cultural and social forces. There have been some incredible, seminal insights by sociologists that help us to understand worldview transformations and illustrate and explain the underlying assumptions behind modern sexual obsessions and permissiveness, which also helps us to see where all of this is likely to take us if current trends hold.

PHILIP RIEFF: THE TRIUMPH
OF THE THERAPEUTIC

In 1966, Philip Rieff saw that our world had become increasingly one in which new needs were being endlessly generated, and any antiquated, restrictive moral codes—any values that have real authority—that stood in the way of satisfying these needs were being discarded. This era was marked by "the triumph of the therapeutic," which became the name of his landmark book. At the center is individualism, ethical relativism, and the worship of self.[2] People long for the spiritual and the transcendent more than old-fashioned religion—to explore through personal journeys and experimenting with alternatives. People are guided not by a desire to know objective truth, but by their yearning for things they attach to "self," such as self-realization, self-fulfillment, self-actualization, self-esteem, self-love, and so on.[3] "Piety toward the self" has become the dominant form of religious devotion, and its fruit is rotten.[4] Said Rieff, "The therapeutic cannot conceive of an action that is not self-serving, however it may be disguised or transformed."[5] As Williams College art historian Michael Lewis notes, Rieff saw broad and devastating consequences tied to this new morality of self: "Instead of being guided by an overarching structure of authoritative values … and instead of striving for 'some communal superior end,' modern culture was rapidly reaching a state in which atomized individuals pursued in isolation their personal sense of well-being."[6]

Rieff's insights on the therapeutic mindset were powerful and prophetic. As Lewis pointed out, he "described the predicament of modern culture in terms so comprehensive, spacious, and authoritative" that they have "become part of the general understanding of things," including among many who have never heard of him.[7] The implications of this therapeutic orientation to culture and the self have been clearly documented by sociologists looking at changes in marriage and directly related to areas such as divorce, procreation, child-rearing, and sex, even where they do not invoke Rieff.

For example, in the groundbreaking *Habits of the Heart*, published in 1985, Robert Bellah and several coauthors identified a now-dominant therapeutic orientation to marriage and marital obligations. The view that previously held sway saw marriage as existing within a framework—including established roles and obligations—that could not be changed to suit preferences and involved the denial of self.[8] Here is an excellent passage that summarizes the therapeutic orientation:

> Respondents had difficulty when they sought a language in which to articulate their reasons for commitments that went beyond the self. These confusions were particularly clear when they discussed problems of sacrifice and obligation. While they wanted to maintain enduring relationships, they resisted the notion that such relationships *might involve obligations that went beyond the wishes of the partners. ...* They had few ideas of the substantive obligations partners in a relationship might develop. ... It was not that they were unwilling to make compromises or sacrifices for their spouses, but they were *troubled by the ideal of self-denial* the term "sacrifice" implied. If you really wanted to do something good for the one you loved, they said, it would not be a sacrifice. Since *the only measure of the good is what is good for the self,* something that is really a burden to the self cannot be part of love. Rather, if one is really *in touch with one's feelings,* one will do something for one's beloved only if one really wants to, and then, by definition, it cannot be a sacrifice. ... They clung to an optimistic view in which love might require hard work, but could *never create real costs to the self.*[9]

The applications to understanding how those who have adopted it will view not only marriage, but sex, are obvious, as are the connections to Rieff's views on the therapeutic mindset.

In 1996, Barbara Dafoe Whitehead applied this to understanding the nature of the "Modern Divorce Culture." A new way of thinking about marital dissolution—what Whitehead called "expressive divorce"—had emerged. It was a product of the "inner revolution" that Rieff described. In it, divorce is a kind of personal journey of self-exploration and liberation, guided not by moral authority and demands but by psychological counseling, whether the advice sought is that of a professional counselor or a pastor. If marriage is just a vehicle for self-fulfillment, when it fails to deliver, divorce becomes another means toward the same end. The focus is on psychological health, development of the self, and personal identity, rooted in "expressive individualism."[10] In this view, it makes sense that one not only could, but *should*, leave a personally limiting and "stifling" marriage—even where no egregious wrong has been committed by the spouse and the couple may even still love each other. No relationships or rules can be truly good if they limit the development of one's authentic self.

These insights about the nature of marriage and divorce continue to inform relevant scholarship. For example, Andrew Cherlin, a widely respected family sociologist at Johns Hopkins University, uses the term "individualistic marriage," which represents "an important break with the meaning of marriage in the past" to capture much of the same reality. He describes the overall context within which Americans contemplate marriage, saying that "being emotionally satisfied was more important. Feeling that you were meeting your obligations to others was less central; feeling that you had opportunities to grow as a person was more central." Cherlin looked at the nature of marital advice from popular magazine articles starting in the 1960s. One of the key themes he mentions is "'self-development,' the belief that each person should develop a fulfilling, independent self instead of merely sacrificing oneself to one's partner."[11] Cherlin discusses this without mentioning *The Triumph of the Therapeutic*, but it permeates this analysis, as it does Whitehead's and Bellah's.

All of these trends must be reflected in our understanding of sex, including its connection to marriage. The degree to which the therapeutic mindset rejects authority also undermines a Christian understanding of sex and marriage. As a pastor once explained to me, "Marriage and sex must be authorized from an external reality, not just self-authenticated."[12]

PITIRIM SOROKIN: SENSATE CULTURE

The great Harvard sociologist Pitirim Sorokin's magnum opus was a four-volume set, published between 1937 and 1941, entitled *Social and Cultural Dynamics*. Thankfully, he was kind enough to distill a shorter version of this massive work in *The Crisis of Our Age*.[13] Sorokin wanted to identify the basic forms of culture that animated the great civilizations in history and the shifts among them. We could refer to these as "cultural mentalities." Every element of each culture and its society is unified by a central understanding of the ultimate source of all truth, reality, and value.[14]

In brief, in the Western world up until about the end of the twelfth century, reality, truth, and value were to be found in the Christian God, and every particular flowed from that. This is clear in looking at medieval laws, architecture, art, and economics. Then the idea began to emerge that, as Sorokin put it, "true reality and value is sensory. Only what we see, hear, touch, smell, taste and otherwise perceive with our senses is real and has value." At first, this blended with the older, God-centered view into an organic unity that believed both/and. Sorokin said, in this period, "true reality is partly supersensory and partly sensory."[15] For example, we need facts *and* the sacred, logic *and* theology, empirical science *and* the Scriptures and Christian doctrine, to understand reality and to live well.

However, argued Sorokin, over time the focus on the senses increasingly took over and the realm of the sacred shrank, pushing God to the margins. Sorokin, regarding our current era, said, "True reality and value is sensory. ... The major principle of our modern sensate culture is 'this-worldly,' secular, and utilitarian."[16] Religion is not disappearing, it is simply becoming more secularized, less culturally important, treating much of the previous substance of religious faith as mere superstition. The overarching principles of truth and value are shaped by *relativism*: "Everything becomes relative. ... A thing may be good today and bad tomorrow." It all varies according to "the individual, the group, and the period." Sensate people, he observed, have "a negative attitude toward any absolute whatsoever." Increasingly, "skepticism, cynicism, and nihilism" become prevalent. Beyond this, we naturally see the rise of values that are hedonistic, utilitarian, and instrumental. We seek pleasure, judge things solely by their usefulness, and believe that our personal ends justify whatever means we use to pursue them, even when those "means" are other people. Sorokin quotes the ancient saying we find condemned in Scripture (1 Corinthians 15:32b; see also Isaiah 22:13, Luke 12:19) to epitomize the sensate outlook: "Let us eat, drink, and be merry, for tomorrow we die."[17]

Ultimately, a sensate culture degrades people, ironically reducing human life itself to relativity valued only on utility. Lamented Sorokin, "Stripping man of his divine charisma and grace, sensate mentality, ethics and law have reduced him to a mere electron-proton complex or reflex mechanism devoid of any sanctity or end-value."[18]

That this would include an increased sexual obsession was obvious, and Sorokin discussed the increasingly erotic dimensions in art and literature.[19] The latter certainly points to the rise of pornography, which he tackles in his 1957 book, *The American Sex Revolution*. There, he gives an overview of what he described as an increasingly sex-obsessed and permissive culture, asserting that it was "changing the lives of men and women more radically than any other revolution of our time."[20] The book, which seemed extreme to many at the time, now appears mild. It is remarkable that he penned this several years before the 1960s sexual revolution began in earnest. Few today would deny the accuracy of his claim that "every phase of our culture has been invaded by sex. Our civilization has become so preoccupied by sex that it now oozes from all pores of American life."[21]

As Russell Nieli observed, "Hardly a page of *The American Sex Revolution* is dated, and readers today will look repeatedly at the publication date for reassurance that the book was actually written during the supposedly tranquil years of the Ozzie and Harriet era."[22] Sorokin predicted what Dennis Hollinger noted regarding our modern condition in 2009: "Sex has become an industry. ... Sexuality and sexual imagery is used to sell products, enhance Nielsen ratings on TV, sell movies and books, achieve a certain image in sports and entertainment, and provide people with products and symbols that lead them to believe that they are sexually normal and sound."[23]

To get a sense of how amoral much modern discussion of sex has become, consider how a couple of sociologists chose to assess the "hookup culture" of casual sex common at American universities. In her book *American Hookup*, Lisa Wade found much to praise in hookup culture. She says it provides students with a "joyous sense of liberation and the belief that they have the right to indulge their desires and no reason to feel shame." Students "get to explore the whole range of sex options ... and, thanks to effective, available birth control, they get to do so with much fewer unintended pregnancies and early marriages."

They can enjoy different options and "relish novelty."[24] Wade's only real moral disapproval focused on gender inequality, not being welcoming to homosexuals, and the need for hookup relationships to be "kinder and safer." Prominent family sociologist Andrew Cherlin also gives hooking up a positive spin. He adds to Wade's list of positive outcomes that hookups offer sex without interpersonal commitments that might interfere with personal goals.[25]

The world of hookups—only one of many bits of flotsam downstream of the sexual revolution—and Wade's views on it exemplify Sorokin's depictions of and predictions regarding sensate culture, in addition to the triumph of the autonomous self that Rieff and others documented.[26]

DAVID RIESMAN: OTHER-DIRECTED CHARACTER AND BEYOND

The Lonely Crowd became an instant classic when it was first published in 1950, making its primary author, David Riesman, the first (and still only) sociologist to grace the cover of *Time* magazine.[27] This book focused on the changing "social character" Americans embraced and sought to instill in their children through our social institutions, including parenting and educational practices. In other words, Riesman and his two collaborators looked at shifts in the fundamental psychological orientation to the world that Americans idealized, which they believed people needed to be socialized into if they were to adapt successfully to society.

Their work was rooted in exhaustive research, including interviews along with content analysis of materials used to teach morals or guide instructors in doing so or that simply showed dominant ideals. Riesman and his coauthors concluded that the social character type that had been dominant in American life since the colonial era, called "inner-directed," was being displaced by one that was "other-directed."

The previous worldview was guided by absolute moral authority, instilled in children early and guiding them to act regardless of pressures from others or the inertia of the past. Riesman and his coauthors used the example of a "psychological gyroscope" to describe what parents and other moral authorities trained children to absorb and admire. As they put it, "This instrument, once it is set by parents and authorities, keeps the inner-directed person ... 'on course' even when tradition ... no longer dictates his moves." Thus, the person "can remain stable even when the reinforcement of social approval is not available."[28] Inner-directedness is exemplified in a book my wife and I gave our sons, *Boys of Grit Who Became Men of Honor*.[29] Published in 1925, it is hard to imagine this book finding a home in today's schools.

The worldview that is now dominant, on the other hand, is one in which being tuned in to and following the dictates of peers and those admired through the mass media is not a pressure to be resisted but a moral imperative. This was the world of *The Brady Bunch*, where popularity and social acceptance was everything and being eccentric and out of step was shunned. Here, the metaphor that Riesman used was a "psychological radar" that enabled people to be "in touch with others," to facilitate "close behavioral conformity" rooted in "exceptional sensitivity to the actions and wishes of others."[30] Riesman noted that this involved an inescapable loss of parental authority, as "students everywhere now begin to resemble each other in basic outlook as well as superficial fads, so that, despite many cleavages, these students are more like each other than any one of them is like his father or mother."[31] No one who lived through teenage fads—from Elvis, Beatlemania, and on through today's transgender obsessions—can doubt the accuracy of this observation.[32] It is not that peer pressure only began to exist in the mid-twentieth century, but that its power became greater. Moreover, bowing to it began to be seen and promoted by those charged with shaping the moral character as healthy and desirable. Seeing children out of step with their peers—being "unpopular" and "not cool"—became a major concern for parents, something Riesman and his coauthors illustrated in numerous interviews. The oversized influence of peers on young people remains a major factor of modern culture.[33]

Following in the wake of Riesman's landmark study, numerous other social scientists—including Robert Bellah, mentioned above—traced changing social character ideals and their socialization beyond the 1960s and '70s. The insights of Ronald Inglehart's *The Silent Revolution* are especially powerful.[34] Qualities he saw increasingly embraced included: a reliance on subjective feelings more than on logic and evidence, an extreme egalitarianism and anti-authoritarianism that scoff at the idea that anyone has "superiors" or should defer to experts in areas of ignorance, a new conformity that is deceptively disguised as freedom and rebellion, and a premium placed on autonomy and self-expression. All these were anticipated by Riesman.

Around the same time, Christopher Lasch identified the dangers of what he called our expanding "culture of narcissism."[35] In a wide-ranging cultural critique, he described ills he saw growing, such as craving acceptance; oversized but fragile egos; hedonism, including sexual permissiveness and a desire for immediate gratification over self-control; rejecting realistic constraints and limits on our aspirations; endemic and chronic anxiety; and a longing for affirmation, personal security, self-fulfillment, and well-being that demands much from others but little from oneself.

Continuing some of the same themes, in 2000 James Davison Hunter published *The Death of Character*. For Hunter, morality has been emptied of all meaning, authority, and significance; the creedal has been replaced by the psychological; feelings have become the arbiter of goodness and truth. In his postmortem he states:

> We say we want a renewal of character in our day but we don't really know what we ask for. To have a renewal of character is to have a renewal of a creedal order that constrains, limits, binds, obligates, and compels. The price is too high for us to pay. We want character but without unyielding conviction; we want strong morality but without the emotional burden of guilt or shame; we want virtue but without particular moral justifications that invariably offend; we want good without having to name evil; we want decency without the authority to insist upon it; we want more community without any limitations to personal freedom. In short, we want what we cannot possibly have on the terms that we want it.[36]

KRISTIN LUKER: WORLDVIEWS OF PRO-LIFE VERSUS PRO-CHOICE ACTIVISTS

In 1984, sociologist Kristin Luker used extensive interviews to explore and contrast the worldviews of early pro-life activists, who were overwhelmingly religious conservatives, with those of pro-choice activists, who tended to be secular, humanistic, or, at best, theologically liberal. All were women. As activists, their commitment to the core beliefs of the "faiths" they represented were well above average.[37]

It is not surprising to learn that the pro-lifers mostly believed sex was only morally allowed within marriage. Pro-choicers thought sex was acceptable outside marriage, even as a recreational activity, provided it protected against the risks of pregnancy and sexual disease, was consensual, and had partners who at least cared about each other. What is more interesting, however, is the ultimate source of these different sex "rules"— their understanding of the meaning, purpose, and place of sex in the natural order. Both sets of activists understood that their sexual norms were integrally connected to their comprehensive understanding of reality.

The typical pro-life activist believed all horizontal human relationships were lived out under and within a vertical relationship to God that had ultimate priority. They viewed sex as inherently *sacred* because God had made it so. Sex outside of marriage was more than potentially risky or a rule violation for which God, nature, or others might rap our knuckles. It was a moral offense that profaned and secularized what was essentially and unalterably holy. Marriage was sanctified by God, as was procreation. Sex had to be understood in light of its unique place within marriage—which was itself viewed as a consecrated relationship—and procreation. For these women, the place, meaning, and purpose of sex was part of a larger design that truly, objectively existed, that all humans lived within, and that no one could modify or reject without consequence. No one could truly be happy or fulfill their best ends and ignore it. The designer was God, who had revealed all this through the Scriptures and his church.[38]

To the pro-choice activists, sex was only *potentially* sacred. To be more exact, it *could* be mystical or transcendent if we chose to make it so. This was dependent upon such factors as personal interpretation, the partners really caring about each other, love of self, security and trust, and sexual experiences of a nature and power that made them spiritual. Sex that was less than transcendent was acceptable, just not ideal. All sexual accountability was horizontal unless one chose to believe otherwise. The moral dimensions were centered on and determined by human perception and, ultimately, the self. As Luker put it, the basic values of the pro-choice activists focused "on the present and on other people rather than on the future and God." Sex was a basic human need, like food and drink. Its purposes were "pleasure, human contact and ... intimacy." The fact that humans were capable of having lots of sex of different kinds across their lifetimes meant Christian limits on it were absurd and oppressive. They limited and harmed people. As with other needs, people's tastes, compunctions, and legitimate opportunities dictated how sexual desires should be satisfied, provided the sex was rendered "safe" by appropriate contraception (unless a couple desired children or were unable to have them), and sexual disease was not a real danger.[39]

On Moral Authority in an Anti-Culture

None of the works I have cited are without flaws, and orthodox believers certainly cannot endorse the destinations that authors such as Rieff, Bellah, Lasch, or Riesman wanted our American culture to travel toward. Each is also far more complex and has more applications than can be considered here. Moreover, the American people have never been uniformly seduced by the dark trends these authors identified. Yet the accuracy of the main lines they agreed on in describing our current predicament—what we are really up against—are profound.

These analyses point to an acute loss of any overarching moral authority beyond the self. This deepening crisis of meaning is made obvious by how the most fundamental aspects of reality are to be determined not factually—through science, observation, or even by reference to the obvious—but by the dictates of subjectively experienced personal identity.

This is abundantly clear in discussions around transgender ideologies. It is common to assert that we not only tolerate but affirm and celebrate—and never openly question—the identities people have adopted, regardless of biological sex. This has extended to firing teachers for refusing to use a student's preferred pronouns and, in some states, even altering birth certificates.[40] Dealing with someone with a fluid gender identity while adhering to affirmation may mean constantly changing the pronouns by which we refer to someone.[41] The array of possible gender identities is extensive, confusing, and growing. This would not surprise Rieff: the therapeutic orientation he described has developed so completely that reality itself must be set aside if it collides with an absolute "right" to radically redefine one's self.

The American Psychiatric Association (APA) relied on an earlier version of the therapeutic outlook when it removed homosexuality from its list of disorders in 1973, declaring that it should only be treated as a pathology if it was "unwanted" and thus produced psychic pain or involved some kind of significant social impairment.[42] At the time, many psychiatrists opposed this shift, and the *New York Times* hosted a debate between Robert Spitzer, who supported it, and Irving Bieber, who believed that homosexuality should still be listed as a kind of malady. Bieber had provocatively asked what the APA's new stance would mean for the treatment of sexual disorders such as voyeurism and fetishism. Spitzer's reply reflects the degree to which perception and self-identity had begun trumping all else in matters of sex even almost fifty years ago.

> Much of the language that Dr. Bieber uses (homosexuals are crippled, there is an injury) represents precisely the definitions that homosexuals now refuse to accept.

Homosexuals are insisting *they no longer want to view themselves this way*. I haven't given as much thought [as Dr. Bieber] to the problems of voyeurism and fetishism, and *perhaps that's because the voyeurs and fetishists have not yet organized themselves and forced us to do that*. But it is true that there probably are some other conditions, and perhaps they include voyeurism and fetishism, which do not meet the criteria [of mental disorders]. I would be for reviewing those conditions as well.[43]

This idea that the self can no longer be held accountable to any fixed moral system or objective realities is a central feature of a collection of perspectives often identified under the umbrella name "critical theory." It is associated with something that Rieff sadly prophesied: an "anti-culture."[44] This anti-culture is what Wilfred McClay—no admirer of Rieff or Bellah—called the "pathology of the unencumbered self."[45] Many people today have no idea how radical the claims being made are. Historical theologian Carl Trueman, an admirer of Rieff's work, made the following incisive observations about this in an article addressing so-called queer theory:

The purpose of critical theory is not to establish anything at all. Rather, it is to *destabilize as potentially oppressive any claim to transcendent truth or value*. Its target is the destruction of all metanarratives. ... All previous metanarratives have, for good or ill, attempted to *provide the world with stability, a set of categories by which cultures can operate*. ... The metanarrative of the death of metanarratives does the antithesis of this: It serves only to *destabilize everything*. It is the quintessential ideology of the *anti-culture*, opposed to any and every form of transcendent authority."[46]

Is this talk of anti-culture far afield from something as seemingly simple as premarital sex? Not at all. Consider the implications of teaching biblical sexual ethics to those who have adopted such a mindset—hyper-relativistic and focused on radical moral autonomy, including a perceived right to redefine self and reality. Contradictorily, this mindset also yearns for constant affirmation and approval and is beset with anxieties and sensitivities.[47] Add to this a world increasingly defined by social media—not parents, pastors, or even peers, but influencers who are detached voices on the Internet. Ours is a society in which devotees of this anti-culture demand to be kept safe from counter views and absolute truth claims that represent the rank bigotry of the unenlightened.

Let us further contemplate the degree to which this worldview is embraced most by teens and young adults. This world is not an easy milieu in which to help singles comprehend and follow a biblical sexual ethic that requires self-sacrifice and the restraining of natural impulses, no matter how clear the scriptural texts are. Have all young evangelicals embraced anti-culture? No—but many have, a lot do not know the degree to which they have, and almost all are profoundly impacted by it.

Too often, church leaders approach sex outside marriage as if they were still living in a culture where facts and values have objective standing regardless of our feelings, what we imagine or desire for ourselves, the views of our peers or those we admire, and what popular consensus is. Leaders who take this view see singles as breaking the rules because they do not know or understand biblical norms, or because they do but do not accept them, have carved out limited exceptions to them, or just fall into temptation. This may still be true for some teens, but it is less by the day.

The nature of what we are confronting is far deeper. It is rooted in the very understanding of moral authority, reality, identity, and liberation that is thick and pervasive throughout every element of our culture. This is the water we swim in. It is a culture where the biblical sexual ethic is not simply wrong; it is immoral, oppressive, enslaving, and even evil. This is not just a cultural crisis; it is a spiritual one, with dark forces at work armed with powerful tools of seduction and intimidation. It is the epitome of what the prophet Isaiah describes: They "call evil good and good evil ... put darkness for light and light for darkness ... put bitter for sweet and sweet for bitter" (5:20). Christians cannot be protected or sealed off from this anti-culture, at least not entirely.

We can only help Christians who are swimming in the water of anti-culture if we understand the contemporary worldview overall and in its particulars. We must learn to speak with Christians who think this way so that they can see not just *what* they think but also *how* they reason. Together, we need to understand and question what has taken root in our thinking so that we can turn from it. We must set against the anti-culture the only fully true "metanarrative" of the created order: God and the people he has made in his image and set apart for himself, revealed in the word of God.

From Ethic of Covenant to Ethic of Consent

In our current anti-culture, people are not without absolutes. This, of course, is inconsistent with the "first principle" of relativism, which is that there are no absolutes. But the notion that there are no absolutes is itself an absolute; it is self-refuting and impossible to prove or live out consistently. The certainty that it is evil to press moral claims on others, but only *some* moral claims, is another. This means constantly changing and confusing lists of "sins" and ways of categorizing their nature and seriousness, without much critical deliberation. At times, whether something is "bad" may even depend on what category of person does it.

In the world of sexual practices, the key absolute appears to be consent. Any sexual act is acceptable if the parties agree, without coercion or deception, to engage in it. If the sexual activity is purely individual (for example, involving auto-eroticism or inanimate objects), moral objections to them are viewed as laughable.

Dale Kuehne has identified many of the features of the therapeutic, sensate, and anti-culture orientations as they pertain to sexual relationships and marriage under the label "iWorld."[48] In distinguishing the iWorld from the one of traditional marital obligations it replaced, and versus an ideal world rooted in deeper, richer relationships that he proposes, Kuehne makes the following simple but powerful observation: "Sexual relationships are now governed by consent rather than a covenant."[49] These represent the center points of two vastly divergent sexual ethics: an ethic of consent versus an ethic of covenant.

Stanley Grenz has accurately described the covenantal understanding in which marriage, and with it sex, are not only private but public realities sealed and defined by mutual oath. This view of marriage is not only the biblical view but is embraced across cultures and religions, as any competent cultural anthropologist could attest. If marriage "is not merely a private covenant but ... made within the context of the social community," then societies across time "have expressed the public interest" in it by regulating it. It follows then, says Grenz, that there is also "a public dimension of the sex act in addition to its very private nature." In fact, all societies show their concern with sex by regulating both marriage and it. This includes setting "some limitations on the practice of the sex act."[50] This conception of sex and even marriage has been substantially eclipsed. Its decline is evidenced not only in broad acceptance of premarital sex, including multiple partners, but in the epidemic of pornography, the explosion of premarital cohabitation, the high rates of births out of wedlock despite abortion on demand and widely available contraception, liberal divorce attitudes, and high rates of marital dissolution—most of which are not justified by grave covenantal violations. As Kuehne notes,

> Mutual consent rather than a marriage contract ... is the new moral foundation for sexual relations. As a result, sexual relations have been disconnected from marriage and procreation. The decision to have children is now a choice separate from having sexual intercourse. Even the personal health consequences of engaging a wide variety of sexual partners are regarded as an acceptable result of freedom of choice. The results of individual relational choice on children, parents, spouses, and third parties are considered of secondary importance to the happiness and autonomy of the individual adult. Marriage still exists, but only insofar as both marriage partners wish it to exist.[51]

To be sure, there remain a lot of wrinkles and complexities in the consent ethic. For example, in the highly regarded General Social Survey (GSS), the majority of Americans continue to denounce extramarital sex. However, the GSS also shows that majorities are either comfortable with existing no-fault divorce laws—by which the marital covenant can be erased by only one spouse without cause—or actually think that divorce should be *easier* than that.[52] Meanwhile, if a couple *agrees* to having an "open" marriage in which each partner is free in some ways to have other sex partners, most Americans appear to at least tacitly condone this. Consent, even in marriage, seems to clearly overrule covenant.

Various writers, unwilling to drop completely the idea that sex should be something more than mere consensual recreation, often add additional preferences that identify various sorts of nonmarital sex as being more "noble." That was obvious in Luker's pro-choice activists. A more recent example of this is pastor Bromleigh McCleneghan's book *Good Christian Sex*.[53] In it, she denounces lust, infidelity, rape, and mistreating one's partner as "sexual sins." However, when pressed by an interviewer, she still could not name any sex acts as being absolutely wrong so long as true "mutuality and consent" were present.[54]

No matter how it is sliced, the ethic of consent leaves a wide range of activities and types of relationships open beyond fornication. The frontiers are already proving to be expansive. We see this with polyamory—simultaneous sexual relationships between any number of people of varying sexual orientations and gender identities—which McCleneghan specifically makes room for in her theology of sex.[55] Certainly, any fetish is easily justified, and brisk sales of increasingly responsive, life-like sex robots testify to this.[56] The legalization of incest among close family members, provided they are considered consenting adults, is a distinct future possibility. All of this makes objecting to old-fashioned "fornication" seem downright trivial and silly—a fact that is not lost on single evangelicals. Many a pastor or parent has heard the refrain: "Well, at least I'm not as bad as (fill in the blank)."

How Bad Is It?

As Richard Weaver famously declared in a book of the same name, "ideas have consequences."[57] Before we close out this chapter, I would like to briefly demonstrate that this is certainly true of the poisonous ideas we have considered so far, which appear to have brought forth some terrible sexual results, at least from the perspective of those viewing these unfolding realities from within a biblical moral framework. Without addressing some of the most terrible or exotic sexual manifestations of these worldview transitions, we can track their impact through the increasing acceptance and practice of basic things such as sex outside of marriage, promiscuity, nonmarital cohabitation, and the use of pornography over time.

WIDESPREAD ACCEPTANCE AND PRACTICE
OF SEX BETWEEN UNMARRIED ADULTS

Up until the 1950s, sex between unmarried persons was widely condemned, and promiscuity was especially discouraged. Premarital sex was usually between partners headed toward marriage.[58] This changed dramatically during the sexual revolution of the 1960s.

In 1994, a group of prominent sociologists released a large, landmark volume detailing American sexual activity, including their number of sex partners.[59] By looking at groups born during successive decades, they could compare those who were more influenced by the sexual revolution as young adults to the generation that came before them.

Among those born from 1932 to 1942, the oldest would have been twenty-eight in 1960, and the youngest would have been eighteen. Most of this group would not have been strongly impacted by the sexual revolution as young adults. But among those born in 1943 to 1952, all would have been at least somewhat affected by it. Even the oldest member of this age group was turning eighteen in about 1961, while the youngest turned eighteen around 1970. And certainly, among those born from 1953 to 1962, all came to adulthood following the sexual revolution.

Figure 2–1 looks at the percentages that claimed to have had *five or more* sex partners between the ages of eighteen and thirty.[60] Since during most of this period the average age at first marriage was in the early twenties, for most of these respondents, at least one of these sex partners was a spouse.[61] But, except for occasional adultery, the "other four" were mostly nonmarital. This graph clearly shows the impact of the sexual revolution. Among these people born from the Depression into the Baby Boom, not only was sexual promiscuity climbing but the old "double standard" between males and females was already beginning to decline. In fact, the impact of the sexual revolution was greatest among single women.

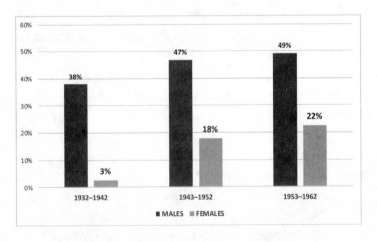

FIGURE 2–1: FIVE OR MORE SEX PARTNERS BETWEEN
THE AGES OF 18 AND 40 —MALES VS. FEMALES IN
THREE BIRTH COHORTS (*LAUMANN ET AL 1994*)

Laumann and his coauthors also looked at the number of sex partners people had *prior* to age eighteen. Here, they were able to look not only at the age groups we have already considered but those born from 1963 through 1972. Results are shown in Figure 2–2.[62] Notice that the sexual activity of those under eighteen increased a lot as we move from the oldest folk into those who spent more of their life during and after the sexual revolution. Early teen marriage remained quite uncommon, so this activity is overwhelmingly premarital sex.[63] Over time, the percentages with no sex partners before age eighteen declined, while the percentages of those with more than one sex partner increased. Again, the sharpest rises in promiscuity were among females.

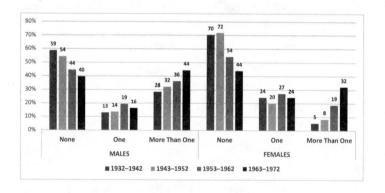

FIGURE 2–2: NUMBER OF SEX PARTNERS
BEFORE AGE 18—MALES VS. FEMALES, IN FOUR
BIRTH COHORTS (*LAUMANN ET AL* 1994)

From this data, the movement toward more sex outside marriage has been developing for decades. In teaching college, I have lost count of the number of times I have been told, "Things haven't changed all that much among teens and unmarried adults, we just talk about it more now." Claims such as these are false.

The Youth Risk Behavior Survey (YRBS) has been conducted by the Centers for Disease Control and Prevention (CDC) on huge representative samples of ninth- through twelfth-grade students in American public and private schools since 1991.[64] On the one hand, the YRBS shows that more youth are waiting until their senior year or even until after high school to begin having sex than was true in 1991. For females, the percentage of those who had sexual intercourse by the spring of their senior year declined from 62 percent to 52 percent, and for males from 69 percent to 48 percent, between 1991 and 2019.[65] Promiscuity among high school youth who have become sexually active is also declining. Among those who had engaged in sexual intercourse, in 1991, 63 percent of females and 77 percent of males claimed to have had more than one sex partner by the spring of their senior year, compared to 60 percent and 63 percent, respectively, in 2019. The percentages for three or more partners among those who had engaged in sexual intercourse among high school seniors changed from 46 percent to 38 percent among females, and from 61 percent to 42 percent among males, during this time period.

This decline in sexual activity among high school students over the past three decades is good news, of course. However, our relief over "only" about half of those who remain in high school through the twelfth grade engaging in sexual intercourse by the spring of their senior year, and that "only" about four in ten of sexually active seniors have done so with three or more separate people, says a lot about how much our expectations about sex among teenagers have changed since the 1960s. Meanwhile, the majority of those who refrain from sex during high school end up engaging in sex outside marriage within a few years of their graduation.

The National Survey of Family Growth (NSFG) is also conducted under the auspices of the CDC,[66] using large samples of males and females from teen into middle age who are surveyed separately in multiyear cycles released every other year. Here, I look at the most recent release, which encompasses interviews conducted from 2017 through 2019. Figure 2–3 shows the number of partners with whom the respondent has had sexual intercourse for those who have never married from eighteen to thirty-two years of age.

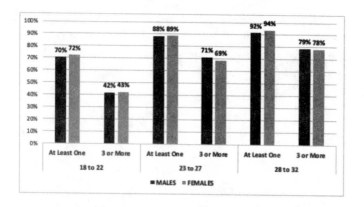

FIGURE 2–3: NUMBER OF SEX PARTNERS FOR
NEVER-MARRIED, BY GENDER AND AGE (*NSFG* 2019)

As Figure 2–3 shows, the overwhelming majority of those who have never married from eighteen to twenty-two have had at least one sex partner, and more than four in ten have had three or more. For those twenty-three to twenty-seven, about 90 percent have had at least one sex partner, and roughly seven in ten have had three or more. By ages twenty-eight to thirty-two, over 90 percent of singles have had sex, and about eight in ten have done so with three or more partners.

Let us also consider the number of sex partners for those who were married but never divorced. Except for the few who have committed adultery, all but the one sex partner (their spouse) involved premarital sex.[67] In the NSFG, among currently married but never divorced respondents, 79 percent of males and 67 percent of females had at least one sex partner other than their spouse. In fact, 62 percent of males and 45 percent of females have had three or more sex partners other than their spouse. In America, not only is it rare to marry as a virgin, but the vast majority have not even restricted their sexual relationship to the person who ultimately became their spouse.

On attitudes about the morality of sex between unmarried consenting adults, the biblical view has been mostly abandoned. Gone are the days when unmarried couples checking into hotels had to fake being married. For example, the GSS has asked, since 1972, if respondents considered sex between unmarried adults to be morally wrong.[68] Figure 2–4 shows the percentages giving the answers "not wrong at all," "sometimes wrong," "almost always wrong," and the biblical answer, "always wrong," by decade.

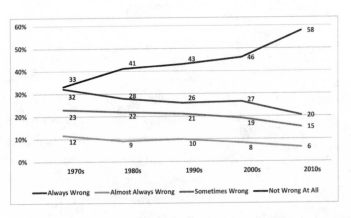

FIGURE 2–4: VIEWS ON SEX BETWEEN UNMARRIED
MEN AND WOMEN, BY DECADE (GSS 1972–2018)

Notice that over this time period, every answer but "not wrong at all" declined steadily. In the last decade there has been an especially dramatic shift. In fact, looking at specific years, by 2018, 62 percent had selected "not wrong at all," while "always wrong" was chosen by a meager 18 percent. Looking at this by age is even more depressing. For all surveys over the past decade combined, only 13 percent of respondents under thirty thought sex between unmarried men and women was "always wrong," and 66 percent selected "not wrong at all." Yet even among those sixty years and older, only 41 percent said "always wrong." The biblical position now faces the twin challenges of being both extremely countercultural while suffering from being decidedly "uncool."

LIVING TOGETHER

Cohabitation, typically defined as a couple living together in sexual union without being married, has exploded. As Figure 2–5 details, according to the U.S. Census, the number of couples[69] more than tripled between 1996 and 2019. Things may be even worse, since the methods used for measuring cohabitation since 1996 probably undercount this demographic.[70] This is a staggering increase.

This represents a long trend of increasing cohabitation, from scarce and frowned upon to unexceptional and acceptable. Prior to 1996, cohabitation was measured indirectly by including unmarried people of the opposite sex sharing housing rather than determining more directly that couples were sexually cohabiting. This produced estimates that were higher than if today's methods were used.[71] Yet even though the older numbers were inflated a bit, census estimates for the number of cohabiting couples for 1960 were only 439,000, and for 1970, 523,000. By 1980, the number of couples was 1,589,000—meaning the number of cohabiting couples more than tripled between 1970 and 1980 alone.

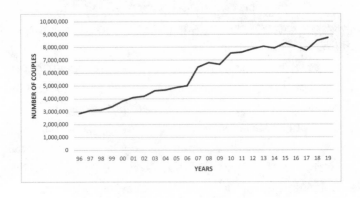

FIGURE 2–5: OPPOSITE-SEX COHABITING COUPLES
IN THE UNITED STATES (*U.S. CENSUS CURRENT
POPULATION SURVEY* [*CPS*] 1996–2019)

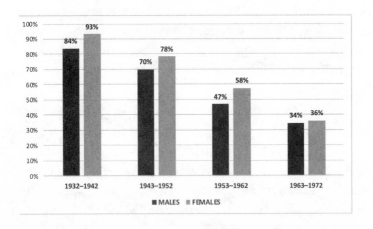

FIGURE 2–6: PERCENTAGES WHOSE FIRST SEXUAL
LIVING TOGETHER WAS MARRIAGE RATHER
THAN COHABITATION AMONG FOUR BIRTH
COHORTS, BY SEX (*LAUMANN ET AL* 1994)

The data presented by Laumann and coauthors likewise underscores the aggressive, long-term trend toward cohabitation. They look at how often the first sexual "living together" experience for Americans was marriage rather than cohabitation. Figure 2–6 shows this by birth group, demonstrating that over time fewer Americans started out living together in marriage, as they increasingly began with cohabitation instead.[72]

The NSFG likewise shows how common cohabitation has become. For example, Figure 2–7 shows the percentages who have cohabited at least once by age group. Clearly, more people cohabit as they get older.

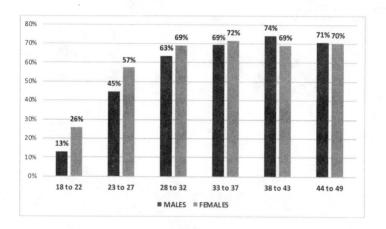

FIGURE 2–7: PERCENT WHO HAVE COHABITED AT
LEAST ONCE, BY GENDER AND AGE (*NSFG* 2019)

Going beyond what is shown in Figure 2–7 is even more alarming. Among those who have ever cohabited in the 2019 NSFG, 44 percent of males and 36 percent of females have done so more than once, including 54 percent of males and 44 percent of females who are thirty-eight to forty-nine years of age. Solid estimates are that, as of 2016, about 70 percent of all marriages were preceded by cohabitation.[73]

In 2019, among younger people, cohabitation outnumbered marriage significantly. This has been true for some years. Figure 2–8 shows census data on this for 2019.[74] Whether it is the male partner, or female partner, who is being surveyed, for those under twenty-five, cohabitation is more common than marriage. In these census figures, numbers are rounded and presented in thousands (for example, 821 stands for 821,000).

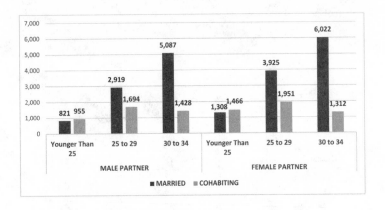

FIGURE 2–8: OPPOSITE-SEX COHABITING COUPLES
IN THE UNITED STATES, BY AGE GROUP AND
PARTNER SURVEYED, IN THOUSANDS (CPS 2019)

Cohabitation is widely accepted. It is now the norm in film and television that the first step following romantic engagement is sleeping together followed by cohabitation. Meanwhile, as cohabitation rates climb, marriage rates keep falling precipitously and are at record lows.[75] A 2016 Gallup poll found that two-thirds of Americans, including 72 percent of millennials, approved of cohabitation.[76] Gallup polls show a sharp increase in support for cohabitation over the past two decades. For example, for years Gallup has asked national samples if cohabitation should be treated before the law "as valid, with the same rights as traditional marriage." This goes well beyond just saying it is morally acceptable to do it. Yet the percentages agreeing with this latter statement went from 27 percent in 1996 to 67 percent by May 2020.[77]

This has radically shaped young people's future expectations. No longer does the typical young man or woman dream of dating, falling in love, getting engaged, then married, before finally creating a home together. In the NSFG, respondents who were not currently married or cohabiting were asked if they thought they would cohabit in the future. Figure 2–9 shows the responses.[78] The overwhelming majority of younger Americans who might get married in the future see cohabitation as a likelihood or possibility, and few flatly reject it.

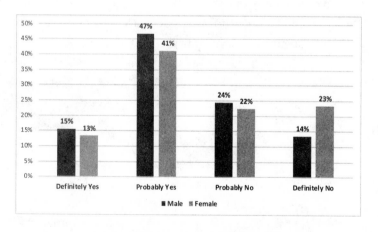

FIGURE 2–9: FUTURE COHABITATION LIKELY?
NEVER-MARRIED AGES 15 TO 27, BY GENDER (*NSFG* 2019)

Pornography

Another practical effect of the anti-culture is the modern scourge of pornography. Available with seeming anonymity on the Internet around the clock in any type and intensity, including not only video but virtual reality and even sex robots, erotica has evolved dangerously beyond the worn-out scraps of *Playboy* that baby boom kids passed furtively on the playground.

The reality of pornography is constantly changing. Yet reliable sources such as Statista, from 2005 through 2014, estimate that 13 percent of computer web searches, and 20 percent of searches using mobile devices, contained pornographic content. These are conservative estimates, as many porn searches do not use obvious terms. Percentages have gone down over the years not because porn searches have declined but because the Internet user base has become broader and larger over time. In fact, as of 2014, about 87 percent of men and 29 percent of women between the ages of eighteen and thirty-five viewed porn at least once a week.[79] In 2019, *Pornhub* reported about fifteen million visitors per day that year—84 percent of the time using mobile devices. In addition to what was already there, 6.83 million new porn videos were uploaded.[80] This is staggering. Pitirim Sorokin's predictions about the continual growth of pornography in modern society have been powerfully vindicated.

The widespread acceptance of and involvement in fornication, cohabitation, and pornography are consistent with the cultural shifts identified by Rieff, Sorokin, Bellah, Lasch, Luker, and others I have discussed. We have truly become a culture in which sexual ethics, as in so much of our moral framework, has no higher authority than self and perhaps the shifting social consensus. It is as Pitirim Sorokin was fond of saying, citing the ancient maxim of Protagoras: "Man is the measure of all things."

Conclusion

Ours is a sex-saturated and sex-obsessed culture that has long divorced sexual expression from an ethic of covenant rooted in committed marriage. We continually push the frontiers of depravity and sensuality. This is enabled and encouraged by a pervasive worldview that promotes human moral autonomy, self-fulfillment, narcissism, and relativism, and that feeds the self and its ever-expanding "needs." It is a remarkably difficult landscape within which to teach and defend the biblical sexual ethic. Unmarried believers are traveling through its toughest terrains. They need support, honesty, and compassion, not compromise and truth-shading.

Paul played a key role in establishing a faithful church with a strict sexual ethic amid a culture as sensual as our own. He did not shrink from being totally honest with his fellow believers about the nature of the cultural world they were living in. If some of the words and observations in this chapter seem a bit rough, consider his powerful observations from the book of Romans on the pagan world, where the rejection of God led to sexual immorality rooted in the kind of willful twisting of human thought and passion I have chronicled here:

> For the wrath of God is revealed from heaven against all ungodliness and unrighteousness of men, who by their unrighteousness suppress the truth. ... For although they knew God, they did not honor him as God or give thanks to him, but they became futile in their thinking, and their foolish hearts were darkened. Claiming to be wise, they became fools. ... Therefore God gave them up in the lusts of their hearts to impurity, to the dishonoring of bodies among themselves ... [and] God gave them up to dishonorable passions. ... And ... God gave

them up to a debased mind to do what ought not to be
done. ... Though they know God's righteous decree that
those who practice such things deserve to die, they not
only do them but give approval to those who practice
them. (Romans 1:18–32)

As we have seen, Paul did not dodge the truth about sin issues
among Christians, including sexual immorality. In fact, he could
be quite blunt about it: "It is actually reported that there is
sexual immorality among you. ... And you are arrogant! Ought
you not rather to mourn?" (1 Corinthians 5:1–2a).

Reviewing what we have seen about transformations in
worldview and practices related to sex in modern America, it
makes sense to ask, "How are evangelicals doing?" If Paul wrote
a letter to evangelical churches today and addressed our fidelity to biblical sexual morality, would he have a similar, brutal
assessment? As we shall see in chapters 3 through 5, the honest,
unvarnished answers to these questions are not the ones I wish
I could give. Most evangelicals, especially those who are under
fifty, have succumbed to worldly attitudes and practices regarding sex outside of marriage. Paul would probably speak to evangelicals today about sexual immorality as harshly as he did to
the Corinthians. This would be for their benefit, not to crush
them but rather to call them to repent of and turn away from
these destructive paths for their good and for God's glory. Let us
begin our survey of the state of the modern evangelical church
by examining what evangelicals believe about sex.

3

FROM COVENANT TO CONSENT
IN THE PEWS (PART 1)

WHAT AMERICAN EVANGELICALS BELIEVE
ABOUT SEX OUTSIDE MARRIAGE

There is no sin so odious, but love to it, and frequent using it, will do much to reconcile the very judgment to it; either to think it lawful, or tolerable and venial: to think it no sin, or but a little sin and easily forgiven.

Richard Baxter, A Christian Directory

I'm done splitting my sexuality into pieces, tying my identity to a word that has no medical definition but devastating social implications. ... Virginity is just another way that people in power talk about who's in and who's out of favor with Church, that we set up winners and losers in a Kingdom supposedly of equals. ... I'm done blanketing all sexual experience outside of marriage as sin. ... I'm done with Christians enforcing oppression in the name of *purity*.

Emily Maynard, "The Day I Turned in My V-Card,"
Prodigal Magazine

Early Christianity was marked by a strong adherence to countercultural sexual ethics that was at times remarkable. Living among pagans in the Roman Empire, in a culture marked by unashamed eroticism and widespread acceptance and practice of sexual immorality, followers of Christ were known for their strict chastity.[1] No, Christians did not always live up to these aspirations (see 1 Corinthians 5:1). For example, we know by comparing wedding dates with the baptismal records for first children that, even in colonial-era Puritan congregations, women were often already pregnant at marriage. Many courting or engaged Puritan couples "jumped the altar" and, when this happened, fellow believers were often gentle in their reactions compared to something like adultery, without modifying their stance against fornication.[2] However—unless our brothers and sisters hundreds of years ago were able to miraculously avoid pregnancy without contraception more than sexual libertines do today when it is widely available—we know that fornication, especially promiscuity, was not the norm for unmarried people in these Christian communities.

In fact, a common error Christians made was not to treat scriptural teaching on sex lightly but to look at all sexual activity with deep suspicion—as inevitably stained even within loving marriages.[3] One of the early church fathers, Tertullian, stated that "marriage and adultery ... are not intrinsically different but only in the degree of their illegitimacy."[4] As we have seen, that was a terrible mistake. Thankfully, few modern believers view sex this way. However, the fact that sincere and wise theologians and pastors could err in that direction illustrates how important and explicit God's teachings against fornication really are. The Bible unambiguously and earnestly insists that Christians pursue chastity in our emotional affections, thoughts, and deeds. That includes abstinence outside marriage and monogamous faithfulness in marriage.

Evangelicals today err in the opposite direction of the leaders of the ancient church. Fornication is seen as no big deal.

Our congregations are populated by saved sinners who are at various points in their sanctification and doctrinal understanding. If the culture is declining, of course we will see similar trends in our churches. Evangelicals are not isolated from the larger world. Hopefully we are reaching out to unbelievers and by God's grace drawing many into committed relationships with Christ and his people. Repentant sinners come with baggage and often start at ground zero in terms of their doctrinal and biblical understanding. And committed Christians fail. We need to be both idealistic and realistic in evaluating the sexual faithfulness of evangelicals.

Even so, widespread disobedience to Christian teaching on sexual immorality among evangelicals would be a massive failure calling for sober reflection and repentance. If professed evangelicals do not adhere to biblical teachings about fornication markedly better than liberal or nominal Christians, and certainly more than those without clear religious commitments, we are dishonoring God, jeopardizing the spiritual health of our churches, and wrecking our witness to those outside the faith. There is no excuse for having a casual attitude toward rampant fornication among evangelicals. "So great a cloud of witnesses" (Hebrews 12:1) is looking on—our Christian forebears and our many steadfast brothers and sisters across the world today. So many of these have practiced difficult faithfulness to God's high standards for sexual holiness in the face of much tougher cultural headwinds than we in America are dealing with.

We cannot separate sexual purity from other forms of moral integrity to which Christians are called. It will not do to pay attention to all the sins on the lists we see in places such as Mark 7:21–22, 1 Corinthians 6:9–10, Galatians 5:19–21, and 1 Timothy 1:8–11, except any we choose to exclude, such as fornication. God does not allow us to pick and choose how and when to honor him with obedience. Besides, sexual immorality always has other sins wrapped up in it. Lust, idolatry, hedonism, and lack of self-control are part of sexual immorality, and sins such as greed, dishonesty, swindling, and even theft usually are too. Consider what John says: "Everyone who makes a practice of sinning also practices lawlessness; sin is lawlessness" (1 John 3:4).

What follows here and in the next chapter is a compressed look at how evangelicals are doing in their beliefs and practices in the areas of sex outside marriage, relative to others. We will then look at factors associated with higher or lower levels of faithfulness to biblical sexual values and behavioral norms. In this chapter, we will look closely at beliefs about fornication. In chapters 4 and 5, we will look at practices.

In doing so, I will make use of data from the General Social Survey (GSS) and the National Survey of Family Growth (NSFG), and I will pull in other sources as they are helpful.[5] This means laying out critical facts using charts and percentages not only in this chapter but in the two to follow. Please don't be discouraged by this. I assure you that this data tells a story, and I will be communicating that story to you as we move along.

Before moving on, I should clarify how I am defining and measuring "evangelical," without getting into unnecessary detail or all of the controversies about the word. This term is hotly contested and exceptionally difficult to pin down. It is like so many things we deal with in life—we know one when we see one but cannot always say exactly what it is.

Defining "Evangelical"

First, I am assuming that "evangelicals" are historically orthodox Protestants, with a high view of the accuracy and ultimate authority of the Bible, rather than relying more on experience, human reason, and church tradition to define what they believe. These are Christians who emphasize that the only way to salvation from sin—the only way to eternal life in heaven—is through repentance and faith in the Lord Jesus Christ. They accept that all human beings are sinners and need salvation. Evangelicals believe that people who have become true Christians endeavor to grow in holiness and obedience to God by his grace, a life in which all believers will need forgiveness regularly. Finally, evangelicals emphasize that it is the duty of believers to support spreading the gospel through evangelism and missions. These elements I have outlined here have been called the "doctrinal markers" by which denominations and individuals are defined as "evangelical."[6]

Second, in the GSS and NSFG survey data used here, I have employed a highly regarded measurement approach, often called RELTRAD, to distinguish evangelicals from other Protestants and from Catholics. This uses respondents' denominational affiliations to categorize them, classifying Protestants as mainline, evangelical, or in historically black Protestant churches such as the African Methodist Episcopal Church or the National Baptist Conference.[7]

There are weaknesses to relying on denominational affiliations to classify respondents.[8] For example, though there are key and historically rooted differences between black Protestant churches and those classified as "evangelical Protestant," many people in both sets of churches hold substantially to the doctrinal beliefs outlined above. Though their numbers are declining rapidly, there are still some people with evangelical beliefs in mainline churches. Moreover, there are many who affiliate with evangelical churches whose beliefs and lifestyles are out of alignment with those of the church and denomination they are attached to. These and other pitfalls are why it is necessary to measure other aspects of religious beliefs and commitments when looking at the sexual views and practices of evangelicals, as I do here.[9]

However, the fact is that pastors, church leaders, parachurch workers, parents, and many others in evangelical churches deal with the congregations they are in and with all of the individuals in them. They do not have the right to narrow down their responsibility to a subset of ideal, "purer" evangelicals within their fellowships. Therefore, they need to be informed accurately about the range of sexual beliefs and practices that might exist among the people in their churches. We get at that best by looking at denominational affiliations rather than only relying on individual doctrinal commitments.

One of the things we need to look at is just *how many* of the people in our churches embrace what we reasonably regard as standard, faithful evangelical behavior and beliefs. We need to know this as it relates to fornication and any other aspects of their religious lives that might affect whether they accept and practice sexual immorality. By looking at factors such as the subjective importance of God and religion, church attendance, views about the Bible, and so on, we can understand, within our evangelical churches, what people are neglecting and what the effects of that are upon their sexual chastity.[10] We can see what differences commitment to solid evangelical doctrines and practices actually make and the level of problems that might remain even when folks are embracing those things. Then perhaps we can discover what else we can do to help errant members better understand, accept, and follow biblical teachings about sex. We can do this better if we classify them as evangelical, simply because they are part of churches that fit the definition, and then look at the impact of their religious ideas and practices on their sexual lives separately.

Beliefs About Sex between Unmarried Adults

In dealing with both beliefs and practices, we will tackle three key areas that give us a good handle on how evangelicals are doing in the area of fornication: sex between unmarried adults, cohabitation, and pornography. Throughout, we will look not only at whether people are affiliated with an evangelical denomination or group but at their gender, education, age, marital status, income and social class, church attendance, view of Scripture, and whether they claim to have been "born again" through salvation in Christ.

We will begin by revisiting a GSS question from the last chapter: "If a man and woman have sex relations before marriage, do you think it is 'Always Wrong,' 'Almost Always Wrong,' 'Sometimes Wrong,' 'Not Wrong at All'?" Dealing exclusively with voluntary heterosexual relationships between adults, it gets everything else out of the way, such as homosexuality or underage sex, and we can learn a lot by seeing how evangelicals respond to it. Throughout, I looked at "Always Wrong" as the only biblical response to this question. There were some who were uncomfortable with fornication but who hedged and selected "Almost Always Wrong." I treated "Sometimes Wrong"

and "Not Wrong at All" as liberal answers.[11] The results of that
are summarized in Figure 3–1.

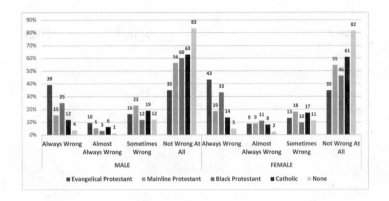

FIGURE 3–1: VIEWS ON SEX BETWEEN
UNMARRIED ADULTS, BY RELIGIOUS
AFFILIATION AND GENDER (GSS 2010–2018)

The differences between religious affiliations are highly statistically significant.[12] Evangelical and black Protestants are clearly
more likely than others to hold to the biblical position that sex
between unmarried adults is always wrong. Yet *most* of them
do not. In fact, 60 percent of black Protestant males selected
"not wrong at all," as did 35 percent of evangelical males, while
the percentages for females were 46 percent and 35 percent,
respectively. This has deteriorated over time. For example, in
the combined GSS for the 1970s, 51 percent of evangelicals
overall had supplied "always wrong" and only 20 percent "not
wrong at all."

To really understand what is going on with evangelical
beliefs about sex between unmarried persons in ways that can
be applied to the actual situations we might be dealing with, it is
important to look at them in detail rather than only as a whole.

Some of us are in predominantly well-off and highly educated churches, while others are among those who are less educated and wealthy. Our churches may be predominantly black, white, or Hispanic. A youth worker may be more involved with males or with females. An adult Sunday school teacher might be ministering to those who are divorced, or who have never been married, and so on. Let's explore these subgroups, starting with some basic demographic variations.

EVANGELICALS: DEMOGRAPHIC FACTORS

Age, marital status, and gender. The picture gets more dismal when we look at breakdowns by age and marital status. Here, Figures 3–2 and 3–3 show this, focusing just on evangelicals and combining the "always wrong" and "almost always wrong," and the "sometimes wrong" and "not wrong at all" answers to simplify the picture.

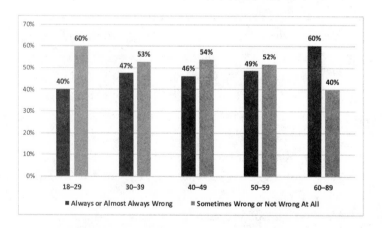

FIGURE 3–2: VIEWS ON SEX BETWEEN UNMARRIED
ADULTS, EVANGELICALS ONLY, BY AGE (GSS 2010–2018)

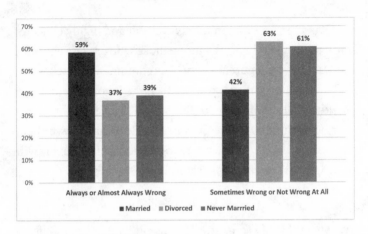

FIGURE 3–3: VIEWS ON SEX BETWEEN
UNMARRIED ADULTS, EVANGELICALS ONLY,
BY MARITAL STATUS (GSS 2010–2018)

The age differences are significant overall, but clearly the most important distinction is between the youngest and the oldest group, with those of middle age being similar. Younger evangelicals are clearly more liberal than older ones, especially in refusing to declare fornication is "always wrong," advancing the notion that it is only "sometimes wrong."

Marital status also makes a significant difference. Those who are single and divorced are much more sexually permissive than married ones.[13] This suggests that evangelical churches are facing major issues promoting orthodox views on fornication among those professed believers who are most likely to be facing this temptation—divorced and never-married adults, especially those who are younger.

Marital status difference among evangelicals is *not* simply because single believers tend to be younger than the married. I included the last twenty-five years of the GSS to get enough cases to compare the differences by marital status within age groups.[14] Within each age group, there were highly significant differences in views on premarital sex by marital status. For example, among those eighteen to twenty-nine, 50 percent of married respondents said that sex between unmarried adults was "always wrong," compared to 32 percent of singles. Among those thirty to thirty-nine, the same comparison was 50 percent versus 30 percent. Even among younger believers, single evangelicals were much more likely than married ones to claim that fornication was always or usually acceptable.[15]

Of course, gender must be considered. Among evangelicals in the 2010 through 2018 GSS, however, gender differences in views on premarital sex were not significantly different.

Race and ethnicity, education, and income. Among evangelicals there were no significant differences between white and black respondents on the acceptability of premarital sex. There were also no differences between Hispanic and non-Hispanic respondents on this issue.

Another basic demographic distinction is educational level. It made sense that a college education would make a difference. However, among evangelicals, those who had completed four-year college degrees or higher were not significantly different from those who had not.

Finally, let us consider income. Here, I grouped family income in constant dollars into five groups—under $25,000; $25,001 to $50,000; $50,001 to $75,000; $75,001 to $100,000; and over $100,000. There were no significant differences in views on premarital sex by income.

EVANGELICALS: RELIGIOUS COMMITMENTS

It is vital that we consider religious practices that demonstrate faith commitment. Most of us recognize that in our churches people can vary quite a bit in their degree of practical dedication and involvement. Obvious aspects of this are church attendance, a high view of the Bible, and being converted through repentance of one's sins and placing one's faith in Jesus Christ for salvation.[16]

Church attendance. Church attendance is an extremely important factor. The writer of Hebrews strongly admonished believers not to neglect the assembly of the saints (10:25). The pattern clearly laid down in Scripture, even before Christ, was that believers gather once a week. This was clearly affirmed in the New Testament (Acts 20:7; 1 Corinthians 16:2; Revelation 1:10). Yet in the combined 2010 through 2018 GSS, only 52 percent of evangelicals said they attended church weekly or more often. Another 18 percent said they did so between one to three times a month. Three in ten attended less than that.

Figure 3–4 shows breakdowns in views on the morality of fornication among evangelicals with different levels of church attendance.[17] The differences between those who attended church about weekly or more and those who attended less often are significant and stunning.

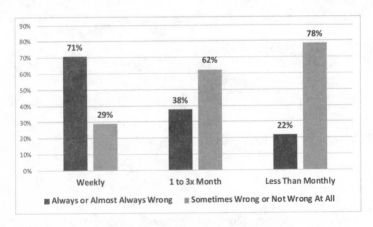

FIGURE 3–4: VIEWS ON SEX BETWEEN
UNMARRIED ADULTS, EVANGELICALS ONLY,
BY CHURCH ATTENDANCE (GSS 2010–18)

Regular church attendance is obviously important to supporting biblical sexual ethics. To be fair, I should note that it is associated with more conservative perspectives on premarital sex across other Christian religious groups as well, not just evangelicals. But it is among regular, weekly church attenders that we most clearly see evangelicals embracing what the Scriptures teach. For example, if we look at those who attend church about weekly or more, only 27 percent of Catholics say premarital sex is "always wrong," and 41 percent say it is "not wrong at all." The comparable percentages for mainline Protestants are 33 percent and 33 percent. Even for black Protestants, only 41 percent of weekly church attenders say premarital sex is "always wrong," and 34 percent say "not wrong at all." So, it is the weekly church-attending evangelical Protestants that really stand out in this area.

Still, it is disappointing that in the period from 2010 through 2018, only 60 percent of those who sit in evangelical churches every week fully embrace the biblical teaching on fornication. This means that about four in ten weekly churchgoing evangelicals do not believe that fornication is always wrong. Close to one in five say that it is not wrong at all.

Views on the Bible. Evangelical churches consistently believe Scripture is the word of God, totally without error in the original manuscripts, authoritative, and that believers should live their lives submitted to and affirming all it teaches. But how do those who attend those churches actually view the Bible?

The GSS asks respondents to choose: Is the Bible the "actual word of God" to be "taken literally, word for word," "the inspired word of God but not everything in it should be taken literally, word for word," or is it just "an ancient book of fables, legends, history, and moral precepts recorded by man"? (Here and elsewhere, I will label these options "literal," "inspired," and "fable.") Among evangelical Protestants in the combined 2010 through 2018 GSS, all ages combined, 61 percent chose the "literal" option and 39 percent selected the "inspired" option. These two views of the Bible were associated with significantly different outcomes on the item about premarital sex beliefs. Those with the literal view were much more likely to hold to the biblical teaching on premarital sex. Fifty-five percent of them said it was "always wrong," while only 23 percent said it was "not wrong at all." Only 25 percent of those with the inspired view of Scripture said premarital sex was "always wrong," but 48 percent of them selected "not wrong at all."

Even though holding a stronger view of the Bible helps, it is discouraging to see that 45 percent of those who claim to believe the Bible is the literal word of God do *not* fully accept its clear, repetitive, urgent denouncements of fornication. Embracing one idea but not the other is puzzling, logically contradictory, and ought to be a cause for real concern among evangelical leaders.

Views on conversion. Another key issue that too many evangelical church leaders overlook is whether the members of their churches have actually repented of their sins and expressed their faith in Jesus Christ. The GSS has asked the following question in every survey since 2004: "Would you say you have been 'born again' or have had a 'born again' experience—that is, a turning point in your life when you committed yourself to Christ?" This corresponds to clear teaching in one of the most famous passages in the Bible (John 3:1–8). Here are excerpts from verses 3, 5, and 7: "Truly, truly, I say to you, unless one is born again he cannot see the kingdom of God. ... Truly, truly, I say to you, unless one is born of water and the Spirit, he cannot enter the kingdom of God. ... Do not marvel that I said to you, 'You must be born again.' "

It would be hard to name a more central tenet of evangelical doctrine than the necessity of a complete spiritual conversion to faith in Christ, described as being "born again." We would not expect those who sit in church services and yet resist this teaching to think and act consistently as people under the authority of Christ. It is surprising to find out how many evangelical Protestants were unable to affirm this statement in the GSS. Taking the last decade of the GSS, from 2010 through 2018, only 75 percent of evangelical Protestants affirmed that they had been born again and were committed to Christ.

Happily, 88 percent of those who held that the Bible was the literal word of God claimed that they had experienced rebirth, as did 90 percent of those who attended church at least weekly. Percentages of evangelical Protestants who said they were born again were significantly lower among those who were never married (70 percent) compared to those who were divorced or separated (76 percent) or married (81 percent). Only 68 percent of evangelicals ages eighteen to twenty-nine said they had been born again, compared to 77 percent or higher for all older age groups.

So how does this relate to sexual beliefs and practices? For both evangelical males and females, those who said they had been born again were significantly more likely to say that fornication was always wrong. Overall, 50 percent of those who had been born again affirmed the latter, compared to only 13 percent of those who did not confirm they had been born again. Meanwhile, 63 percent of the latter group said that fornication was "not wrong at all," compared to only 27 percent of those who said that they had been born again.

Combining church attendance, views on the Bible, and being born again. Now, let us pull together these last three factors. Based on what we can see in the GSS, only about four of every ten professed evangelical Protestants clearly reject fornication. For those who attend church every week, have a high view of Scripture, and have experienced the new birth, this rises to 68 percent. Another 9 percent said it was "almost always wrong." Only 12 percent answered "not wrong at all." By contrast, those who viewed the Bible as only "inspired," did not attend church at least weekly, and were not born again were far more liberal on the morality of sex between unmarried adults. Only 6 percent said fornication was "always wrong," and 71 percent said it was "not wrong at all."

Promoting regular worship, a high view of Scripture, and true conversion is essential in the struggle to impart and preserve a biblical understanding of sex. These are things churches need to emphasize, especially with those who are single and younger. These elements provide a foundation to communicate, and see believers embrace, a biblical sexual ethic. More importantly, they regularly connect believers to the Lord—through church, the living word, and a personal relationship with Christ—and to the strength, motivation, and understanding he wants to give them to help them to resist the enticing, sinful ideas that pour in from every side of our wayward and lost culture.

What about "romance"? Before moving on to the next section, let us deal with an issue that often comes up in discussions among evangelicals regarding the ethics of consensual sex between unmarried adults, namely whether sex between singles is morally acceptable so long as they are committed romantically to each other.

In late 2020, Pew Research released the results of a survey of 3,998 respondents conducted in October 2019. Among the items were two that asked about the acceptability of sex between unmarried adults. One specified the condition "who are in a committed relationship" and the other item asked explicitly about those who are *not* in a committed relationship. The latter was identified as "casual sex." The percentage of evangelicals saying that fornication was "never" acceptable dropped from 47 percent for casual sex to 41 percent for committed relationships. Meanwhile, the percentage saying it was "always" acceptable went from 12 percent for casual sex to 21 percent for committed relationships. Catholics, mainline Protestants, and black Protestants were similarly less accepting of casual sex compared to sex within committed relationships.[18] Overall, evangelicals remained less accepting of premarital sex than these other groups, but relational commitment still affected their judgment of the sinfulness of fornication.

Beliefs About Cohabitation

Well-known actor Chris Pratt announced in early 2019 that he was moving in with his new fiancée, Katherine Schwarzenegger. They have both identified themselves as born-again evangelicals; Pratt even declared his faith on *The Late Show* and stood up for his church when it was attacked for refusing to affirm same-sex marriage. In fact, their desire to follow Christ was given as the main reason they did not move in together until they were engaged and Pratt's first marriage had officially ended in divorce. They believed that sexually living together was only a sin if they were not committed to eventually marrying. This appeared to be accepted by many evangelicals at the time.[19] Were the views of Pratt and Schwarzenegger, and their evangelical admirers, unusual among professed born-again believers? Apparently not.

Shortly after this news broke, Pew Research released a major report on marriage and cohabitation conducted in June 2019 that included the results of a survey of a cross-section of

9,834 Americans. This included asking respondents if "they think it acceptable for an unmarried couple to live together." Possible answers were: "Acceptable, even if they don't plan to get married"; "Acceptable, but only if they plan to get married"; and "Never acceptable."[20] On another, they asked about whether it would be better for society if cohabiting couples eventually married versus staying together without marriage. Their breakdowns of religious groups are close to those I have typically used here but not exactly the same. Although some key details about evangelicals versus others were not in the report, the researchers at Pew provided me with some additional information on the first of these items when I requested it.[21]

Results for the first item are shown in Figure 3–5, on whether cohabitation is acceptable even without plans to marry. Differences are very significant. White evangelicals are least likely to affirm this, with black Protestants the second least likely to do so. However, it becomes less encouraging when we consider additional details provided to me by the researchers. Of both white evangelicals and black Protestants, 23 percent said cohabitation was acceptable if the couple planned to marry. Only 41 percent of the former, and 30 percent of the latter, completely rejected cohabitation. Most white evangelicals and black Protestants do not embrace the biblical view that most Americans overall used to accept a few decades ago.[22]

Thankfully, 78 percent of white evangelicals and 69 percent of black Protestants asserted that it is best that cohabiting couples eventually marry. Members of other religious groups mostly did, but few of those with no religion agreed.[23] Figure 3–6 shows this.

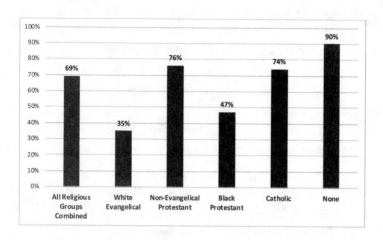

FIGURE 3–5: PERCENT SAYING COHABITATION
IS ACCEPTABLE EVEN WITH NO PLANS TO
MARRY, BY RELIGIOUS AFFILIATION (*PEW* 2019)

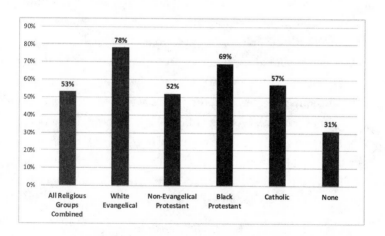

FIGURE 3–6: BELIEVE THAT SOCIETY IS BETTER
OFF IF COHABITERS EVENTUALLY MARRY,[24]
BY RELIGIOUS AFFILIATION (*PEW* 2019)

Not surprisingly, the Pew study found that liberal views on cohabitation were stronger among younger respondents. For example, on this last item, 55 percent of those eighteen to twenty-nine, and 50 percent of those thirty to forty-nine, said it did not matter if cohabiters eventually married. Only 35 percent of those who were sixty-five or older felt that way.[25] On the acceptability of cohabitation, 78 percent of those eighteen to twenty-nine, and 71 percent of those thirty to forty-nine, said it was acceptable even with no marriage plans, compared to 63 percent of those sixty-five and older. Only 8 percent of those eighteen to twenty-nine, and 12 percent of those thirty to forty-nine, said it was never acceptable, compared to 20 percent of those sixty-five and older. We can assume that while the percentages will vary, this trend will hold among evangelicals as well.[26]

The National Survey of Family Growth does not ask much about cohabitation beliefs but instead focuses on behavior. However, it does have one question about cohabitation that evangelicals should pay attention to, which I touched on briefly in the last chapter. For obvious reasons, respondents who were currently married or cohabiting were *not* asked this: "Do you think that you will (ever/ever again) live together with a man (woman) to whom you are not married?" This question is not just asking if the respondents think it is morally acceptable, but *if they see themselves doing it.* The options were "Definitely No," "Probably No," "Probably Yes," and "Definitely Yes." Recall that the age range is fifteen to forty-nine. Figure 3–7 compares religious groups on this item.

The fact that evangelical Protestants and black Protestants were least likely to say "definitely yes" and more likely to say "definitely no" is nice but a small comfort. Figure 3–7 represents

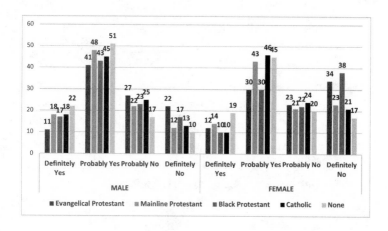

FIGURE 3–7: PERCENTAGES WHO THINK THEY
MIGHT COHABIT IN THE FUTURE, BY RELIGIOUS
AFFILIATION AND GENDER (*NSFG* 2019)

what any faithful evangelical ought to view as a disaster. Among unmarried evangelicals who are not already cohabiting, only about one in five males and a third of females under the age of fifty have categorically rejected engaging in cohabitation. Meanwhile, over half of these males and more than four in ten females are either planning to cohabit or open to doing so. We must consider that we also have, as we shall see in the next chapter, many evangelicals who are currently cohabiting or who are married but cohabited in the past. Such a blasé acceptance of the inevitability or possibility of cohabitation among evangelical singles should be a cause for deep concern among Christian leaders and parents.

In looking at beliefs about sex between unmarried adults, we broke down evangelicals into subgroups to get a more detailed picture of factors associated with greater or lesser acceptance of sexual immorality. This is helpful in applying these facts to people in our churches, who may not represent the overall aver-age. For example, which unmarried evangelicals who are not already cohabiting are open to doing so in the future—those who go to church regularly or who do not? Or is this a bigger problem in churches for people with more or less wealth or education, who attend church more or less often, and so on?

The NSFG does not measure prayer frequency or view of the Bible, and as we have seen, this item excludes those who are married. However, we can consider how evangeli-cals' responses vary by age, gender, educational level, income, and church attendance. We can also compare those who are divorced versus those who have never married. Finally, we can consider the impact of the importance respondents place on their religion in their daily life.[27] In looking at breakdowns within the evangelical camp, I have combined the last two cycles of the NSFG, giving us enough respondents to have a sufficient number of people within each subgroup to give us valid comparisons.

EVANGELICALS: DEMOGRAPHIC FACTORS

Gender and age. Gender differences were large and highly statistically significant. Twenty-one percent of males selected "definitely no" versus 36 percent of females. Meanwhile, 39 percent of males chose "probably yes" versus 29 percent of females. Both genders had 11 percent indicate "definitely yes." Females are more likely to reject cohabitation, though most do not.

Next, let's look at different age groups. To aid in clarity, I will only be looking at those who said, "Definitely No." Figure 3–8 lays this out for us.

There were statistically significant variations across age groups. Clearly, the crisis here deepens at younger ages.

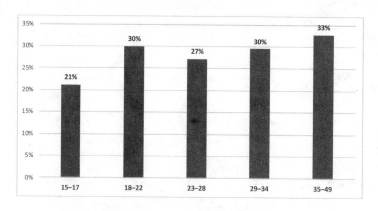

FIGURE 3–8: THINKS THEY MIGHT COHABIT IN THE
FUTURE, "DEFINITELY NO" ANSWER,
EVANGELICALS ONLY, BY AGE
(*NSFG* 2015–2017 AND 2017–2019 COMBINED)

However, there was not a majority within any of these age groups that said "definitely no"; not even close. These responses by single and divorced evangelicals should concern every pastor, parent, and youth worker in American evangelicalism.

Race and ethnicity, education, and income. There were no significant differences in future plans for cohabitation between black, white, and Hispanic evangelicals.

Another basic demographic distinction is educational level. Based on what we know about college education, it made sense that this would make a difference. Among evangelicals—both males and females—those with bachelor's degrees were significantly less likely than those with less education to anticipate cohabiting in the future.[28] For example, 36 percent of those with bachelor's degrees answered "definitely no," compared to 27 percent of those with less formal education.

In the NSFG, household income is measured in terms of percentage of the poverty limit. I grouped respondents into five groups, from those "at or below" the poverty line to those whose household income was 501 percent of that or higher. Among evangelicals, household income was not significantly associated with plans for future cohabitation.

EVANGELICALS: RELIGIOUS COMMITMENTS

Church attendance. Church attendance is typically a vitally important factor in explaining variations in acceptance of various types of sin within religious groups. Results for evangelicals on future cohabitation plans are shown in Figure 3–9. Since church attendance varies significantly by gender (see below), as does anticipating future cohabitation (see above), I reported the results here separately for males and females. The relationship between church attendance and possible plans about future cohabitation were highly statistically significant for both genders.[29]

On the one hand, weekly church attenders, both males and females, were much more likely to say "definitely no" to cohabitation. However, the fact that among even weekly church attenders only about half of females and one-third of males rejected cohabitation is alarming.

Just as disturbing is how few evangelicals actually attend church weekly. Among females, percentages for age groups eighteen and older ranged from 41 percent to 49 percent and were 47 percent overall. Even among those fifteen to seventeen, who would normally attend with their families, only 53 percent did. Among males the situation was even worse. For age groups eighteen and older the percentages ranged from 33 percent to 44 percent, 50 percent for those fifteen to seventeen, and 40 percent overall.

Importance of religion to everyday life. Next, consider respondents' opinions on this item: "Currently, how important is religion in your daily life?" Options were "Very," "Somewhat,"

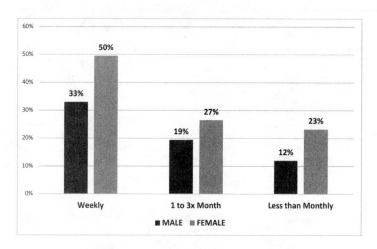

FIGURE 3–9: PERCENTAGES WHO THINK THEY
MIGHT COHABIT IN THE FUTURE, "DEFINITELY
NO" ANSWER, EVANGELICALS ONLY, BY
GENDER AND CHURCH ATTENDANCE, (*NSFG*
2015–2017 AND 2017–2019 COMBINED)

and "Not" or "Refused" or "Don't know." Almost all never-married evangelical Protestants selected "Very" (64 percent) or "Somewhat" (32 percent), so I restricted analysis to those two. The results are shown in Figure 3–10. Since among evangelicals females are significantly more likely than males to consider their religious faith to be very important (69 percent versus 59 percent), these results are reported separately for males and females. While the differences are large and significant for both genders, the results are still disappointing.

Combining church attendance and importance of religion. Weekly church attendance is, of course, strongly tied to rating religion as "very important" in one's daily life. Among evangelicals, for males, 89 percent of weekly church attenders rate religion as "very important," compared to 57 percent of those who attend church one to three times a month, and 34 percent of those who attend less than that. Among females, the

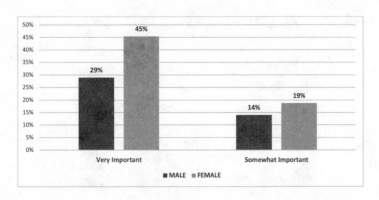

FIGURE 3-10: THINKS THEY MIGHT COHABIT IN THE
FUTURE, "DEFINITELY NO" ANSWER, EVANGELICALS
ONLY, BY GENDER AND SELF-IDENTIFIED
IMPORTANCE OF RELIGION TO DAILY LIFE
(*NSFG* 2015–2017 AND 2017–2019 COMBINED)

respective percentages are 91 percent, 65 percent, and 40 percent. Of course, keeping our faith "front and center" is one fruit
of remaining in regular fellowship. Moreover, we would expect
those who regard their faith as important in their daily lives to
worship with God's people weekly.

The role of church attendance is most important, but rating
religion as very important makes a difference too. The lowest
percentages rejecting future cohabitation were those who *both*
attended church less than weekly and rated religion as only "somewhat" important—males, 10 percent; females, 18 percent. Yet even
in the highest group, only 35 percent of males and 49 percent
of females, who both attended church weekly and rated religion
as "very important" said "definitely no" to future cohabitation.

The situation is grave, with even apparently committed young
evangelicals being open to and even expecting to cohabit in
the future. As a college professor of sociology tackling these
issues in evangelical college classrooms since the late 1980s, I

have increasingly seen pushback from students on this issue, as cohabitation becomes more widely accepted. As I explored in depth in a recent *Christianity Today* article that I cited earlier, which included interviews with a range of evangelical pastors, this is being noticed by church leaders who are struggling to find ways to help young evangelicals understand why cohabitation is wrong and should be rejected by serious professing believers.[30]

Beliefs About Pornography

The impact of pornography is not restricted to things that encourage, normalize, or otherwise shape sex between consenting unmarried adults. Married people often use it. Pornography itself can promote, celebrate, and depict a wide range of forbidden sexual activities, some extraordinarily perverse. Pornography is a major element in the sexual lives and consciousness of contemporary singles, it encourages fornication, and given what the Scriptures teach about lust in the eye, for example, it is a major form of sexual sin among married and singles alike. It is important that we tackle beliefs about it here, before looking at the actual use of porn in the next chapter.

The NSFG does not address opinions about pornography. The GSS does so only every now and then, and not in ways that would be particularly helpful here. The only consistent item used in it asks respondents whether pornography laws should make it illegal for everyone, only those under eighteen, or no one. While this shows evangelicals in recent years are more likely than others to want to restrict it for everyone, this does not get at the issue we need to address.[31]

On June 5, 2018, Gallup released a poll addressing the moral acceptability of pornography. Although it did not distinguish specific religious groups, it measured how respondents rated the importance of religion. The more important people considered religion to be, the less likely they were to accept pornography, and the differences were large. In 2018, only 22 percent of those who said religion is very important thought that pornography was morally acceptable, compared to 50 percent who rated religion as only "somewhat" and 76 percent who said it was "not very" important. Overall, the Gallup study showed that acceptance of porn is rapidly and steeply increasing, especially among males, the single, and the young. Acceptance of pornography increased by 6 percent between 2017 and 2018 among those who rate religion as very important. Among singles it had increased by 15 percent, and among males eighteen to forty-nine years old, 14 percent in that one-year period.[32]

The best recent data we have on views about pornography from evangelical Protestants is *The Porn Phenomenon*, a 2016 report rooted in a partnership between the Barna Research Group and the Josh McDowell Ministry.[33] Data was collected in mid-2015 from 2,771 participants using four online surveys, including teens and young adults, older adults, and senior and youth pastors. The researchers used a standard Barna measurement to compare "practicing Christians" to others. This label refers to those who attend church at least once a month, consider their faith very important to their lives, and identify as Christian.[34] "Practicing Christians" is not the same as the designation of "evangelical Protestant" I have been using here, and it includes in the definition factors I prefer to measure separately, such as church attendance and the importance of religion to one's daily life. However, it does help us to get a pretty good idea of what our more committed evangelical members are likely to be thinking on this issue. Generic evangelical Protestants, whether they attend church regularly or consider their religious faith to be very important, are probably not going to be *more* conservative on this issue than Barna's "practicing Christians."

Figures 3–11 and 3–12 summarize findings across age group on two items—whether porn is morally wrong and whether it is bad for society.[35] This may be the most optimistic data we have looked at so far in this chapter. Practicing Christians are

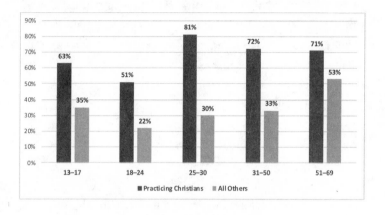

FIGURE 3–11: PERCENTAGES WHO BELIEVE
PORNOGRAPHY TO BE MORALLY WRONG, PRACTICING
CHRISTIANS VERSUS OTHERS, BY AGE (*BARNA* 2016)

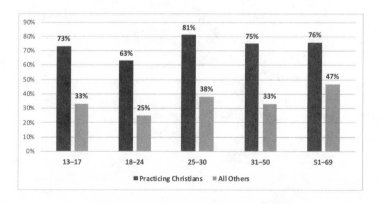

FIGURE 3–12: PERCENTAGES BELIEVING PORNOGRAPHY
TO BE BAD FOR SOCIETY, PRACTICING CHRISTIANS
VERSUS OTHERS, BY AGE (*BARNA* 2016)

much more likely to view pornography as both immoral and destructive. Those under twenty-four are more liberal on the issue than those over that age, but interestingly, young teens are less comfortable with pornography than those eighteen to twenty-four years of age. Overall, however, almost 4 in 10 practicing Christians thirteen to seventeen, and half of those eighteen to twenty-four, do *not* view pornography as morally wrong, which is very concerning.

This study does not break down marital groups or the sexes by their religious views. However, women are a lot less comfortable with porn than men, and married people are more morally opposed to it than the never-married or divorced.[36]

Conclusion

Evangelicals who are serious about adherence to biblical sexual ethics in our churches could look at the beliefs about fornication, cohabitation, and pornography in this chapter and see the glass as half empty or half full. How tempting it is to do one or the other partly depends on which issue and subgroup we are focused on. Of course, knowing these details and breakdowns helps us to be more effective regardless, as we target our redemptive efforts based on wisdom and a clear vision of the specific realities in front of us.

However, the right approach is neither the half-full nor the half-empty one. Since when does being grateful for the sheep that are healthy and secure give us good reason to not be passionately concerned for so many who are sick and in danger? Conversely, what happens to us and our fellow believers, including our families and congregations, if we become so despondent about and focused on those embracing error that we fail to value and nurture those who are safely grazing in our pastures?

In Paul's first letter to the Corinthians, he not only had to call out serious sexual sin, but he also had to face down professing believers who were taking pride in and defending what even pagans found abhorrent (1 Corinthians 5:1–13). He did not turn a blind eye or sugarcoat their sin; he doubled down with clear teaching about sexual immorality (1 Corinthians 6:9–20). But then Paul moved on. He gave them detailed practical instruction, encouraged them to greater unity and use of their spiritual gifts (1 Corinthians 12:1–31), penned some of the most powerful words on love ever expressed in human history (13:1–13), and finished with a powerful teaching on the resurrection (15:12–56). At the end of this last discourse, he helped them lift up their eyes with hope: "But thanks be to God, who gives us the victory through our Lord Jesus Christ. Therefore, my beloved brothers, be steadfast, immovable, always abounding in the work of the Lord, knowing that in the Lord your labor is not in vain" (1 Corinthians 15:57–58).

What we have seen in this chapter is that the beliefs of a large portion of evangelicals have drifted quite far from the clear teachings about sexual immorality laid out in the Scriptures, moving steadily toward the widespread acceptance of nonmarital sex that characterizes modern culture. We would expect the sexual behaviors of evangelicals to follow. As we shall see in the next chapter, that is precisely what has happened.

FROM COVENANT TO CONSENT IN THE PEWS (PART 2)

HOW SEX AMONG UNMARRIED EVANGELICALS COMPARES TO OTHER RELIGIOUS GROUPS

A significant cultural shift has occurred among Christians in recent generations regarding sexuality. My experience with Christians under thirty-five is that many are unashamedly sexually active in their serious relationships. There is growing confusion about what the Bible means when it refers to sexual immorality.

David White, *God, You and Sex*

We knew God wanted us to remain pure so we did everything we could to avoid the temptation ... until one night when things got a little crazy and we had sex. It was the first time for both of us and we felt incredibly guilty. For the next few weeks we asked for God's forgiveness and spent time reading the Bible together to come to a better understanding of how God wants us to experience our sexuality. It became clear and obvious to us that God wants nothing more than for us to feel good and be happy. We realized that having sex made the two of us very happy. Since then we've been having sex.

Female evangelical student quoted in Dennis Hollinger,
The Meaning of Sex

It is unlikely that so many evangelicals could depart from sound biblical beliefs about sex and cohabitation to the degree documented in the last chapter without having their practices follow. It makes sense that if evangelicals think sex outside marriage is morally acceptable, then many will engage in it. If large proportions of unmarried evangelicals say they are open to cohabiting in the future, or even definitely plan on doing so, then we can expect that many evangelicals will be sexually living together out of wedlock or have done so already. If we are moving from a sexual ethic of covenant to an ethic of consent in evangelical churches, then we ought to see more consensual sex outside the covenant of marriage. As we saw toward the end of chapter 2, ideas do have consequences.

In this chapter, we will look at evangelical *practices* in the area of sex between unmarried persons in comparison to those of other and no religious affiliation. In doing so, we will consider the same three basic areas as in chapter 3: sexual activity, cohabitation, and pornography. Most of my information will come from the National Survey for Family Growth (NSFG), but I will also use other sources such as the General Social Survey (GSS) and Barna Research.

In this and the next chapter, we will also consider questions I have encountered in many years of teaching that people may be puzzled by. Is it true that sex among young singles is actually declining? Is most of the sexual activity reported by evangelicals simply the sowing of wild oats from before they committed their lives to the Lord? Is it true that evangelicals often turn to forms of sexual activity other than intercourse to maintain their virginity, or that trying to do so is likely to be successful? Are men really a lot more sexually active than women? When evangelicals cohabit, is it mostly after they are formally engaged or at least have definite plans to marry? The big question is: Do those from churches that still mostly hold to conservative teachings on sexuality, such as evangelicals and Catholics, really do better, in practice, than those from mainline denominations? If so, how much better?

Fornication

SOME PRELIMINARY CONSIDERATIONS

Everything but vaginal intercourse. As we have seen, fornication can be defined as sex between unmarried persons. Beyond that, we often see unmarried believers using a kind of hair-splitting casuistry to defend an "everything but sexual intercourse" approach to premarital sex. It is a kind of moral "weaseling." "Everything but" encompasses other forms of mutual sexual stimulation—such as fondling and oral and anal sex—that might be considered morally acceptable based on the notion that only intercourse is truly forbidden. The same reasoning is then applied to masturbation.

Former President Bill Clinton used this type of justification to claim that he did not "really" have sex with Monica Lewinsky after being forced to admit that he had received oral sex from her. Research shows that, as of 2007, the majority of college students agree with this claim—eight in ten, compared to about half that closer to the era of the Clinton presidency. Only about

10 percent or less viewed manual sexual stimulation as "real" sex, and even fewer included arousing female breasts this way. Again, this has shifted a great deal over time—toward viewing these other forms of sexual play as "not really sex."[1]

Scholars who have studied the sexual reasoning and practices of professed Christians have explored this phenomenon. Questions about "how far is it OK to go" are really quite common, with many professed unmarried believers answering "pretty far"—even among those who do object to premarital intercourse.[2] As David White asserts, based on almost twenty years of counseling Christians struggling with sexual behaviors as part of Harvest USA ministries, "Many millennial Christians think only intercourse really counts."[3]

Dennis Hollinger tackles this issue in depth, noting numerous fallacies in this reasoning. First, such activities naturally lead to full physical union and, at the least, physical titillation leading toward it. Setting aside activities as deeply problematic as anal sex, even engaged couples should hold off mutual sexual fondling until marriage, given that these activities naturally lead to sexual intercourse. As for recreational activity of this sort between those without even tentative plans for future covenantal commitment, it is, in essence, nothing more than using one's partner for self-gratification rooted in lust.[4] Over time, the law of diminishing returns kicks in, and even if a couple seeks to stop short of sexual intercourse, that becomes increasingly hard to avoid.[5] This powerful, common sense principle rebukes believers who imagine they can play with fire without being burned. This includes the high risk of contracting sexually transmitted diseases (STDs) from activities such as oral sex, which few even think about trying to protect themselves from.[6] Besides, the ultimate test of the moral rightness of any action for believers should not be "what can I get away with without technically sinning?" but "what is most pleasing and glorifying to God?"[7]

In this chapter focusing on sexual practices of unmarried evangelical believers, we will be looking not only at intercourse but oral and anal sex as well. Including all of these sex acts is critical to understanding the sex lives of unmarried people. Be assured that I will avoid unnecessary graphic detail.

Data on sexual fondling, or manual stimulation, that provides breakdown for evangelicals is hard to come by. That means that overall estimates of sexual activity are a bit lower than they would be if the latter was included, since some young singles have only engaged in this.

Teen sex. Technically, anyone from ages thirteen through nineteen is a "teenager." However, our focus will be on teens from fifteen to seventeen years of age. This is because one is considered a legal adult for most things by age eighteen in almost every state in America. As for the lower side of this age limit, fifteen is the youngest about which we have sufficient, current data on evangelical sexual activity. However, we will be able to consider a little survey data from items that ask respondents about their sexual activity prior to age fifteen.

I should also note that, despite popular conceptions, teen sex is not necessarily unmarried. Though few get married today at age fifteen (as one of my grandmothers did), older teens more often wed. So, in considering teenage sex, I will exclude any ever-married persons.[8]

Finally, it has been widely publicized that teens are less sexually active today than they were almost a quarter century ago.[9] The assertion is accurate but often misconstrued, as we touched on briefly toward the end of chapter 2. For example, in 1995, 60 percent of high school students surveyed by the YRBS had engaged in sexual intercourse at least once, compared to only 38 percent in 2019. However, that is all high schoolers between the ninth and twelfth grades combined, and then only up until the spring of their senior years. These young adults are not opting out of premarital sex more now than before; they are just delaying it, often until after their high school years are over. So, for example, in the 1995 YRBS, 71 percent of high school seniors had engaged in sexual intercourse at least once, compared to 57 percent in 2019—much higher numbers and less of a drop. And the last cycle of the NSFG, which has comparable numbers as the YRBS for teens, shows the percentage of those who have never married but have had sexual intercourse hitting 62 percent by age nineteen and 73 percent by age twenty.

We have the same number of unmarried young adults having sex by twenty that, in 1995, had engaged in sexual intercourse by the time they finished high school. The fact that young people are waiting longer to begin having sex than a couple decades ago is indeed good news, and it is important to point this out. Delaying sex until later is certainly preferable to having sex at very young ages. It is not the same thing, however, as teens increasingly embracing abstinence until marriage, as a value or a practice. The vast majority do not.

SEXUAL INTERCOURSE

Let's start by looking at the number of sexual partners for never-married respondents, by major religious group and age. Since never-married respondents decrease in number dramatically going into middle age, I will stick with those ages fifteen to thirty-two. I have divided them into fifteen to seventeen (teens), eighteen to twenty-two (young adults) and twenty-three to thirty-two (younger adults to early middle age). To aid clarity,

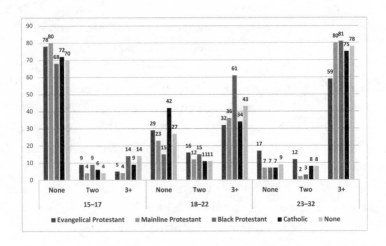

FIGURE 4–1A: PERCENTAGES WITH DIFFERENT
NUMBERS OF OPPOSITE SEX PARTNERS OVER
LIFETIME, BY RELIGIOUS AFFILIATION AND
GROUP, MALES ONLY (*NSFG* 2019)

each gender is presented in a different graph. I am using, again, the last NSFG cycle.[10]

As Figures 4–1A and 4–1B show, evangelicals did better than others among those eighteen and older. Among teens, not so much—among both males and females, overall differences for those fifteen to seventeen are not statistically significant, while the others are. Still, by eighteen to twenty-two, among evangelicals only 29 percent of males and 37 percent of females claimed to have had no sex partners and, for males and females respectively, 32 percent and 37 percent admitted to having had three or more. By the twenty-three to thirty-two age group, among evangelicals only 17 percent of males and females both said they had had no sex partners, and roughly six out of ten of each

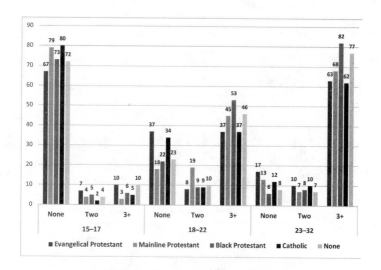

FIGURE 4–1B: PERCENTAGES WITH DIFFERENT
NUMBERS OF OPPOSITE SEX PARTNERS IN THE
LIFETIME, BY RELIGIOUS AFFILIATION AND
AGE GROUP, FEMALES ONLY (*NSFG* 2019)

admitted to having had three or more. Thus, those who remain single well into their twenties and early thirties are usually very sexually active and even promiscuous.[11]

An even more alarming picture emerges when one looks at the percentages of all people—regardless of current age or marital status—who have ever had sex, who had their first sexual intercourse at very young ages. Figure 4–2 shows, for example, that among never-married evangelicals who have ever had sexual intercourse, a third began at age fifteen or younger, almost one in five at fourteen or younger, and almost one in ten at age thirteen or less.[12] Those percentages are this bad despite, as we have seen, more teens delaying sex until they are older than was true some years ago.

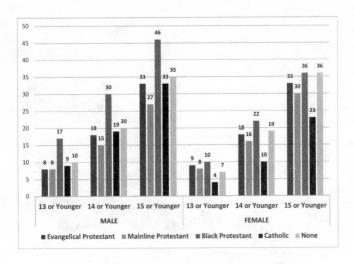

FIGURE 4–2: PERCENTAGES WHO HAD FIRST
SEXUAL INTERCOURSE AT VERY YOUNG AGES, *ALL*
RESPONDENTS WHO HAVE EVER HAD SEX, BY
RELIGIOUS AFFILIATION AND GENDER (*NSFG* 2019)

Next, consider those who are married and have never been divorced or widowed to compare how well members of different religious groups have confined sexual activity to only their own spouse. Here, I look at all relevant NSFG respondents twenty-three through forty-nine. Results are shown in Figure 4–3.

Although overall differences for both genders are statistically significant, Figure 4–3 shows that among males, overall married evangelicals have not done appreciably better than Catholics or mainline Protestants in restricting sex to their spouse only or having high numbers of sex partners. Among females, Catholics did better than evangelicals, but both did better than any of the other three groups.

Here are a couple discouraging facts: Among married evangelicals only about a third of females and a fifth of males had only ever had sex with their spouse. Roughly six in ten men and more than four in ten women have had three or more sexual partners other than their spouse.

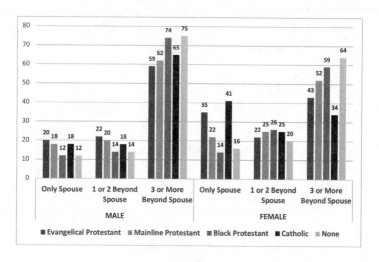

FIGURE 4–3: PERCENTAGES WITH DIFFERENT
NUMBERS OF OPPOSITE SEX PARTNERS
FOR CURRENTLY MARRIED WHO HAVE
ONLY MARRIED ONCE, BY RELIGIOUS
AFFILIATION AND GENDER (*NSFG* 2019)

Is this just "sowing wild oats" prior to conversion? When I
have shared this kind of information with college and church
classes over the years, I am often asked an excellent question:
How much of this evangelical premarital sexual activity is due
to adult believers having sown their "wild oats" prior to coming
to a true, saving faith in Christ? Answering that question with
precision is extraordinarily difficult. In my survey of evangelical
college students that I discussed in the introduction to this book,
all of them had stated clearly—before they were admitted to the
college—that they were followers of Christ and willing to abide
by our rules on sexual activity. Most eventually chose to engage in
premarital sex anyway. We also saw, in chapter 3, how many were
embracing permissive sexual views while being professing evangelicals at the same time. Still, how could we determine precisely,
even there, when a believer has truly converted and how much
of their sex outside marriage preceded or followed that point?[13]

I have been able to get a pretty good idea by analyzing the General Social Survey. This looks at the religious affiliations that respondents had when they were sixteen years of age. It does this by classifying them on a "fundamentalist-to-liberal" spectrum and by more specific religious affiliations that they had at that age.[14] When I have looked at measures of sexual activity and numbers of sexual partners among never-married respondents by religion at age sixteen, I have not seen any evidence that those from conservative Protestant homes are doing better than those from other, liberal or moderate, Protestant or Catholic homes.[15]

Of course, some (though not all) of these who were in more conservative churches at age sixteen may have consciously left the faith and then returned after having engaged in sex. Some of you may know of such cases. However, the GSS also enables us to see how many never-married respondents have had sex within the last year. In the 2010–2018 combined GSS, 71 percent of never-married evangelicals had sex within the last year. Over half, 58 percent of them, had sex once a month or more, and 35 percent at least weekly, in the past year. They did no better than mainline Protestants. More importantly, it is hardly likely that substantial percentages, much less majorities, of those who had been sexually active in the past year converted to the evangelical faith and then renounced this sexual activity prior to being surveyed.

For many years, usually in response to inquiries from students or attendees at presentations I have given, I have looked for evidence that high rates of premarital sex among evangelicals are largely due to the wild oats that many sowed before committing themselves to Christ and becoming professed evangelicals. This has always been important to me because of my own conversion story, as I did enter evangelicalism from a sinful life outside of it. Sad as it has made me, I have concluded that, while taking account of one's life prior to salvation is a factor in many individual lives—including my own—it does not do much to explain the current state of the evangelical church as a whole. It is certainly a factor, but not the major one.

ORAL AND ANAL SEX

Many Christian leaders are hesitant to address oral and anal sex among singles, but for the sake of our young people, we must. To start, we will just identify the percentages who have engaged in these behaviors. Figure 4–4 deals with oral sex; figure 4–5 looks at anal sex. We will look at never-married evangelicals in the three age groups we used earlier (fifteen to seventeen, eighteen to twenty-two, and twenty-three to thirty-two).

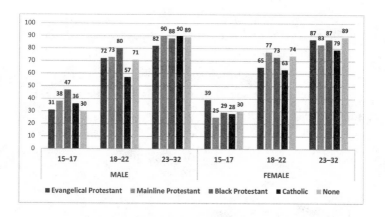

FIGURE 4–4: PERCENTAGES OF NEVER-MARRIED
WHO HAVE EVER ENGAGED IN ORAL SEX WITH
THE OPPOSITE SEX, BY AGE, GENDER, AND
RELIGIOUS AFFILIATION (*NSFG* 2019)

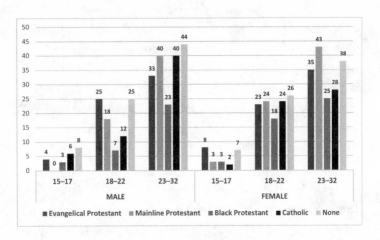

FIGURE 4–5: PERCENTAGES OF NEVER-MARRIED
WHO HAVE EVER ENGAGED IN ANAL SEX
WITH THE OPPOSITE SEX, BY AGE, GENDER
AND RELIGIOUS AFFILIATION (*NSFG* 2019)

Overall, Figures 4–4 and 4–5 are a mixed bag for evangelicals. Never-married evangelicals do not consistently do better than the others.[16]

Do evangelical singles engage in oral or anal sex to maintain their "virginity"? Sometimes researchers have explored something called "technical virginity" with regard to manual stimulation or oral sex. The term refers to singles who use "alternative" forms of sexual enjoyment so they can still think of themselves as a "virgin."[17] On the one hand, we have already seen that many young people do not think that sex other than vaginal intercourse is "real sex." On the other hand, there really is not much evidence that many evangelical young people use, for example, oral sex to maintain technical virginity.[18]

That among evangelical teens about four in ten females and three in ten males admit to engaging in oral sex should concern us deeply. Among young single evangelical adults, oral sex is now the norm. That about one in four of those eighteen to

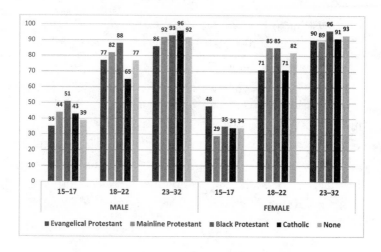

FIGURE 4–6: PERCENTAGES OF NEVER-MARRIED
WHO HAVE EVER ENGAGED IN ANY OR ALL OF THE
FOLLOWING WITH THE OPPOSITE SEX—VAGINAL
INTERCOURSE, ANAL OR ORAL SEX, BY AGE, GENDER,
AND RELIGIOUS AFFILIATION (*NSFG* 2019)

twenty-two, and about a third of evangelical singles twenty-three
to thirty-two, have engaged in something as dangerous as anal
sex is hard for many pastors to accept. It is long past time for the
professing evangelical church to seriously tackle the prevalence
of engaging in these "alternative" forms of sex.

PULLING IT TOGETHER

Figure 4–6 measures whether respondents have ever had *any*
or *all* of the following: vaginal intercourse, anal sex, or oral
sex. It is not clear that evangelicals here are doing consistently
better than the other religious affiliation categories. Moreover,
among evangelical teens, about one-third of males and close
to half of females have engaged in some kind of sexual activity.
More than seven in ten of those eighteen to twenty-two have

become sexually active in some fashion beyond just sexual fondling. For those still single at ages twenty-three to thirty-two, the percentages approach nine in ten.

The overwhelming majority of evangelical singles engage in sex outside marriage. Large percentages are extremely promiscuous. We are a long way from the chastity taught by the Bible and evidently practiced more faithfully by early Christians during the notorious sexual corruption of the Roman Empire. For the good of God's people and the testimony of the gospel, it is long past time to admit how bad things are and prayerfully consider how to tackle this issue.

Cohabitation

In looking at the actual practice of cohabitation among evangelicals compared to others, we need look no further than the NSFG. This survey explores this in detail. Given that cohabitation tends to emerge more among those who are older, and we do not see how these relationships end until later in life (we will see that below—whether the partners split up, marry, and so on), in dealing with cohabitation, I focus here on age groups starting at twenty-three up through forty-nine. This starts at an age for respondents to be old enough, and have the personal freedom, to make this type of decision.

First, Figure 4–7 illustrates the percentages who have ever cohabited by religious affiliation, age, and gender. Although overall differences are statistically significant for all but ages twenty-three to twenty-eight among males, comparing evangelicals with others produces mixed results, and the former do not stand out as doing consistently better. Except for males twenty-three to twenty-eight, large majorities of professed evangelicals across all age groups have cohabited at some point.

It is interesting that among evangelicals twenty-three to thirty-four, much higher percentages of females have cohabited (42 percent of males versus 57 percent of females among those twenty-three to twenty-eight and 62 percent versus 72 percent among those twenty-nine to thirty-four), but the trend begins to reverse among the oldest group (72 percent versus 68 percent). I do not have a full explanation for this. Some of this could be due to the tendency for women to link up with men who are older but not the reverse.[19] That is, more women twenty-three to twenty-eight cohabit with men who are twenty-nine to thirty-four—who cohabit more than men who are twenty-three to twenty-eight—and so on. That would drive the percentages of women in one age group closer to the percentages of men in the next higher age group.

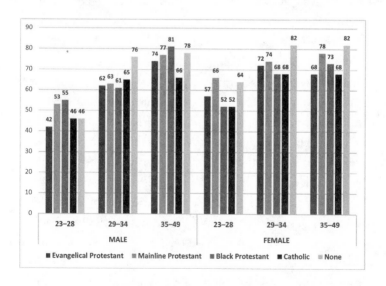

FIGURE 4–7: PERCENTAGES WHO HAVE
EVER COHABITED, BY AGE, GENDER, AND
RELIGIOUS AFFILIATION (*NSFG* 2019)

As a quick follow-up—what percentages have had more than one partner? For evangelicals twenty-nine to forty-nine, 16 percent of males and 21 percent of females had lived with two partners, while 18 percent of males and 11 percent of females had lived with three or more.[20] Among evangelicals, by middle age, four in ten males and one-third of females had cohabited with more than one partner. In percentages taking on two or more cohabitations, male evangelicals did worse than mainline Protestants and Catholics, while female evangelicals did worse than black Protestants and Catholics.

What percentages of married respondents lived with their current spouse prior to marrying them? Differences among the denominations are statistically significant. On the one hand, in each age group and gender evangelicals were least likely to have done so. On the other hand, among married evangelicals between 59 percent of males and 53 percent of females had.

What about marital plans among cohabiters? We recall from chapter 3 that many evangelicals believe that cohabitation is acceptable if marriage is intended. Numerous times, evangelicals have suggested to me that evangelical cohabitation is normally at the front end of intended marriages. Is this true?

One item in the NSFG asks whether those who are currently cohabiting believe they will marry their partner. The options are definitely yes or no, or probably yes or no. Among evangelicals, only 54 percent of males and 56 percent of females said "definitely yes." Among males, this was not much different than among black Protestants or Catholics, and it was worse than the 70 percent of mainline Protestants who answered this way. The percentages of cohabiting female evangelicals who said "definitely yes" were higher than for the other religious affiliations.[21]

Another NSFG item asks those who are currently cohabiting if they were formally engaged at the time they moved in together. Options included "yes," "no but definite plans to marry," and "no." For males, only 9 percent were engaged with another 22 percent saying they had definite marriage plans. For females, those percentages were 16 percent and 21 percent respectively. Neither were consistently more likely to give these answers than those in other religious affiliations.

Given the evidence in the NSFG, we cannot say that most evangelicals who move in with their lovers are engaged or even planning to marry. This data shows that, unfortunately, evangelical cohabiters who end up married are about as likely as others to be subject to "sliding or deciding." This phenomenon, which is well documented, highlights the degree to which many cohabiters who go on to marry begin their relationship with ambiguous ideas about what it means, which are often different for each partner. Then they are carried forward by inertia into marriage ("sliding" into it) rather than clear decisions leading to marriage ("deciding"). Partners who might have decided not to marry for any host of reasons end up marrying because of this inertia, leading to more troubled marriages. It is as if they are saying, "Heck, we already live together, everyone expects us to get married, so I suppose we might as well."[22] This is not a good beginning for marriage.

Figure 4–8 looks at outcomes of first cohabitations. Did the relationship end in marriage or not? Did it dissolve, with or without marriage? Here, I focus only on those twenty-nine to forty-nine, as this provides time for more respondents to see how their first cohabitation ended up. As this graph makes clear, most first cohabitations did not end well. For example, among evangelicals, first cohabitations dissolved one way or another for 70 percent of males and for 66 percent of females.[23] Black Protestants had the highest rate of dissolutions. There was no clear advantage for evangelicals.

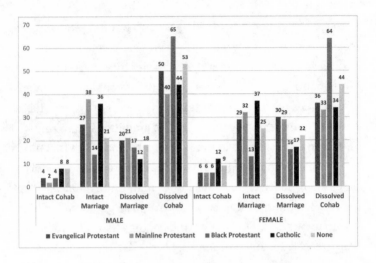

FIGURE 4–8: AMONG EVER-COHABITERS, HOW
FIRST COHABITATION ENDED UP SO FAR, 29–49, BY
GENDER AND RELIGIOUS AFFILIATION (*NSFG* 2019)

I have been told that evangelicals should start treating cohabitation essentially as marriage without the license. The data we have looked at show that there are very real differences between the two that should not be overlooked. Cohabitation overall is less stable and less committed than marriage.

The general conclusions to be reached from the facts on cohabitation we have looked at so far are simple. Evangelical Protestants cohabit about as much as most other religious people. Compared to the latter, evangelicals are not aimed more toward marriage when they cohabit, nor are their final outcomes clearly superior. They do better in most respects than those of no religious affiliation, which is a glimmer of a silver lining.

Pornography

In the last chapter we looked at data from the 2016 pornography attitude and usage survey done by the Josh McDowell Ministry and Barna Research partnership. Recall that they used the designation "practicing Christians," which, though encompassing many evangelicals, was not identical with the latter. However, we would expect evangelicals overall to do worse on average, not better, than practicing Christians on sexual matters.[24]

Figure 4–9 summarizes findings on the percentages actively seeking out pornography at least monthly. Practicing Christians do much better. However, as the researchers noted, active believers are more motivated to hide this behavior and so the true percentages are almost certainly higher, although it is difficult to know by how much. The way their report packages the data, it combines gender and age differences.[25]

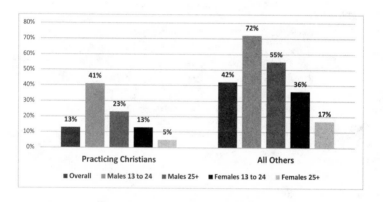

FIGURE 4–9: PERCENTAGES ACTIVELY
SEEKING OUT PORN AT LEAST MONTHLY,
BY AGE AND GENDER (*BARNA* 2016)

Other findings of interest are that, among all those of any age who actively seek out pornography, practicing Christians are more likely than others to say that they have tried to stop using it at some point in the past—16 percent versus 9 percent. They are more likely to be currently trying to stop—19 percent versus 9 percent. They are also more likely to experience guilt when they use pornography—about one-third versus one-fifth. However, notice that the majority of practicing Christian porn users are not feeling guilty about it and have made no effort to stop.[26]

Active users were also asked to choose from three options. Each one, and the percentages selecting each, for all ages and both sexes combined, are shown in Figure 4–10. Clearly, most practicing Christians did not express a clear desire to quit using porn completely.[27]

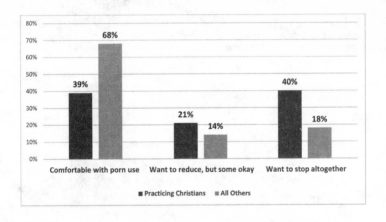

FIGURE 4–10: PERCENTAGES OF ACTIVE PORN
USERS EXPRESSING ONE OF THREE DESIRES
RELATED TO THEIR PORN USE (*BARNA* 2016)

In C. S. Lewis's *The Great Divorce*, there is a scene where a ghost is trapped in purgatory. He has the opportunity to enter heaven but is controlled by a lizard, representing sexual lust, that sits on his shoulder and constantly whispers in his ear. An angel asks for permission to kill the lizard and thus free this tormented soul forever. The lizard is begging in the ghost's ear to be kept alive, promising to behave himself in the future. The ghost pleads with the angel to postpone killing the lizard a little

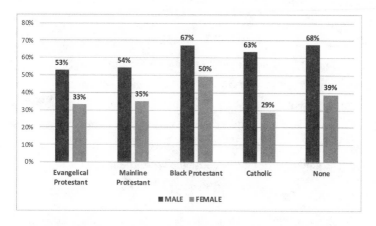

FIGURE 4–11: PERCENTAGES VIEWING PORNOGRAPHIC
FILM WITHIN LAST YEAR, NEVER-MARRIED 18–44, BY
RELIGIOUS AFFILIATION AND GENDER (*GSS* 2010–2018)

longer, insisting that it can be controlled and managed. Finally, with great agony, the ghost gives the angel permission to kill the lizard. Not only is the man gloriously freed, but the lizard is transformed into a beautiful, powerful stallion, which the ghost (now a real person filled with joy) rides into the "everlasting morning."[28]

Too many believers struggling with porn addiction are trying to manage it by resorting to half measures rather than taking the radical actions of confession and accountability that are necessary to abandon pornography completely. As a result, they never know real joy and freedom in Christ. It appears that roughly six of ten practicing Christian porn users are still opting to keep that lizard alive. In so doing, they are being held back from all God has for them, including all the true joy they could know in their sex lives as God intended them, and it, to be.

Finally, there is a standard item in the GSS that asks respondents if they have viewed an X-rated movie in any format in the last year. Figure 4–11 compares the percentages answering "yes" by religious group and sex, for those who have never married and are eighteen to forty-four, for 2010 through 2018.

The data show that single males were more likely to watch a pornographic video than single females. Evangelical percentages were lowest overall but not by much compared to Catholics and mainline Protestants. Also, for males and females, evangelical and mainline numbers were almost identical, and for females, Catholic percentages were the lowest.

Conclusion

This chapter has set forth challenging, even disturbing, facts about sexual activity, cohabitation, and usage of pornography among professing evangelicals overall, and as compared to other religious groups including those of no religious affiliation. It is no wonder that evangelicals are widely denounced as hypocrites when they oppose same-sex marriage. The charge, so far as I can see from data such as these, is just.

Nor is it surprising to see evangelicals try to resolve the glaring contradiction between the unrepentant practice of fornication by majorities of believers and denouncing homosexual relations. The problem is that the resolution seems to be softening our stances across the board, rather than humbly but effectively addressing our sexual licentiousness.[29] Our gospel witness is being damaged by our sexual practices, as is our moral compass. We are becoming more like the world, rather than having a transformative and prophetic impact on it in the crucial area of sexuality, as in so many other aspects of life.

This chapter has not been easy for me to write. I take no pleasure in laying out such dismal facts about people I love so much. Yet I know our God is jealous for the holiness of the church, which is in turn tied to his amazing, undying love and incredible plan for us. We must never lose sight of that or place our ultimate confidence and hope in anything else. Our assurance in his love for us should enable us to be honest about these difficult realities and lead us to repentance and a renewed zeal for sexual holiness, rooted in knowledge and walked out with patience and grace.

In the next chapter, we will look at sexual activity among evangelical Protestants in more detail, focusing on important differences among them. This will include standard demographic breakdowns: gender, race and ethnicity, education, and income. Most importantly, we will consider variation by religious commitments such as prayer, church attendance, applying faith in everyday life, and views of the truth and authority of Scripture. The layout will be similar to chapter 3. This will demonstrate the benefits of faithful versus lukewarm Christianity and provide useful information that will aid those who want to help their churches and fellow believers be more successful and committed in the pursuit of biblical chastity.

FROM COVENANT TO CONSENT IN THE PEWS (PART 3)

HOW DEMOGRAPHIC FACTORS AND RELIGIOUS DISCIPLINES AFFECT THE SEX LIVES OF UNMARRIED EVANGELICALS

[Jesus] again exhorts them to be earnest and careful in keeping the grace which they had received, for the carelessness of the flesh can never be sufficiently aroused. And, indeed, Christ has no other object in view than to keep us "as a hen keepeth her chickens under her wings" ... lest our indifference should carry us away, and make us fly to our destruction. In order to prove that he did not begin the work of our salvation for the purpose of leaving it imperfect in the middle of the course, he promises that his Spirit will always be efficacious in us, if we do not prevent him.

John Calvin, commentary on John 15:4

We are to study and implement schemes that motivate one another in godly living. ... We must give thought to how we can be of help to other believers. ... This alone provides an excellent reason to come to church and other Christian gatherings: that we may be of benefit to others, encouraging them and taking a care that they are standing firm as the day of the Lord approaches.

Richard D. Phillips, commentary on Hebrews 10:24–25

I t is clear to anyone involved in evangelical church life that some evangelicals strongly believe their faith ought to inform how they live each day, while others do not think about God much outside of religious contexts. Some accept the Bible's claims about its authority and accuracy, while others try to find work-arounds for the parts they do not like. Should we expect the same levels of sexual chastity among professed believers at different levels of seriousness and personal commitment? Not at all. This is addressed pointedly by Jesus in Revelation 3:15–16: "I know your works: you are neither cold nor hot. Would that you were either cold or hot! So, because you are lukewarm, and neither hot nor cold, I will spit you out of my mouth."

No one who is "half in and half out" of the faith should expect to live a transformed life. That principle is true generally, but especially in an area such as sex, where the cultural contest is intense and the pull of the flesh is—for most of us—so strong. Chastity is not automatic, even for those redeemed by God. It comes only to those who abide in Christ (John 15:5) and who are faithful in partaking of the assembling of his people (Heb 10:24–25), by his grace.

In speaking to pastors in a range of denominations and geographies, I have learned that many find the situations in their congregations to be different than the norms I wrote about in the last chapter. For example, if they serve believers who are wealthier and better educated, there is usually less sex outside marriage, even if it happens a disappointing amount. However, in evangelical churches located in areas marked by poverty and low education, the situation may be far worse. It is important to understand the differences these things make.

In this chapter we will consider the association of demographic factors and religious commitment to having sex outside of marriage, living together and, briefly, using pornography among professing evangelicals.[1] We will not go into every aspect of fornication, pornography, and cohabitation that we covered in the last chapter. It will suffice to deal with major measurements that provide us an accurate picture of how the various demographic and religious commitment issues impact illicit sexual activity.

Fornication

DEMOGRAPHIC FACTORS

In examining the impact of demographic factors, let's look at whether never-married respondents have ever engaged in intercourse, in any of the three forms of sexual activity we have been considering, or all of these; and whether they have had three or more opposite-sex sexual partners over their lifetime.[2] Throughout, I focus on those fifteen to thirty-two divided into three groups: fifteen to seventeen, eighteen to twenty-two, and twenty-three to thirty-two, using the NSFG. Knowing how sexual activity among singles in our churches varies demographically helps us to understand and adjust to local variations, knowing that a less educated and poorer church might not be the same as a wealthier and more educated congregation. The basics were covered here: gender, education, income (measured as a percentage of poverty level, as discussed in chapter 3), and race and ethnicity.

Within evangelical churches, there were no significant differences on any of these sexual activity measures in any of the age groups between white, black,[3] and Hispanic respondents. The only differences among income groups were among those eighteen to twenty-two wealthier singles, who were more likely to have had intercourse or anal sex. These are not critical realities.

The educational comparison focused on those with or without at least bachelor's degrees, restricted to those twenty-three to thirty-two since the younger age groups would not have had ample time to complete a four-year college degree. For every measured sexual activity, those with bachelor's degrees were significantly less likely to have engaged in it. Differences are as follows: intercourse, 71 percent versus 91 percent; any or all of our three types of sexual activities, 80 percent versus 92 percent; and having three or more sex partners during their lifetimes, 50 percent versus 72 percent.

Most never-married evangelicals have been sexually active in one way or another, whether or not they have bachelor's degrees. However, it is especially interesting that, given all the discussion of the "hooking up" culture on college campuses, single evangelicals who have completed at least bachelor's degrees are so much less sexually active than those who have not. Those serving in churches with less people who have at least college degrees will, all other things being equal, face more issues with those involved in their churches being sexually active.

Finally, gender differences were considered. Interestingly, there were no significant gender differences for any of these sexual activity measures within any of the age groups. As we saw in chapter 2, the old sexual double standard in which men could "sow wild oats" while women were expected to remain abstinent until marriage, or at least be less promiscuous, is dead. This also means that there are no reasons to separate men from women when looking at how factors such as demographic differences or variations in religious commitment impact sexual activity.

RELIGIOUS DISCIPLINES

We'll look now at the relationships between unmarried sexual activity and church attendance and the self-identified importance of religion in everyday life using the NSFG. It is important to know how much the basic disciplines, experiences, and practices that evangelical churches emphasize are actually associated with sexual faithfulness. Church attendance and keeping our faith front and center daily are both things that the Scriptures teach and that we emphasize the value of in our churches. Knowing if these are associated with better outcomes and to what degree they make a difference can help us better encourage people to engage in them as part of our ministry to those who are struggling sexually.[4]

Church attendance. If church attendance were edible, we could refer to it as a "super food." Attending church regularly—particularly weekly or more—is significantly associated with lower levels of sexual activity among never-married evangelicals, with just a few exceptions. This can be seen clearly in Figure 5–1.

Among those eighteen to twenty-two and twenty-three to thirty-two, weekly church attenders have significantly lower percentages who had ever engaged in any of the sexual activities measured. For those fifteen to seventeen, weekly church attenders only had a significantly lower percentage of those who "ever had sexual intercourse." For the "three or more sex partners" measure, few teens hit this number so early in life, yet even here notice that the percentages for weekly attenders are half those of those who attend church less than monthly.[5]

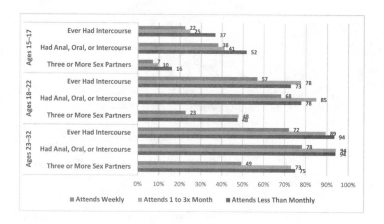

FIGURE 5–1: VARIOUS DIFFERENCES IN SEXUAL
ACTIVITY AMONG NEVER-MARRIED EVANGELICALS,
BY CHURCH ATTENDANCE AND AGE (*NSFG*
2015–2017 AND 2017–2019 CYCLES COMBINED)

Although it is encouraging to see how much better the singles who attend church weekly are doing, it is obvious that even among these, a lot of intervention is called for. After all, 68 percent of weekly attending singles who are eighteen to twenty-two have engaged in some kind of sexual activity—almost six in ten of them intercourse. It is worse for those twenty-three to thirty-two. One in four of weekly church-attending singles ages eighteen to twenty-two, and half of those ages twenty-three to thirty-two, have had three or more sex partners already. To say the least, these are not very comforting realities.

Importance of religion to everyday life. Next, there is the NSFG item asking, "How important is religion in your daily life?" As in chapter 3, I focus on the two answers supplied by 95 percent of never-married evangelicals: "very" and "somewhat." Figure 5–2 shows singles who rate their religion as "very important" have significantly lower percentages in every measure examined here.

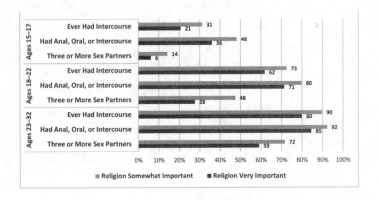

FIGURE 5–2: VARIOUS DIFFERENCES IN SEXUAL ACTIVITY AMONG NEVER-MARRIED EVANGELICALS, BY SELF-IDENTIFIED IMPORTANCE OF RELIGION IN DAILY LIFE AND AGE (NSFG 2015–2017 AND 2017–2019 CYCLES COMBINED)

Again, the results are still disappointing, even if they show the value of believing it is important to apply our faith to our daily lives. For example, among singles ages twenty-three to thirty-two, about six in ten of those who gave the "very important" answer had still had three or more sex partners in their lives, and about eight in ten had had intercourse, and even more at least one of the three types of sex.

Combining church attendance and importance of religion. As documented in chapter 3, church attendance and considering religious faith to be very important are strongly linked. The best results are seen when the two go together. For example, 70 percent of evangelical singles aged twenty-three to thirty-two who attend church weekly *and* consider their religion to be very important have had sexual intercourse, compared to 82 percent of those who attend church every week but only consider their religion to be somewhat important and 91 percent of those who rate their religion as very important but do not attend church every week. This pattern exists in every age group with each of our measures of sexual activity. Church attendance and people keeping their religion front and center in their daily lives work much more powerfully together than apart. Both matter.

However, overall, even for the "best" evangelicals in terms of these religious commitments, the statistics on sexual activity are disheartening. Still, it is good to see that those maintaining these commitments—especially for those at younger ages—are more likely to be sexually faithful. When singles want to apply their faith to their lives and are regularly in worship, parents and church leaders are much better positioned to teach and disciple them, and singles are better able to hear and care about that instruction and assistance. It is difficult to teach and encourage those who are not actively part of churches and do not try to apply their faith daily as part of a commitment they have consciously made to follow the Lord.

Cohabitation

In looking at cohabitation, I focus on those ages twenty-three to forty-nine. This provides time for more respondents to get old and independent enough to cohabit if they want to. It also allows us to keep the analysis simple and focused. I provide a brief overview of outcomes associated with each factor I discuss, looking at the amount of cohabitation including serial cohabitation, and the extent to which evangelicals who are cohabiting view it as truly premarital rather than just living together.

DEMOGRAPHIC FACTORS

Men are not likely to have ever cohabited, but if they have, they are significantly more likely to have done so with three or more partners. About half of each gender who is cohabiting says they definitely plan to marry.

In comparing those with and without bachelor's degrees, there were no significant differences in whether cohabiters had definite plans to marry. However, those with bachelor's degrees were significantly less likely than those without them to cohabit or to do so three or more times.

Regarding racial and ethnic differences, Hispanic respondents were the most likely to cohabit and white respondents the least. However, white respondents were most likely to have done so three or more times, while black and Hispanic respondents were not different on this measure. There were no significant differences among white, black, and Hispanic respondents who did cohabit in whether they planned on marrying their partner.

Income mattered quite a bit. Poorer evangelicals were more likely than those who were better off to engage in cohabitation and to do so three or more times. Among those who were cohabiting, poorer respondents were less likely to say that they had definite plans to marry their partners.

RELIGIOUS DISCIPLINES

Church attendance. Figure 5–3 breaks down cohabitation outcomes by church attendance. Evangelical weekly church attenders are significantly less likely to cohabit. If they did cohabit, they were more likely to indicate they had definite plans to marry their partners and were less likely to go on to have three or more cohabitations than those who attended church less than monthly.[6]

The good news is that attending church is associated with much lower levels of cohabitation and, if it occurs, with mainly better outcomes. The bad news is that there is still a lot to be concerned about even among evangelicals who are faithful in coming to services. Even though they do comparatively better, weekly church attenders who cohabit—and half do—still have bad outcomes. Attending church regularly does help point people toward glorifying God with their living, but that alone is not always enough.

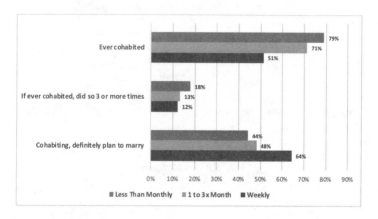

FIGURE 5–3: VARIOUS COHABITATION DIFFERENCES
BY CHURCH ATTENDANCE, EVANGELICALS 23–49
(*NSFG* 2015–2017 AND 2017–2019 CYCLES COMBINED)

Importance of religion to everyday life. Figure 5–4 shows the differences on our three cohabitation outcomes among evangelicals by self-identified importance of religion. Clearly, this is not as powerful a factor as church attendance. However, those who considered religion very important were significantly less likely to cohabit or to do so three or more times.

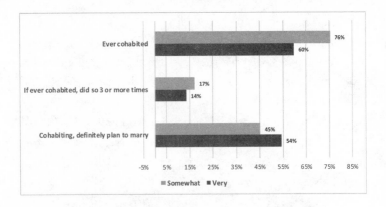

FIGURE 5–4: VARIOUS COHABITATION DIFFERENCES
BY SELF-IDENTIFIED IMPORTANCE OF RELIGION
IN DAILY LIFE, EVANGELICALS 23–49 (NSFG
2015–2017 AND 2017–2019 CYCLES COMBINED)

Bringing together church attendance and the importance of religion. Once again, we see the value of these two aspects of religious commitment being combined. For example, only 50 percent of those twenty-three to forty-nine years of age who both attended church weekly *and* considered their faith to be very important had ever cohabited, compared to 62 percent who attended weekly but only considered their faith to be somewhat important, 71 percent who considered their faith very important but attended church only one to three times a month, and 78 percent who also rated their faith very important but went to church less than once a month. While it is still disappointing that half of those who show the most commitment in these two areas still end up cohabiting at some point, these religious investments matter. Keeping these commitments puts evangelicals in a better position to receive the teaching and support they need to make more biblical choices.

Pornography

Recall from the last chapter that there is one GSS item that asks about watching a pornographic film within the past year. I looked at this briefly, checking first our demographic factors and second our various religious commitments. Analyses were restricted to never-married evangelicals between the ages of eighteen and forty-four in the GSS combined for 2010 through 2018.[7]

Demographically, men were significantly more likely to have watched a porn film in the past year—43 percent versus 35 percent. Black respondents were significantly more likely to have done so than white non-Hispanic respondents (42 percent versus 31 percent), but Hispanic respondents least of all (26 percent). Those without a college degree were significantly more likely to have done so than those with one (34 percent versus 22 percent).

Weekly church attenders were significantly less likely to have viewed a pornographic video. This held up for both genders. In fact, among males, the difference between those who attend weekly and those who do not was 31 percent versus 54 percent, while for females it was 15 percent versus 35 percent.

Conclusion

In this chapter we covered some basic demographic factors that contribute to the variations in the percentages participating in sexual immorality in chapter 4, in order to help you to understand how and why the local conditions you live in may vary from the averages. But the most important thing I want to communicate with the hard facts in this chapter is this basic, potent idea: *commitment matters.*

Those who attend church regularly and who strive to live out their Christian faith daily clearly do better in pursuing biblical chastity. I have seen this in interviews with evangelical pastors—for example, those whose church members exhibit a generally higher level of basic commitment to the life of the congregation and who say they apply their faith throughout the week find themselves counseling cohabiting couples a lot less.[8] Unfortunately, body parts cut off from the circulatory system grow weak. Churches and pastors cannot nourish and support those who refuse to participate in services or take their faith seriously. Often I have spent many hours laboring over a weekly Sunday school class only to find myself thinking, "The people in this church who need this the most almost never come." Low commitment of those who claim to be part of our churches is discouraging to our pastors and teachers and destructive to those they are trying to serve.

In the next chapter, we will consider the philosophical and theological currents among young evangelicals that help to drive this abandonment of biblical sexual ethics. This will show the specific ways that the trends in chapter 2 both manifest themselves among and subvert evangelicals. Turning the tide among evangelicals toward sexual faithfulness means understanding and confronting these sinister, sometimes subtle and sometimes brazen, theological and worldview errors.

6

THE THEOLOGICAL AND PHILOSOPHICAL ROOTS OF SEXUAL LIBERALISM AMONG EVANGELICAL SINGLES

Conversion and sanctification are the renewing of the mind, a change not of the substance, but of the qualities of the soul. It is the same with making a new heart and a new spirit—new dispositions and inclinations, new sympathies and antipathies; the understanding enlightened, the conscience softened, the thoughts rectified; the will bowed to the will of God, and the affections made spiritual and heavenly: so that the man is not what he was—old things are passed away, all things are become new; he acts from new principles, by new rules, with new designs. The mind is the acting ruling part of us; so that the renewing of the mind is the renewing of the whole man, for out of it are the issues of life, Prov. 4:23.

Matthew Henry, commentary on Romans 12:2

> The fact that fewer than one out of five born-again adults hold a biblical worldview highlights the extensive decline of core Christian principles in America.
>
> George Barna, American Worldview Inventory 2020

Some years ago, I was conversing with a young evangelical college student about her struggle to have meaningful conversations about personal morality with many of her peers. "As soon as I try to point out that the Bible teaches us that something is sin, I get back almost immediately, 'Don't judge me. Who are you to judge?'" Of course, that always brought the conversation to a screeching halt. It was as if she was being told, "Stop trying to make me feel guilty with this legalism. I feel okay about what I am doing. God loves me anyway. Stop telling me about the rules." This kind of interaction did not unfold in dialogues with her classmates about heinous crimes such as human trafficking, murder, or rape. Rather, it happened when discussing sins where all the participants consent and are happy if they are not made to suffer guilt or get into trouble. These were sins that were widely accepted, "not a big deal," and supposedly victimless, such as getting drunk, smoking pot, or cheating on exams. Commonly, it was sins such as having sex with a significant other, getting an abortion, or surfing porn sites.

Shutting down discussions about personal morality may also involve misusing another biblical text, wrenched out of context from John 8:7—"Who are you to throw stones?" Of course, we should always offer correction in humility, gentleness, and after honest self-reflection, including making sure that we sincerely desire the sinner's restoration and welfare (Matthew 7:3–5; Galatians 6:1). Pointing out that something a brother or sister is doing is a sin that any believer should flee from is not the same as censorious pride. It is not necessarily elevating oneself over another. Yet, as many who have tried to urge a fellow believer to repentance for sexual sin—even doing so gently and lovingly—have seen, he or she often respond by personally attacking the admonisher as a legalist and hypocrite. Sociologists have a technical term for when wrongdoers use this tactic to deflect guilt and continue their actions: condemning the condemners. This is one of several "neutralization techniques," which are rationalizations employed to break the power of moral norms that try to restrain illicit behavior and induce guilt.[1]

When people condemn the condemner, they make the accuser's failings and supposed ill motives (not objective truth and their behavior) the "real" issue. Jesus warned us about this when he stated that those bent on sin may respond to "pearls" of biblical wisdom by trampling them under their feet before attacking us (Matthew 7:6). Many of us have done this and had it done to us. However, in recent years, condemning the condemner has become more acceptable, and shrill, particularly on social media. Our online content reeks of "but what about *them*?" arguments to defend wrongdoing.

Sadly, many evangelicals today who are members of solid churches, and who honestly view themselves as Bible-believing, selectively neutralize the clear moral teachings of both their churches and the word. They filter the Bible through hazy lenses of subjectivism, emotionalism, and relativism. They manufacture qualifications and exceptions that reflect the larger cultural milieu, not sound doctrine. They turn from evaluating their conduct and actions by the fixed and unerring teachings of the Bible to calculations based on human standards of assessment and comparison. Too often, they treat those who challenge them to greater faithfulness as enemies rather than, as the

Scriptures teach, great friends (Proverbs 27:6). Unsurprisingly, this leads them to feel better about themselves than they probably should, while setting all words of remonstration at a distance. This cuts them off from correction, leaving them to their sin. When sinners say they have no sin, their sin remains (John 9:41; 1 John 1:8, 10).

These interpersonal dynamics unfold within, and are generally consistent with, a larger worldview in which God is most honored and pleased when they are comfortable, happy, and secure rather than when they are honestly striving to live according to his righteous commandments. Too often, evangelicals tie this to a view of God's mercy that nullifies the fearsome gospel demand that "if anyone would come after me, let him deny himself and take up his cross daily and follow me" (Luke 9:23) and the difficult pursuit of holiness "without which no one will see the Lord" (Hebrews 12:14). This understanding of God turns the basic disciplines of the Christian life, including simple moral obedience and accountability to spiritual leaders and others, into mere rituals and legalisms rather than necessary practices for our spiritual health, just as nutritious food and clean water sustain our physical bodies.

These ideas have left many single believers in a convoluted and dangerous predicament. They face not only natural sexual temptations but great cultural pressures to succumb to the sin of fornication. Although it will lead to many negative consequences down the line, including alienation from God and greater enslavement to deception as well as material and interpersonal damage, in the short term it often appears that they can indulge their sexual desires without guilt or penalty. Because these ideas are often accepted without inspection or argument by almost everyone they know, or at least by most people they are close to and really listen to, it is hard to know how to free believers from these sins.

In this chapter, we will explore the theological and philosophical roots of the widespread and growing embrace of sexual liberalism in evangelical churches. Although our focus will be on singles, we must recognize that these worldview assumptions, tendencies, habits, and beliefs are well represented across all relationship statuses. After all, every married person is a former single, and for those who are younger and wedded, their singleness is recent. We must also acknowledge that what we see among the young today is a direct product of all that they have been taught and exposed to. Many older evangelicals may also recognize that they have embraced similar thoughts and deeds and, hopefully, learned and matured in their Christian walk. Those of us who raised the current generation of young people, or taught them as new believers, are not solely culpable for the sad state of affairs we looked at in the last two chapters.[2] But we must recognize our share of the blame if we are to move forward to a better place.

In the process of exploring these dangerous modes of thinking that have overtaken so much of the evangelical church, we will see how much the mindsets that have infiltrated the evangelical churches are "baptized" versions of the cultural trends that we explored in chapter 2. The therapeutic mentality; sensate truth and ethics promoting relativism, utilitarianism and hedonism; expressive individualism; the pursuit of radical autonomy and self-fulfillment; the elevation of subjective experience; the difficulty in finding anything to condemn in what is mutually consensual and pleasurable; a hatred of institutional constraints while, paradoxically, being hypersensitive to the cues of peers and the broader, ever-shifting culture—it is all there. The insights of Rieff, Sorokin, Riesman, Inglehart, Bellah, and Hunter about modern culture are all represented in the mindset that has become dominant, especially among young people, in modern evangelicalism.

In this chapter we will focus on three basic insights, coming from three very different types of scholars and professional orientations, that will help us to see how the larger trends described in chapter 2 have manifested themselves in the worldview of many evangelicals. Each of these insights overlap to some extent but are better seen as complementary and mutually reinforcing. Together, these insights capture and even document vital segments of the destructive intellectual currents, contrary to the historic Christian faith, currently sweeping through the evangelical churches. Some of these currents detach believers from sound biblical thinking about the nature of God and humankind, the purpose and meaning of existence, and the value and sanctity of human persons. Others promote deficient ideas about sin, salvation, and sanctification, as well as increasingly questioning the very existence, and ultimate source of, absolute moral truth, including the clarity and authority of scriptural teaching. Still others directly undermine faithful Christian commitment. They come together in complex ways, but all flow ultimately from the old tendency to elevate the self over God.

The three thinkers we will consider are the famous German Lutheran theologian, Dietrich Bonhoeffer, and two contemporary figures who are both Christians—sociologist Christian Smith and social researcher George Barna. We will also look at applicable reflections from young evangelical singles, a textbook on issues of Christian sexuality written by two well-known evangelical marriage and family scholars, a revealing item from the National Survey of Family Growth, and select findings from the American Worldview Inventory (AWVI) administered recently to a national cross-section of two thousand adults ages eighteen and older by Barna and his colleagues. We will also consider findings on the worldview perspectives of students at conservative evangelical high schools and colleges from the PEERS (Politics, Economics, Education, Religion, and Social Issues) test created and administered by the Nehemiah Institute.

From there, we will follow up with some additional insights, consistent with those of these three men, making some connections directly to sexual liberalism, associating belief and practice. These will include another brief look at the importance of daily application of faith, our understanding of the nature and authority of Scripture, and evidence of having accepted the need for repentance and faith by being born again and trusting in Christ alone (John 3:3–18).

Three Pivotal Insights

CHEAP GRACE

In interacting with those caught up in sexual sin, and indeed in many other habitual transgressions, most pastors find themselves dealing with something that can be hard to dislodge. As we will see, this is an issue that concerned believers from the earliest days of the Christian church. It is the problem of antinomianism—the idea that God's grace eliminates our need to live under moral rules, making most sins "no big deal." The apostle Paul's famous question, "Are we to continue in sin that grace may abound?" (Romans 6:1b), was directed at this error. Ultimately, antinomianism leads believers to treat the forgiveness of God secured for us by Christ as a kind of celestial "get out of jail free" card. Sometimes people take this to mean that sin is not really sin at all. At other times, they use this to treat select moral failures lightly, not responding to them with deep sorrow or serious struggle.

Antinomianism is a major problem among modern evangelicals and in many ways reflects that sensate mindset in which sexual sin is evaluated based on its perceived impact on people, or lack thereof, rather than as an offense against a just and holy God.[3] Tied to this, a kind of therapeutic restoration to wholeness and self-acceptance replaces godly guilt followed by repentance and a renewed pursuit of holy living by the grace of God.

As a young believer coming out of my "hippie" lifestyle, antinomianism was a major issue for me. I thank God for mature believers who dissuaded me from believing that God's mercy could ever be a license to sin. I had to learn, often the hard way, that God would not wink at me treating sin lightly, that he loved me too much to let me get away with flippant apologies without real regret or any ongoing commitment to change.

What I am talking about here is the "cheap grace" that Dietrich Bonhoeffer so famously warned us about in his magnificent book *The Cost of Discipleship*—something he connected to a weakened, flaccid church that had lost its holiness and spiritual power:

> Cheap grace is the preaching of forgiveness without requiring repentance, baptism without church discipline, Communion without confession, absolution without personal confession. Cheap grace is grace without discipleship, grace without the cross, grace without Jesus Christ, living and incarnate. Costly grace is the treasure hidden in the field; for the sake of it a man will go and sell all that he has. ... Such grace is *costly* because it calls us to *follow*, and it is grace because it calls us to follow *Jesus Christ*. It is costly because it costs a man his life,

and it is grace because it gives a man the only true life. It is costly because it condemns sin, and grace because it justifies the sinner. Above all, it is *costly* because it cost God the life of his Son: "ye were bought at a price," and what has cost God much cannot be cheap for us. Above all, it is *grace* because God did not reckon his Son too dear a price to pay for our life, but delivered him up for us. Costly grace is the Incarnation of God.[4]

As Bonhoeffer made clear, true grace from God is not cheap at all. It is costly. It demands everything from us but gives us everything in return. Bonhoeffer captures perfectly the balance of how the Christian walk can be both receiving a free gift and living a life of deeply committed service to the one who gave it. It is both liberating and disciplined, free and ruled, having the hope and motivation to ask forgiveness again and again while having that mercy bear real, tangible fruit of obedience and growth in holiness. The apostle Paul lays out the reasoning that Bonhoeffer seems to follow in Romans 6. He shows that a proper understanding of our union with Christ is the antidote to the deadly poison of antinomianism. We "who have died to sin" should not continue to "live in it" (6:2). We should instead live in a new reality in which we have "died to sin" and now live "to God" (6:10). Paul admonishes us not to let "sin therefore reign in [our] mortal bod[ies]" to "obey its passions" (6:12). Living "not under law but under grace" (6:14b) does not mean we are now free to indulge in sin but rather that sin should "have no dominion over" us (6:14a). Sanctification, whereby we are liberated from being slaves to sin in order to become slaves to Christ, is a necessary and natural fruit of true salvation (6:16–22). We who are in Christ can give up the temporal but deadly pleasures of sin joyfully, knowing that we now have something infinitely better, namely "the free gift of God" which is "eternal life in Christ Jesus our Lord" (6:23).

On the one hand, we are saved by grace through faith in Jesus Christ. Our sins are forgiven because we have been credited with his perfect righteousness, our sins atoned for by the blood he shed for us as he took our punishment upon himself on the cross. On the other hand, those who truly receive this grace ought to earnestly pursue holiness and obey his commands, however imperfectly, by his grace. Moreover, we do not view this forgiveness as an excuse to sin because, by the power of the Holy Spirit, we ought to *hate* sin. This balance, which we see clearly in the New Testament, is lost to much of the evangelical church today.

Jerry Bridges, the late evangelical writer and Navigators staff member, brought these concerns to the modern church in his magnificent best-seller, *The Pursuit of Holiness*. As Bridges points out, a key problem facing believers "is that we have misunderstood 'living by faith' (Galatians 2:20) to mean that no effort at holiness is needed on our part. In fact, sometimes we have even suggested that any effort on our part is 'in the flesh.' " A diminished regard for holiness is rooted in a view of sin that is "more self-centered than God-centered," along with other deficient views of God that make him much smaller than, to put it mildly, he really is.[5]

Bridges says the way we categorize sin substitutes—sometimes subtly but other times quite brazenly—our reason and cultural biases for God's word.[6] As Sorokin said those of sensate culture would do, we have made "man ... the measure of all things."[7] We treat some sins as not all that serious, and any concerns about them as "nit-picking legalism." This second-guesses God and trivializes his infinite knowledge and perfect goodness. It also fails to recognize the snowball effect as "little sins" compound and become bigger and more deadly over time, as the list of what we excuse grows exponentially.[8] As we have seen, this happens not only in the lives of individuals but in the trajectory of Christ's church as a whole. Widespread acceptance of premarital sex has led to the normalization of cohabitation and now, increasingly, the growing acceptance of homosexuality and even transgenderism.

A fascinating NSFG survey item labeled, humorously, "YNOSEX," asks singles who have never had sexual intercourse to give their reasons for abstaining.[9] Certainly, many of those who had sex—and so were not asked this question—believed that what they did was morally wrong and may have even repented for it. And yet, among evangelical teens fifteen to seventeen who had refrained from sex, only 44 percent gave "against my religion or morals" as their primary reason for abstaining. Among singles eighteen to twenty-two, who had held off on having sex longer, 59 percent did, rising to 64 percent for those twenty-three to thirty-two.

The biggest reason evangelical virgins gave for not having sex, beyond morals, was not having found the right person or the right time to have sex in the relationship they were in. The rest gave utilitarian reasons, mostly concerned about pregnancy or sexual disease. Almost half of evangelical teens who had not had sex admitted they would like to but lacked opportunity or were only trying to avoid practical consequences. Given the right person and the right protection, they said they would willingly commence sexual activity.

These results do not reflect an evangelical church in which most singles, or even most virgin singles, overwhelmingly want to honor God and keep his commands in the ways they use their bodies. I praise God for that core of young believers who are striving for abstinence, failing or not, because they are motivated to obey God and they trust his greater wisdom in their lives. They are the true countercultural teens, carrying on the difficult pursuit of sexual chastity in line with God's word. However, most evangelical teens appear to have drunk deeply of a "cheap grace" approach to Christianity that does not recognize the urgency of the pursuit of holiness.[10]

MORALISTIC THERAPEUTIC DEISM

In the landmark book *Soul Searching: The Religious and Spiritual Lives of Teenagers*, sociologist Christian Smith, with Melinda Lundquist Denton, supplemented extensive survey data with in-depth interviews from 267 teens in 45 states from rural, suburban, and urban areas, to discover the main lines, and big picture, of "adolescent religion and spirituality."[11] They famously summarized the dominant view of God among American teenagers as "Moralistic Therapeutic Deism" (MTD). Although they never cited Philip Rieff, nor did they draw on any of Robert Bellah's relevant insights, concepts consistent with the works of these sociologists permeate their discussion of MTD. Sorokin is not cited either, but the results he predicted of sensate culture appear to be everywhere in MTD.[12] Smith and Denton outline the "creed" of MTD as the following:

> 1. A God exists who created and orders the world and watches over human life on earth. 2. God wants people to be good, nice, and fair to each other, as taught in the Bible and by most world religions. 3. The central goal of life is to be happy and to feel good about oneself. 4. God does not need to be particularly involved in one's life except when God is needed to solve a problem. 5. Good people go to heaven when they die.[13]

Smith and Denton go on to outline more specific concepts in this view of religion and the spiritual life. First, people should try to be "good, moral persons," which is mostly about being kind, pleasant, trying to be healthy, being responsible and respectful, trying to be successful and improve oneself.[14] What about God? The deity certainly exists and created the world, including a moral order. However, God is not personally involved in our private lives. Tellingly, this is especially true about "affairs in which one would prefer not to have God involved. ... God keeps a safe distance."[15] Lastly—and here the ghost of Philip Rieff really asserts himself—religion is ultimately "about providing *therapeutic benefits* to its adherents."[16] What about obedience, struggle, and spiritual discipline? Say the authors:

> This is not a religion of repentance from sin, of keeping the Sabbath, of living as a servant of a sovereign divine, of steadfastly saying one's prayers ... of building character through suffering, of basking in God's love and grace, of spending oneself in love for the cause of social justice, etcetera. Rather, what appears to be the dominant religion among U.S. teenagers is centrally about feeling good, happy, secure, at peace. It is about attaining subjective wellbeing, being able to resolve problems, and getting along amiably with other people.[17]

Ultimately, this is an "instrumental view of religion." Belief in God is a means to various personal ends. It "helps you do what you want."[18]

MTD is also averse to saying that any particular religious ideas are right or wrong. In practice, this leads to an underlying religious relativism. Echoing the college student's observations that I noted at the outset of the chapter, "Who am I to judge?"

was a constant response to different beliefs and practices.[19] Right
on its heels was a sentiment that I hear constantly as a Christian
college professor: "There is no right answer."

I received a paper some years ago from a Christian student
on Aztec cannibalism, a hideous practice that was unbelievably cruel and carried out on a wide scale. Without flinching
from the reality of it, this young person pointed out, at some
length, that though this seems like a terrible thing to us modern
Americans, so long as Aztecs were comfortable with the practice, we could not absolutely condemn it. I have almost gotten
used to this kind of cultural relativism from young evangelicals.
It requires little imagination to see how easily this is applied to
our own widespread sins, including the sexual ones that our
culture likewise broadly participates in and accepts. If murder
followed by cannibalism can be justified in this manner, then
everything else can, including fornication. It is the old saying,
"Different strokes for different folks,"[20] gone wild.

The authors make clear that when young people embrace
MTD, they are not joining some altogether new religion.
They still consider themselves to be evangelicals, or Catholics,
Methodists, Buddhists, Mormons, Jews, and so on. What they
mean is that, among those teens that are at all connected to religion, MTD is increasingly "colonizing many established religious
traditions and congregations."[21] Some absorb the whole package,
others assimilate various components of it. Regardless, they
integrate it with their existing faith traditions. In this respect,
MTD is "a parasitic faith."[22] This means the religious and moral
teaching and symbols of the host faith are fundamentally altered,
while much of the trappings remain. And like parasites often do,
they make the formerly healthy body sick and weak.

What about evangelical Protestants? The authors say that,
at least at some points though not necessarily all, most of the

resistance to MTD comes from evangelicals and Mormons, but those who resist represent a sliver of the whole and are not dominant, even among conservative Protestants.[23] One stunning fact is that out of the 267 teens they interviewed, only 47 ever mentioned "being a sinner," a mere 13 talked about "obeying God or the church," 12 mentioned repentance, and only 9 said they loved God. How many mentioned the idea that God was "holy"? Literally, *two*. "Loving one's neighbor?" Three. No one brought up anything related to self-discipline, nor did any mention sanctification.[24] And yet, roughly 15 percent of these interviewees (forty) would have been members of an evangelical Protestant church, and roughly 27 percent (seventy) would have described themselves as either born-again, evangelical, fundamentalist, or charismatic.[25]

Here are some representative quotes from interviews with conservative Protestant teens that crystallize MTD well:

> "God is ... like someone that'll always help you go through whatever you're going through. When I became a Christian I was just praying and it always made me feel better."

> "Religion is very important, because when you have no one else to talk to about stuff, you can just get it off your chest, you just talk [to God]. It is good."

> "He believes in forgiving people and whatnot and he's there to guide us, for somebody to talk to and help us with our problems. Of course, he doesn't talk back."[26]

Although this book, and these interviews, focused on teenagers, Smith and Denton point out forcefully that MTD is well represented among American adults as well. In fact, teens primarily have absorbed and learned this from older believers.[27] This point was made in an excellent *Gospel Coalition* essay entitled "Moralistic Therapeutic Deism: Not Just a Problem with Youth Ministry." The author, Brian Cosby, cites Kenda Creasy Dean's *Almost Christian: What the Faith of Our Teenagers Is Telling the American Church*,[28] to make this telling point: "American teenagers have bought into MTD, not because they have misunderstood what the church has taught them, but precisely because it is what the church has taught them."[29]

Catholic scholar Leroy Huizenga has an even more ominous observation about MTD. It is, he says, in many respects a practical gnosticism, especially in its emphasis on a therapeutic deity who serves us—the central role of subjectivity and feeling—and in making Jesus a kind of "mascot for its ideology." It is obviously antithetical to the gospel.[30]

Those who embrace MTD can view themselves as "good evangelicals" while being, at the same time, wholly prepared to absorb sexual liberalism in belief and in practice. It is centered on subjective happiness, comfort, and the self. Many evangelicals who do not embrace MTD have no idea how to argue against it. MTD directly undermines every moral absolute and discourages every spiritual discipline that one would use to combat sexual temptation. It actively discourages any challenges from others from an objective moral starting point, including biblical teaching. Those who preach judgment for sinning against a holy God have no place in the MTD spiritual world.

A sad example of what both Bonhoeffer and Bridges warn against, as well as the essential approach of MTD in evangelical clothing, may be found in a book that has influenced thousands of evangelical college students and seminarians and, through them, those they teach, parent, and counsel. I am referring to *Authentic Human Sexuality* by Fuller Theological Seminary professors and marriage and family therapists Judith and Jack Balswick.

Note that the title alerts us to an approach leaning toward the therapeutic mindset—not biblical but "authentic." This theme is emphasized throughout the book, even though the authors do often accurately identify and summarize biblical teaching on sex. In some ways, this is what makes it so deceptive.

While at points affirming that waiting until marriage to engage in sexual activity is wisest and most consistent with scriptural teaching, the Balswicks also appear to make it one option among others for sincere believers. God's biblical standards are muddled, undermined, and partially "walked back." "Some claim that the Bible doesn't clearly forbid premarital sex like it does adultery, sexual immorality, and prostitution. ... Christian singles are challenged to choose a standard that resonates with *their* values and morality."[31] Following the clear teachings of the Bible becomes the ideal, but not the only legitimate, way for unmarried Christians in romantic relationships to live sexually. They counsel couples to be guided by

> the standard of the person with the strongest *felt* limits ... use Scripture as your guide and recognize your freedom in Christ ... strive for sexual authenticity ... seeking to be congruent with ourselves before God. ... *Mutual empowerment* throughout our sexual journey helps us make decisions that are in the *best interest of self, partner, and relationship.*[32]

The Balswicks' book has a telling section addressed to unmarried evangelical lovers entitled "Guidelines for Sexual Involvement." It opens with the claim, "The Bible is not so clear-cut about engaging in sexual expressions of love. ... We believe it is more helpful for a couple to consider a series of crucial questions about their level of sexual involvement."[33] These questions involve issues such as emotional consequences, the possibility of pregnancy and whether the couple are willing to marry if it occurs, the reactions of and impact upon significant others, the strength of the relationship, whether sex will "enrich the relationship," and a host of similar rationales. All their reasons, whether defined as "right" or "wrong" ones, are rooted in peer reactions, personal perceptions, and subjective feelings while effectively neutralizing clear scriptural boundaries. Preeminently, it is about the needs and feelings of the self and other people, not God's righteous rule.[34]

The Balswicks' overall approach is made crystal clear in this statement, prior to considering various sexual scenarios: "Even though sexual pleasure and enjoyment may be a good reason, it is important to consider the potential impact of sexual involvement for your partner, yourself, and your relationship." They are certainly not calling believers to exercise costly self-control in reverence to a holy and gracious God. It is therefore not surprising that later we find the Balswicks accepting cohabiting to the point that they recommend that churches hold public ceremonies for believers who want to live together but not be married.[35] Treating the clear commandments of God as if they are merely ideals within a range of options carries throughout, trivializing sin and offering cheap grace.

Ultimately, this same logic leads the Balswicks to come down in favor of accepting same-sex marriage, while recognizing man-woman marriage as, again, God's ideal. "The foundational relational principles of covenant, grace, empowerment and intimacy as God's plan for humankind and relational health can be lived out as gay or straight." What matters is "making responsible choices regardless of sexual orientation and identity."[36]

These claims parallel almost exactly what an evangelical lesbian college student confronted me with a few years ago, denouncing my alleged legalism and small-mindedness. Her argument was that while heterosexual marriage was clearly an ideal, we should also accept gay marriage as a legitimate "lesser option" in a sinful world. Her justification for homosexuality is the same one used by many believers, including the Balswicks, for making peace with fornication and cohabitation. There really is a slippery slope.

ALTERNATIVE WORLDVIEWS

Social researcher George Barna is one of the leading figures today in tracking trends across numerous areas of life by measuring behavior and opinions and focusing heavily on religion, spirituality, and worldview. Much of it has to do with the interaction between faith and culture. He is an evangelical, and his approach is heavily rooted in marketing research.

Based on an enormous amount of data and decades of experience and in cooperation with Summit Ministries, Barna classified five competing worldviews. One of these is the Biblical Worldview, which he defines this way:

> Absolute moral truth exists; the Bible is totally accurate in all of the principles it teaches; Satan is considered to be a real being or force, not merely symbolic; a person cannot earn their way into Heaven by trying to be good or do good works; Jesus Christ lived a sinless life on earth; and God is the all-knowing, all-powerful creator of the world who still rules the universe today.[37]

This understanding of a biblical worldview is careful, not fanciful or overreaching. Some might even say it is too minimal. It requires that one believes in the Bible, the existence of a real devil, salvation by grace through faith in Christ alone, Jesus's perfection, and an omniscient and omnipotent God who actively reigns over his creation. These are not to be accepted à la carte but as a package—all together. It clearly represents the basics of evangelical Christianity.

The four other competing worldviews are New Spirituality, Postmodernism, Secularism, and Marxism. While many people fall into one camp or another, there are ideas in each that often have broad appeal.

New Spirituality emphasizes beliefs such as the now-common ideas that religious people pray to the same God even if he goes by different names, that "meaning and purpose come from becoming one with all that is." It also embraces a version of karma—the belief that doing good brings good and doing evil brings evil.

Secularism places a premium on science and rationalism and looks at the material world as "all there is." This worldview focuses on what can be experienced and earned in this life through our efforts.

Postmodernism rejects the idea of objective, absolute truth. It holds that "claims on ultimate reality are subjective by virtue of their context—that is, we are all limited by our experience, and at best we can know only what is true for ourselves." When people talk about "your truth" and "my truth," they are crudely expressing this idea. Postmodernism now also focuses on how the metanarratives (overarching views of reality) of some people oppress others and fail to account for their unique experiences. This ends up emphasizing the destructive roles of capitalism, maleness, and whiteness particularly. Here are some key survey items Barna uses to measure postmodernism: "No one can know for certain what meaning and purpose there is to life. ... What is morally right or wrong depends on what an individual believes. ... If your beliefs offend someone or hurt their feelings it is wrong."[38]

Finally, Marxism emphasizes that private property is not only destructive but encourages greed and other sins and should be eliminated. Marxism encourages the expansion of government over private businesses to redistribute and equalize wealth. It is also explicitly and strongly hostile to religion.[39]

Barna has been warning for years that solid, competent, faithful adherence to the Biblical Worldview is fading among evangelical Christians as well as among professing, practicing Christians more generally. Outside a Biblical Worldview, the ones that hold the most attraction to practicing Christians[40] are New Spirituality and Postmodernism. From the Secularism worldview, many are attracted to being materialistic—that is, finding meaning and purpose in material success.[41]

Interestingly, Barna finds what attracts Christians the most tend to be perspectives that have the most affinity with MTD. It is easy to see how a Christianity compromised by these ideas would embrace sexual liberalism. A god that wants to serve people and make them happy and successful; relativism; viewing established teaching and authorities (particularly those seen as tainted by their gender, ethnicity and "privilege") as inherently suspect; emphasizing subjectivity and personal experience as means of knowing truth; enjoying life in the here and now—these are all consistent with MTD as well as to worldviews such as secularism, the new spirituality, and postmodernism. All of them are used to justify and accept fornication and, increasingly, aberrant views on sexual orientation and identity.

Barna is now, in addition to other hats he wears, the director of research at the Cultural Research Institute (CRI) at Arizona Christian University. Through this entity, in 2020 he released a series of research briefs on worldview issues starting in the early spring into the fall, based on a new instrument called the American Worldview Inventory (AWVI). These were based on data collected using the AWVI with a national sample of two thousand adults (half by telephone and half online), which CRI expects to be the first in a series of annual surveys based on this instrument.[42]

Barna and his associates found that only 21 percent of adults who attend evangelical churches, which "teach that the Bible is the word of God and is reliable and trustworthy in all matters," hold a biblical worldview. Only 19 percent who called themselves born-again Christians"—believing they will go to heaven "only because they have confessed their sins and have accepted Jesus Christ as their savior"[43]—do so. Startlingly, only 16 percent of those that Barna identified as charismatic or Pentecostal held a biblical worldview.[44] Among those who believe that the Bible is the inerrant word of God—a view held by 74 percent of evangelicals and 78 percent of Pentecostals—only 14 percent have a biblical worldview. Among those who describe the Bible as "inspired" by God but containing errors, the latter percentage drops to 2 percent.[45]

Things do not get much better when we dive into the details. Table 6–1 samples some key AWVI findings by category.[46] This includes percentages for those that Barna and his associates identify as evangelicals, as well as those they designate as Pentecostal or charismatic.

Given what we see in Table 6–1, we should not be surprised at what we have found out about evangelical sexual beliefs and behavior in the previous three chapters of this book. Much of it fits the idea of MTD. Thus, we are not surprised to find in another AWVI report that most evangelicals, and a bit over 40 percent of Pentecostals, did not believe that having sex with someone you loved and planned to marry was morally wrong.[47] Obviously, this applies to not only singles struggling with sexual temptation but the parents, peers, fellow church members, and others advising them.

TABLE 6–1: PERCENT *REJECTING* SELECT
BIBLICAL TEACHINGS, EVANGELICALS
AND PENTECOSTALS (*AWVI 2020*)

Worldview Stance	Evan-gelical	Pente-costal
Christ		
"When Jesus Christ was on the earth he was fully human, but he did not sin."	43%	44%
The Holy Spirit		
"The Holy Spirit is not just a symbol of God's power, presence, or purity, but is a real, influential being."	58%	66%
Purpose		
"Success is consistent obedience to God."	53%	48%
Human Nature		
"People are not basically good; we are sinners."	75%	76%
Sin and Salvation		
"Which faith you embrace matters as much or more than simply having some faith."	62%	71%
"People cannot earn a place in Heaven by being good or by doing enough good works."	58%	49%
"[I am] personally certain to have eternal salvation only because [I] have confessed sins and confessed Christ as savior."	28%	45%
The Source and Nature of Truth		
"There are absolute moral truths that apply to everyone all the time."	46%	63%
"God is the basis of truth."	72%	70%
"The Bible is the primary source of moral guidance."	42%	38%
Abortion and the Sacredness of Human Life		
"Human life is sacred."	40%	54%
"The Bible is ambiguous in its teaching about abortion."	44%	49%

Let us consider the topics addressed in Table 6–1 in order. I will occasionally bring in findings provided in other reports from the AWVI and insights from the GSS.

Beliefs about God. Evangelicals seem to be certain about God's existence. We find in the GSS, combining years 2006 through 2018, that 82 percent say that they know he exists, while another 12 percent do but admit to having some doubts. However, the data in Table 6–1 suggests some terrible errors, if not outright heresy, in the beliefs that many evangelicals have about God. Logically, as Barna notes, given what they tend to believe about human goodness, they have elevated humankind while humanizing Jesus and demoting the Holy Spirit.[48] It is no wonder that so many evangelicals set aside God's condemnation of fornication, placing their own "needs" and ideas above God's moral commandments and believing that, in doing so, they make him happy by making themselves happy.

Over 40 percent have a grossly deficient understanding of the Christ they are called to imitate and trust in. This has real ramifications. Evangelicals and Pentecostals either believe that they are called to imitate a God-made man who was at least to some extent sinful, like we are, or they do not believe that our lives should be modeled after Christ. This leads to many deficiencies of understanding in areas we often encourage those facing sexual temptation to rely on. It is no wonder that we see terrible actions rooted in shallow ideas of "What would Jesus do?" (WWJD).

Much Christian strength and hope come not only from trusting in the atonement Jesus made for our sins at the cross but in his imputed righteousness—the merit of his perfect obedience transferred to us. As R. C. Sproul said, "He lived a perfect life of obedience and fulfilled the law for those who put their trust in Him."[49] The power and sufficiency of Jesus's sacrifice on the cross is rooted in his perfection. Jesus was the perfect sacrifice, a willing lamb without spot or blemish. How can evangelicals rely on an imperfect Christ to help, and inspire, them to overcome the powerful temptation of indwelling sexual sin? The answer is they cannot.

We also rely on the indwelling power of the Holy Spirit for real sanctification in the areas of sexual desire as in every other aspect of sin. The Spirit strengthens us; he also convicts us of sin and affirms to us the truth found in God's word (John 16:7–10; see also Ephesians 4:30). The apostle Paul emphatically connected living by the Spirit, being led by the Spirit, as essential to overcoming the flesh, putting to death our sin, and being able to gratefully recognize and rejoice in God as our Father (Romans 8:1–16). Yet we see that most evangelicals and Pentecostals have a heretical view of the Holy Spirit, one which denies him as a distinct Person.

In fact, combined with what we have seen they believe about the incarnate Son, many evangelicals' beliefs about the Trinity are grossly deficient. As Barna notes, many evangelicals "have non-biblical views about the Christian Trinity." To many, Jesus is a sinful man, and the Holy Spirit is just a symbol.[50] If this is true, neither is fully God. As we saw in chapter 1, a basic, orthodox understanding of the Trinity is helpful, if not essential, to having a Christian understanding of marriage, and with it, sex, which reflects the fruitful union of the three Persons who are together our one God.

Beliefs about our purpose in life. In terms of the purpose of their lives, roughly half of evangelicals and Pentecostals do not measure their personal success in terms of obedience to God. In another report, Barna and his associates had 43 percent of evangelicals and 49 percent of Pentecostals say they would *not* affirm that the universal purpose of human beings is to "know, love, and serve God."[51] To be sure, over 90 percent of evangelicals, and almost as many Pentecostals, believe that they have "a unique, God-given calling or purpose,"[52] which is good. However, many do not see this as integrally tied to obeying and serving God in all that he commands. In the face of cultural pressure, personal temptation, and opportunity, many evangelicals simply do not have a foundation that encourages them to set aside their fleshly desires in order to obey and please God, or to even believe that they should try their best, by his grace, to do so. God is simply not first in their lives. They are.

I also looked at a powerful item in the 2008 and 2018 GSS, which asks for a response to this statement: "To me, life is meaningful only because God exists." This summarizes in key ways the central point of Ecclesiastes, and it is clear that its author would have "strongly agreed." Unfortunately, that was true of only 40 percent of evangelicals. In fact, 29 percent did not agree with this statement at all, and 14 percent disagreed with it. If God is not our ultimate source of meaning, if our lives are not truly "hidden with Christ," how motivated are we to "put to death ... what is earthly in" us, including "sexual immorality, impurity, passion, evil desire, and covetousness" (Colossians 3:3–5)?

Beliefs about sin and salvation. In reaching out to believers about fornication, as with every other sin area, we generally want them to have a clear idea of the exclusive claims of Christ upon them. We hopefully teach them that they should honor him with their bodies not as one possible means of salvation, but in a grateful response for what they have been freely given in Christ and in recognition of the subsequent claims God now has on them as their Lord (1 Corinthians 6:20).

Yet what emerges in the AWVI is that evangelicals and Pentecostals have a muddled picture of sin and salvation. Over

60 percent of evangelicals and over 70 percent of Pentecostals reject the idea that true Christianity is the only faith that ultimately matters. Most evangelicals and about half of Pentecostals believe that one can earn heaven through good works. Given the percentages here, at least some believe the latter two things while also holding to the orthodox belief that they themselves are only saved by God's gracious forgiveness of their sins.[53] Clearly, many of those in our evangelical or Pentecostal churches do not have a clear understanding of the gift we have received and what those who have been blessed by it owe in obedience to the one who gave it to us—our Creator God. This gift provides the motivation that enables us to desire, from our hearts, to resist sin, including sexual lust. How can we ask believers who do not understand saving grace at all to reject cheap grace and embrace costly grace?

Elsewhere in the AWVI, we find that 85 percent of evangelicals and 82 percent of Pentecostals agreed with the following statement: "You consciously and consistently try to avoid sinning because you know your sins break God's heart."[54] That motivation is in many ways laudable in that it at least views sin as something that offends God and prioritizes pleasing him. Yet it is offset by, for example, the works-salvation idea we have already seen. It is in the grateful acknowledgement and receiving of salvation, really appreciating it, that we find motivation to search out his will for our lives and by which we seek to live a life worthy of what God has called us to (Ephesians 4:1). Further, what does that mean when we have no clear way to understand just what sin is and what specific sins are?

Beliefs about human nature. Most evangelicals have an inflated perception of human nature, one that is not only at odds with a lot of clear biblical teaching but makes man bigger and God smaller. This compounds the problems caused by an unclear understanding of sin and salvation. For example, if we think we are "basically good" but just damaged in some ways, we can do works that are ultimately and truly good on our own efforts. Moreover, our sinfulness becomes something done to us rather than what we are, in essence, apart from Christ. However, those who know that they came to Christ "dead in the trespasses and sins" (Ephesians 2:1) are more grateful for what they have been freely given and cling to Christ even more. Those who have an elevated view of human goodness are going to be more willing to trust their own judgments and feelings rather than to have a healthy mistrust of their own reason and emotions. Believing that "I am basically good, just a little messed up" is antithetical to a gospel understanding and living—continually turning to Christ in repentance and faith, trusting in him and not ourselves—which is the only way to overcome sexual temptation.

I was not surprised at what the AWVI revealed here. Over many years of teaching, I have had the opportunity to straw poll hundreds of evangelical college students about human nature. Given the basic options, most select "people are basically good."

In reflecting on this finding, I was reminded of a pivotal moment when I was a very young believer in the mid-1970s in the Jesus Movement. During "testimony time" at our large mid-week Bible study and worship, I rose to share about how Jesus had taught me that day, through an incident at work, that "all people were basically good." The response was polite but deadly silent. After the meeting, an older believer took me aside, Bible in hand, and kindly but firmly showed me why Jesus could have never told me that, since it was contrary to his word. It did not take him long to identify numerous clear passages in both Testaments detailing the depth and scope of our inborn fallen natures, what that meant regarding the state of our hearts, and how this connects to the gospel and my desperate need for it. I praise God for that forthright, precious saint.

Beliefs about truth and moral decision-making. Almost half of evangelicals and over 60 percent of Pentecostals do not believe in absolute truth. Roughly 70 percent in both religious classifications rejected the idea that God is the basis of all truth. About four in ten in both groups did not believe that the Bible is our primary source of moral guidance. Note that, once again, all of this makes people and their autonomous judgment—whether through logic, emotion, experience, or some other means—and not God's absolute moral law, the fundamental basis of right and wrong. Of course, we have seen much of this human-centered moral reasoning in the previous three chapters.

Beliefs about abortion and the sacredness of human life. The latter two items in Table 6–1, which show 40 percent or more of evangelicals holding problematic views about the sacredness of human life and abortion as sin, are also relevant to the issue of fornication among evangelicals. First, as we will see in chapter 8, the fuzziness many evangelicals have about the morality of abortion has real, tragic consequences when unmarried evangelical young people, and those who are advising and pressuring them, are dealing with unintended pregnancy.

Second, going beyond the obvious abortion issue, how can we expect professed believers who claim that human beings are not sacred to believe that sex or marriage is sacred? Yet the sacredness of marriage and the marital act is basic to the biblical sexual ethic. This reverence governs how we relate to sex, our bodies, and to our potential sexual partner. Moreover, if human beings are not sacred, what does that say about our view of the God who made them in his image? How can those who claim that the lives of human beings are not sacred ever bow in reverence to the Maker who made them the crown of his creation and submit their bodies to his service rather than using them primarily to gratify themselves?

Generational worldview differences. One 2020 AWVI report overviewed those who were eighteen to thirty-six years of age—whom they identify as millennials—compared to those who were older. Although they did not look at evangelicals separately, the trend—that younger respondents are far less biblical—is almost certainly true for them and not just for everyone else. Thus, we can take the results I have laid out here and assume that, in working with younger evangelicals, the percentage holding to any aspect of a truly biblical perspective is lower. Besides, knowing the overall state of millennials is not only helpful to our outreach but to understanding what younger Christians are getting from their peers. Here are some telling, summarizing quotes from the report:

> Millennials are significantly less likely to believe in the existence of absolute moral truth or that God is the basis of all truth; to believe that human beings were created by God, in His image, and that He loves them unconditionally; pray and worship regularly, or seek God's will for their lives. Yet, Millennials are significantly more likely to wonder if God is really involved in their life, to believe that human life has no absolute value and to believe that having faith matters more than which faith they have.
>
> [Millennials] are less than half as likely as other adults to say that human life is sacred. They are twice as likely to diminish the value of human life by describing

human beings as either "material substance only" or their very existence as "an illusion."

A far smaller proportion of Millennials believe that people are basically good, but their view is unrelated to the sinfulness of humanity. Their perspective is simply that people are less valuable creatures, made neither in the image of God nor imbued with value due to their creation by God and being loved by Him. America's youngest generation simply accepts the existence of humanity without assigning any spiritual or innate value to the human race.[55]

I have compiled a sample of relevant results from this final report in Figure 6–1.[56] These do not bode well for the future unless we can turn things around.

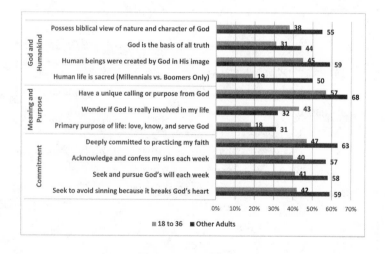

FIGURE 6–1: MILLENNIAL VERSUS OLDER ADULTS
ON KEY WORLDVIEW ITEMS (*AWVI 2020*)[57]

Evangelicals Holding the Line

Is the reality this bleak? What about the many great young people and youth programs so many of us have undoubtedly encountered? The answer, thankfully, is that all the news out there is not bad. Within the ranks of modern evangelicalism are parents, churches, schools, and institutes working with young people, with some degree of success, to impart a more biblical worldview.

One organization that seeks to assist particularly educators, and to track their results, is the Nehemiah Institute. Its PEERS test is another worldview measurement system. The core worldview it seeks to identify and support is "biblical theism," as opposed to moderate Christianity, secular humanism, and socialism. The focus of PEERS testing is more on politics, economics, social policy, and education than the AWVI. It is not administered to random samples but mainly to members of conservative Christian organizations dedicated to promoting a biblical worldview that opt in to have their students, faculty, administrators, or other workers tested to see how well they are doing. Homeschoolers also use it. PEERS has been available since 1987, and well over 110,000 respondents have participated in its testing program.[58]

I obtained the last ten years of PEERS data and separated out the 19,046 ninth- through twelfth-grade high school students and the 5,661 undergraduates at some conservative liberal arts colleges but mainly Bible colleges.[59] Most of these schools require a signed statement of faith from students. These respondents are on average much more conservative than their peers in the wider evangelical world.

As a result, the findings are much more encouraging than what we have seen in the works of Christian Smith, George Barna, and (for opinions on sex) in the GSS. I have provided a summary of key worldview items that are especially relevant to understanding the respondents' theology, views of the human person, and morals—including sexual ethics—in Table 6–2.

TABLE 6–2: PERCENT AGREEING AND DISAGREEING
WITH SELECT WORLDVIEW STATEMENTS,
CONSERVATIVE PROTESTANT HIGH SCHOOL
AND COLLEGE STUDENTS (PEERS 2010–2020[60])

Item	School	Agree	Dis-agree
Human nature, because it continually adapts and changes, has an unlimited potential for progressive development.	High School: College:	43% 42%	46% 43%
Because human nature is constantly changing, values and ethics will also change. Therefore, each generation should be free to adopt moral standards appropriate to their preferences.	High School: College:	9% 15%	84% 76%
All religious belief is strictly personal and should never be imposed on others, particularly on children.	High School: College:	15% 15%	76% 79%
Absolute truth exists in all areas of life and can be known.	High School: College:	79% 72%	14% 17%
An individual can share in the divine nature of God through many avenues other than a personal relationship with Jesus Christ.	High School: College:	13% 18%	83% 75%
Human life as a real and unique person begins at conception.	High School: College:	90% 84%	5% 8%

The concept of family, traditionally understood as father, mother and children (in marriage recognized by the church and the state), needs to be redefined to include other types of committed relationships.	High School: College:	7% 10%	88% 82%
Jesus Christ was, and is, both fully God and fully man, yet remains one person.	High School: College:	92% 90%	4% 6%
The Bible is meant to be a guide or an example to individuals, not an authoritative rule over lives.	High School: College:	20% 28%	74% 66%
All Scripture is inspired by God and is inerrant in every detail as recorded in the original manuscripts.	High School: College:	93% 92%	2% 3%
Because the Bible is inerrant in all areas, learning through science and reason must be understood in light of what the Scriptures say.	High School: College:	85% 81%	7% 9%
Each person has a soul which will live forever after the body dies. This soul will either live in happiness with God in heaven or in torment with the devil in hell.	High School: College:	93% 93%	3% 4%
Premarital sex is always wrong and should not be condoned by society.	High School: College:	90% 85%	5% 8%

PEERS data suggest that, at least in terms of worldviews and attitudes on sexual ethics, there is a subculture within the evangelical world that takes these matters seriously and does a good job imparting biblical theology, anthropology, and morals to contemporary young Christians. Other than the first item in Table 6–2 on human nature, a majority of both sets of students chose the most biblical and conservative options. There were still sizable groups with problematic views on matters such as absolute truth and evolving moral standards, but even accounting for differences in the content and wording of questions and statements, results shown here reflect more consistent biblical worldviews than the national results of the AWVI.

Having the actual data set also enabled me to determine if holding more biblical worldview beliefs in these key areas were associated with rejecting fornication. Not surprisingly, every single item in Table 6–2 was highly associated with the final item about premarital sex, with conservatism or liberalism in one predicting the same in the other. PEERS respondents as a whole, and for high school and college students separately, showed this same association. Views about fornication tend to be organically connected with other aspects of a biblical worldview, as we would expect them to be. For example, overall, 88 percent of those who strongly agreed that absolute truth exists also strongly agreed that premarital sex is always wrong, compared to only 71 percent of those who strongly *dis*agreed that absolute truth exists. And 82 percent of those who strongly agreed that Jesus Christ was fully God and fully man in one person also strongly agreed that fornication is always wrong, compared to only 66 percent of those who strongly disagreed with that statement about Christ.

The Relationship between Belief and Practice in Sex Outside Marriage

Our brief sketch of the status of a biblical worldview, which would in turn support sound Christian beliefs and actions, among various categories of evangelicals, is sobering. What we have discussed so far in this chapter is consistent with the attitudes about sex we saw in chapter 3, and with the sexual activities documented in chapters 4 and 5. We do not see evidence that evangelical believers are reliably guided by the theological understanding laid out in chapter 1, but rather, by the modern Western thought patterns reviewed in chapter 2.

Throughout this book I have affirmed that sex between unmarried adults is morally unacceptable. Above, we looked at the ways in which various theological and philosophical ideas and commitments can create an ideological framework accepting of sexual permissiveness, even among professing evangelicals. However, we have not considered whether, and to what degree, accepting the morality of premarital sex is associated with being more likely to engage in it and to be more promiscuous in doing so.

This has practical implications. If liberal ideas lead to liberal actions, then it is more likely that helping evangelicals have the right beliefs about premarital sex, as well as holding to other Christian doctrines that support the latter, will also help them to be morally chaste, to repent quickly when they fall, and so on. This makes a lot of sense, but we should never assume such things, especially if we have the data to test this hypothesis, which we do. The fact is that in social science beliefs do *not* always predict actions.

The data set for this is in the GSS. Figures 6–2 and 6–3 look at never-married evangelical Protestants ages eighteen to forty-four in the last twenty-five years combined.[61] The differences are highly statistically significant and do show that those with biblical beliefs about fornication are less likely to engage in it and vice versa.

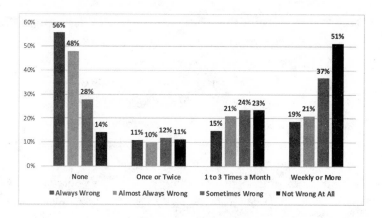

FIGURE 6-2: ASSOCIATION BETWEEN BELIEFS
ABOUT THE MORALITY OF PREMARITAL SEX AND
NUMBER OF TIMES HAD SEX IN LAST YEAR, AMONG
NEVER-MARRIED EVANGELICALS (GSS 1993–2018)

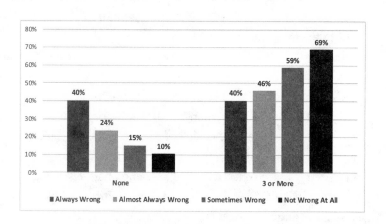

FIGURE 6-3: ASSOCIATION BETWEEN BELIEFS ABOUT
THE MORALITY OF PREMARITAL SEX AND NUMBER OF
OPPOSITE-SEX, SEX PARTNERS SINCE AGE 18, AMONG
NEVER-MARRIED EVANGELICALS (GSS 1993–2018)

This does *not* prove that having liberal sexual beliefs *causes* promiscuous behavior among evangelicals. It is almost certainly

true that the relationship goes both ways and that engaging in fornication will also lead people to become more liberal in their attitudes about it. Moreover, conservative sexual beliefs are not in and of themselves a panacea. Reality is complex. However, these two things—sexual beliefs and sexual actions— are strongly associated. Looking at Figure 6–2, among single evangelicals who believe that premarital sex is always wrong, 56 percent had not had sex in the past year, but among those with the most liberal views on this issue, only 14 percent had none while 51 percent had sex at least weekly. Meanwhile, looking at Figure 6–3, among those who thought premarital sex was always wrong, 40 percent had no sex partners since age eighteen compared to 10 percent of the most sexually permissive evangelical singles. Over two-thirds of the latter had three or more sex partners since age eighteen compared to only 40 percent of the most conservative group.

Conclusion

In this chapter we have seen, mostly through the lenses of Dietrich Bonhoeffer, Christian Smith, and George Barna, that the worldviews of many evangelicals are, in many critical ways, no longer consistent with the historic Christian faith. Rather, they are far more reflective of what Philip Rieff described as the triumph of the therapeutic, what Pitirim Sorokin diagnosed as sensate culture, and as David Riesman saw, a lack of a firm character at the core determined to affirm and live according to timeless principles rather than the shifting dictates of the moment. The characteristics of individualistic, expressive, self-oriented, relativistic, and instrumentalist ways of looking at morals emerge repeatedly. Mutual consent of the "victimless" and "harmless" activities of recreational sex, often justified by considerations such as relational commitment or respect, have replaced the awesome and difficult obligations of marriage as the context in which sexual activity may rightly commence.

Real repentance and renewal among evangelicals in the area of sex outside marriage will involve a lot more than teaching young people about the applicable biblical "rules." Their entire set of theological and anthropological assumptions needs to be brought into harmony with the whole teaching of Scripture as understood by generations in the established doctrines of the church for these rules to make any sense. There needs to be understanding of the nature and relationship of Creator and creation, the relative places of humankind and God, the nature and purpose of salvation, what it means to be in covenant with God, a Christian theology of the body, the nature and purpose of Christian marriage, the existence and knowability of moral absolutes, and the binding character of the moral law witnessed to in both Testaments. We must recapture a view of sex that is set within God's larger revelation of himself and his world, just as a fine diamond is beautifully protected and presented within skillfully crafted jewelry.

We also need to pay attention to the intricate interplay between belief and practice. Liberal sexual beliefs tend to lead to licentious sexual practices, which in turn beget more drifting and decline in those moral ideas. Even people with the best and most sincere beliefs will sin, but when people continue in and justify their sin, this tends to harden their consciences and open them up to deception and confusion (Proverbs 6:27; 28:14; Mark 4:18–19; Hebrews 3:13). Over time, the unthinkable becomes normal. Sin that is not repented of—even and perhaps especially when people redefine it as "a little sin" or "not a sin"— separates us from God (Proverbs 14:12; Isaiah 59:2; Micah 3:4; Ephesians 4:18; 1 John 1:8; James 1:14–15). In that state, believers are even more susceptible to both sexual apostasy and temptation. Like drowning people, they drag down those around them unless the latter are themselves exceptionally well prepared for these challenges. In this way, as Paul warned the Corinthians in 1 Corinthians 5, sexual sin and the toleration of it begins to defile the entire church: "A little leaven leavens the whole lump" (5:6).

Rejection of the clear biblical teaching from God, about sex or anything else, dishonors God. It expresses a lack of faith in him and endangers our souls. It is incumbent on all believers to grow in our salvation by drinking, with the kind of dependence of newborn infants on their mothers, the pure milk of the word of God (1 Peter 2:2).

In addition to understanding and combatting the influences of subversive worldviews, assumptions, and theological errors discussed in this chapter as well as in chapter 2, there are practical and social influences that make acceptance and practice of sexual immorality more likely. We need to learn about these things too. These factors are well-documented in decades of sound research in the social sciences. Wisely using, or responding to, them can help us to become much more effective in supporting those we serve in their difficult, uphill struggles against sexual deception, compromise, and temptation. Let's turn to that now.

SOCIAL INFLUENCES ON SEXUAL ACTIVITY AMONG EVANGELICAL SINGLES

Chastity is the most unpopular of the Christian virtues. There is no getting away from it: the old Christian rule is, "Either marriage, with complete faithfulness to your partner, or else total abstinence." Now this is so difficult and so contrary to our instincts, that obviously either Christianity is wrong or our sexual instinct, as it now is, has gone wrong. One or the other. Of course, being a Christian, I think it is the instinct which has gone wrong.

C. S. Lewis, *Mere Christianity*

Now young people face a social frontier of their own. They hit puberty around 13 and many don't get married until they're past 30. That's two decades of coupling, uncoupling, hooking up, relationships and shopping around. This period isn't a transition anymore. It's a sprawling life stage, and nobody knows the rules.

David Brooks, "The New Lone Rangers,"
The New York Times

Why would evangelicals, who may be in most respects orthodox and who identify with churches that officially embrace biblical teaching on sexuality, choose to turn away from such basic and important Christian moral teachings? What has changed in recent decades that has led to such a sharp decline—where violating these clear regulations is no longer the exception but has become a new norm among evangelicals?

Certainly, the influence of our culture, and the price we increasingly pay for resisting it, is part of the explanation. This is why I devoted chapters 2 and 6 to exploring these very things, including documenting the relationship between our beliefs about sex and committing fornication. Holding to a biblical sexual ethic is increasingly "odd" to our contemporaries. Ways of thinking about the self and sex that encourage what moderns now view as sexual liberation and authenticity have become part of the air we breathe. Our culture is one in which, as Mark Regnerus has noted, sex has become "cheap," in the sense that it is relatively easy to get and is seen by most people as less "costly" economically and socially than it was in the past.[1] Dennis Hollinger accurately summarizes our current situation:

> It is not easy to believe in and live out the Christian meaning of sex. Little around us upholds or reinforces its tenets and ethics. The meaning of sex is not buttressed by public opinion; the major carriers of culture such as film, art, or music; our major educational institutions; public policies of government; and increasingly even portions of the church. Embodying the meaning of sex derived from a Christian worldview goes against the grain of almost everything in our society and culture.[2]

Yet blaming the world—its pressures and seductions working on us to embrace sexual immorality—is not enough. If it were, how would we explain the faithfulness of so many of our predecessors in cultural situations that were far more challenging?

Some General Sociological and Biblical Insights

Both natural reason and the Scriptures teach us that the majority of people *want* to engage in sin. If we are honest with ourselves, we must admit that obtaining sexual pleasure, on our own terms, and making ourselves comfortable doing so, is inherently attractive. Accepting the ways of the world we live in and accommodating ourselves to obtain the rewards that come from conformity, while avoiding the negative repercussions we suffer for refusing to affirm modern sexual morals, sounds tempting. Recall what Jesus taught: ultimately it is not the external things that contaminate us but what so readily flows out of our sinful hearts (Matthew 15:11–20). What are these? "For out of the heart come evil thoughts, murder, adultery, sexual immorality, theft, false witness, slander. These are what defile a person" (15:19–20a). Christians have always had these powerful illicit sexual desires, but why are we acting on and accepting them more now than in the past?

Here, a powerful insight from a major sociological perspective on explaining "deviance"—often called social control theory—is extraordinarily helpful. Theorists in this tradition point out that in trying to explain why people deviate from the norms of social groups they are a part of, we usually start with the wrong question: "Why *do* people do that?" Control theorists say that the right question is: "Why *don't* people do that?" Or to put it another way, "What frees, or releases, them to act on these desires rather than those urges being curbed or channeled toward socially productive ends?"

To control theorists, most deviation involves select people doing what just about everyone would like to do under the right circumstances. This is consistent with what the Bible teaches about our sin nature and its power. Although the theorists fail to appreciate the innate, God-given consciousness and the willful suppression of this by sinful people that Paul described in Romans 1:18–20, they do assume that pursuing illicit pleasure comes naturally to people.

This certainly applies to sexual immorality. The person who chooses to sleep with his girlfriend is not having sexual urges pressed upon him that his chaste fellow church member does not experience. They both have these desires—one acts upon them, the other does not.

Once we can answer "What keeps people from doing that?" we are better able to see why people are succumbing. We are looking for what has damaged, neutralized, reduced, or eliminated those things that ought to have "controlled" those desires. Among control theorists, there is a general understanding that properly functioning society is designed to discourage destructive impulses, redirecting human energy toward positive outlets and goals—both by the restraints and guidance we put outside people and by the moral beliefs and strengths we instill within them. As a result, control theory emphasizes the importance of many things that Christianity encourages—stable families; attentive, firm but loving parenting; active membership in larger moral communities; social institutions that promote virtue; morally-grounded education, and the like. These include having and instilling right beliefs that encourage moral living and protect people from destructive ideas and temptations that lead them to act on harmful desires. Breakdowns in these positive structures, forces, and processes increase deviation.[3]

All of this encourages self-control. Social processes and institutions that impart self-control are central to discouraging deviance, according to social control theory.[4] This quality is also regularly lauded in the Scriptures as a fruit of the Holy Spirit (Galatians 5:23; see also 1 Timothy 3:2; 2 Timothy 1:7; Titus 2:12; 2 Peter 1:6) with warnings against people who lack it (see Proverbs 25:28; 2 Timothy 3:3).

Some social control theorists warn about "social pulls." Typical social pulls include enticements and pressures from wayward friends, social media "influencers," and others through mass media—film, popular music, and the like.[5] A similar idea focuses on "differential association," which emphasizes the power of peer influences—our tendency to conform to those we are closest to, for good or for ill.[6] Negative pulls and associations are most likely to become problematic when a person's surrounding positive forces and structures break down.

In the Scriptures, we find many admonitions regarding the pull of wayward associates and the words of wise counsel, including from parents, urging young people to avoid and resist them. The apostle Paul flatly said, "Do not be deceived: 'Bad company ruins good morals' " (1 Corinthians 15:33). Fostering good associations and avoiding negative ones is also urged in Proverbs 13:20: "Whoever walks with the wise becomes wise, but the companion of fools will suffer harm." And Proverbs 1:8–18 is an urgent warning to heed godly parents while avoiding falling in with companions who are given over to sin.

There is another insight from sociology worth highlighting: there is never just one explanation for complex social phenomena; there are always multiple factors at work. These forces interact with each other, directly and indirectly, in complex ways. There are no simple answers, no magic bullets.

Ultimately, people make choices. They normally do so freely, and they are morally responsible for their choices. When our explanations for why people engage in sexual immorality, or any other sin, fail to acknowledge this, they cease being valid insights into the forces shaping us. Instead, they become excuses, which stand in the way of true repentance and change. We can understand why someone has done something, or why for some people in some circumstances obedience to God's law is more difficult, and we can acknowledge those realities with compassion and humility. However, in all but the most extreme and unusual circumstances,[7] this must not lead us to deny moral responsibility. "But each person is tempted when he is lured and enticed by his own desire. Then desire when it has conceived gives birth to sin" (James 1:14–15a).

Factors Associated with Religious Belief and Practice

We have already seen that church attendance and high levels of commitment to faith are associated with lower levels of sexual activity among single evangelical Protestants in the NSFG. Importantly, it is not mainly becoming sexually active that reduces religious commitment, but the opposite. A 2004 review of empirical research on sexual behavior among adolescents found similar connections between church attendance and overall levels of religiosity with teenage sexual activity.[8] Large controlled studies by Mark Regnerus have also verified both.[9] As if that was not enough, I used controlled research to support the same conclusions about the value of: church attendance, using almost twenty years of GSS data; believing that the Bible is literally true; and being born-again.[10]

Mark Regnerus emphasizes a point I have also made in the last three chapters: just being associated with evangelical churches that emphasize conservative doctrines is not enough. Of course, this does not mean that doctrine and moral beliefs are not important (I have argued quite the opposite). We have seen how important honoring the Bible as true and authoritative is. However, the key elements have to do with a practical commitment to living out the faith in communion with others, applied in church and family settings. Yes, it has to be the right faith teaching the right morals. But without hands-on dedication and involvement in strong churches and families, it is all for nothing. It is in practically living out these obligations day by day that biblical beliefs are learned, embraced, and followed, even in the face of temptation and against the cultural tide.

Regnerus points to a core concept advanced in 1967 by the famous sociologist Peter Berger: "plausibility structures." These are "the networks by which beliefs held by individuals or groups are sustained."[11] They are like the structures that social control theorists discussed and like the strong families, churches, and parenting that the Bible encourages us to build and maintain. Regnerus provides a summary:

> Teenagers who are embedded in religious plausibility structures—usually by way of more active religious involvement and stronger religious commitments—are more likely to make sense of their developing sexuality in religion terms, using distinctly religious motivation to ride out the storm of the adolescent religion-sex culture collision. Forms of religiosity and religious sources of moral decision making, not particular religious affiliations, are the key religious predictions of sexual outcomes. ...

Nearly across the board, religious influence on sexual decision making is most consistently the result of high religiosity rather than certain religious affiliations. ... If you want to know what distinguishes youth who delay sex, who are less sexually active, and who have few lifetime partners, you must look beyond the particular doctrines they espouse, their denominational figureheads, and even any particular oath or attitude they hold, to how immersed they are in religious plausibility structures and how connected they feel to family and friends who are—for lots of reasons—committed to helping them effectively navigate adolescence and its sexual pressures.[12]

Note that Regnerus brings up connections to family and friends. These are also vital ways that young people's religious convictions are built, supported, and enforced. I will touch on the first of these in this next section, and then peer relations after that. Churches can and should work hand in hand with both.

Parenting and the Family

Parents and the family are by far the most important influences on the sexual beliefs and activities of singles, not only when they are teenagers and young adults but later on as well. Not only do they shape the consciences and restrain the behavior of their children, but they also influence religious commitments, provide moral teaching and examples, and play a major role in balancing and guiding peer relationships. There is no getting around it.

FAMILY STRUCTURE: DIVORCED AND SINGLE-PARENT HOMES

The connection between divorced and single-parent families and the higher risk of promiscuity in kids raised in those homes is well-established in controlled studies. The impacts are direct—for example, reduced supervision, loss of (in most cases) a consistent father presence in the home, conflicts tied to stepparent families and transitions. There are also indirect impacts, such as a significant loss of income, geographic transitions, disruptions in extended family and friendship networks, great stresses placed upon the custodial parents, and conflicts over custody and child support.[13] All of this fits easily within the social control theory model—the parenting and family influences that control deviation are not able to function as they should. Indeed, social control theory generally expects much higher rates of deviation among those from single-parent and divorced homes.

In controlled studies, children from divorced homes are not only more likely to begin having sex early, to be sexually promiscuous, and to have children out of wedlock, but they also suffer from a host of problems directly related to the divorce. These problems include low self-esteem, drug and alcohol abuse, delinquency, poor school performance, and weaker relationships with both parents.[14] Stepfamilies and cohabiting households do not typically fare better than single-parent ones; certainly none do as well as children being raised by two married, biological parents.[15] Cohabiting households are notoriously unstable situations,[16] particularly for children following a divorce,[17] and remarriages are more likely to end in divorce than first marriages.[18]

Similar findings continue unbroken in recent years, showing that married biological or adoptive households fare much better than divorced, other single-parent, step-, and cohabiting households in reducing risky, promiscuous sexual behavior and delaying the onset of sexual activity.[19] Virtually all literature reviews in articles dealing with this note the overwhelming volume of research connecting the lack of two married parents, directly and indirectly, with heightened risk of sexual promiscuity and its consequences. Comments like this are common: "Family structure is associated with many youth risk behaviors, such as sexual risk taking, substance abuse, and delinquency."[20] Here is a more specific statement, based on the literature:

> Over the past two decades there has been a large body of research substantiating the powerful influence of the family on adolescent sexual health behaviors and outcomes. In general, studies found that adolescents in married, biological two-parent families are less likely to engage in unprotected sex and early sexual initiation compared to adolescents from single parent, cohabiting stepfather, and married stepfather families. In fact, irrespective of whether it is a low, middle or high-income country, adolescents raised in single parent households have an increased probability of both early sexual debut and pregnancy.[21]

A common rebuttal to these concerns is that children are better off in a divorced situation than enduring a high-conflict marriage. That assertion is usually true.[22] However, most marriages that end in divorce are not categorized as high-conflict, and conflict often continues or even intensifies following divorce. The majority of children of divorced parents do not experience the end of a high-conflict home situation following the separation.[23] This leaves most children of divorce worse off.[24]

Another important issue is how divorces often proceed. The separation can be one part of a long train of multiple household transitions that children of divorce often endure.[25] Increasingly, we are looking not just at the impact of one divorce upon children but cohabitations followed by breakups or subsequent marriages that also dissolve, not to mention steady boy- or girl-friends of the custodial parents who "sleep over." In fact, in the United States today, over 8 percent of children experience three or more partnerships by their mothers by the time they are fifteen years old. In one international comparison, this was three times more common than the next closest nation (Sweden).[26] This kind of childhood was intimately chronicled in J. D. Vance's stunning autobiography, *Hillbilly Elegy,* and the film based on that book.[27] The effects of these multiple transitions on children are devastating, undermining their sexual health and safety in many direct and indirect ways.

Let's look at some data from the NSFG that will help us to see the impact of this even in the evangelical Protestant world. Figure 7–1 looks at teens and young adults in the NSFG.

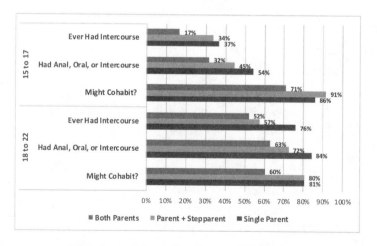

FIGURE 7–1: VARIOUS SEXUAL OUTCOMES BY FAMILY STRUCTURE AND AGE AMONG NEVER-MARRIED TEEN AND YOUNG ADULT EVANGELICALS (*NSFG* 2015–2017 AND 2017–2019 CYCLES COMBINED)

Figure 7–1 shows, in every case, significantly better outcomes for respondents living with two biological married or adopted parents versus other options.[28] Within each age group they are much less likely to have engaged in intercourse or anal or oral sex. They are also less likely to indicate they might consider cohabiting in the future.[29]

To look at the continuing relevance for those who are older, I looked at the GSS. Here, the GSS measured the family structure for each respondent from when they were sixteen years old. Again, this shows those from homes with two married or adoptive parents do much better. They were more likely to have had no sex in the past year and no opposite-sex partners since age eighteen, and they were less likely to have had sex monthly or more in the past year or to have had three or more opposite-sex partners since age eighteen. Moreover, when I controlled for race, education, Hispanic status, and household income, the role of having two biological or adoptive parents was still powerfully significant, for each of these outcomes.[30]

Finally, there is an interesting connection between growing up in a stable two-parent household and church attendance for never-married evangelicals. Among evangelicals overall—with sex, race, Hispanic status, and income controlled for—church attendance is independently and significantly associated with family structure.[31] Thus, those who had two biological parents were more likely to attend church regularly as adults, which as we have seen is also associated with less sexual activity among singles.

PARENTAL BONDS AND SUPERVISION

Key reasons for the negative impact of family disruption upon children are damage to the bonds between children and their biological or adoptive parents, and those parenting on their own finding it harder to adequately supervise their children.

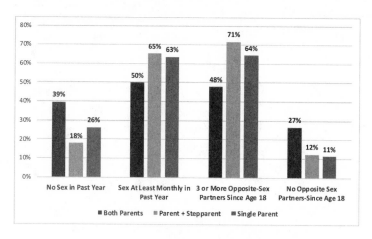

FIGURE 7–2: VARIOUS SEXUAL OUTCOMES BY FAMILY
STRUCTURE AMONG NEVER-MARRIED
EVANGELICALS (*GSS* 2010–2018)

This is worth highlighting. When parents fail to develop strong relationships with their children, or to properly monitor and supervise them, or, even worse, to develop a hostile[32] relationship with them, their offspring are more likely to become sexually active.[33] Another key element of good parenting is simply having high standards of achievement for one's teens. This keeps teenagers busy on positive activities. It also focuses their attention on achieving goals that sexual activity and problems related to it, such as unwanted pregnancy, could undermine.[34]

In fact, as Christine Kim of the Heritage Foundation asserts, "Parents, as teens themselves reveal, are the ones who have the most influence on their children's decisions about sex. Indeed, two-thirds of all teens share their parents' values on this topic."[35] The fact that parents directly impact teenage sexual decisions so much is important. Their intervention can help discourage sexual activity in the earlier years, where the risk for sexually transmitted infections (STIs) and unwed pregnancy—which can potentially lead to lifelong problems—are so high.[36] Their teaching and example also play a huge role in setting patterns for teens that will likely influence their adult lives.

Of course, all this works only if *both* parents disapprove of their teens getting involved sexually and clearly communicate this.[37] Many of us have known "cool" parents who tolerate and even encourage their teenage children's sexual activity. We may also be aware of situations where one parent approves of pre-marital sex and the other does not. There is good evidence that in such cases the outcomes—earlier sexual onset, more sexual partners, higher frequency of oral sex and intercourse, whether the young person has liberal sexual attitudes—are the same as they would be if both parents approved.[38]

In other words, when parents have strong bonds with their children; monitor their activities; communicate, agree upon, and enforce the right values about sex; have high expectations for them; and relate to them in affectionate rather than manip-ulative and hostile ways, teens are much less likely to become sexually active. Doesn't this describe a healthy home?

This helps us to qualify some of what we saw earlier about single- and stepparent homes. Many of us have seen or been a part of single-parent or stepparent families that do a great job with their children. We have also seen terribly run households in which the parents are the married biological or adoptive par-ents of all their children. It is possible in a less-than-ideal single- or stepparent situation to—with thought and effort—provide the children with the parental bonds and oversight that they need. It is harder, but many do it well. This can and ought to include, for divorced persons, making every effort to keep the noncustodial parent involved in the lives of his or her children and for ex-spouses to relate to each other in mature ways. For those who are married and raising their own offspring, this is wonderful but, in itself, not enough. The commitments of parenting, the self-sacrifice that is often required to focus energy on the children and to provide a healthy and orderly home environment, to monitor kids, and to set and enforce reasonable limits, is still critical.

We must remember that some married parents are facing challenges that are as, or more, difficult than dealing with single parenthood or blended families. Severe illness, long and unavoidable geographic absences, demanding work schedules, believers married to unbelievers with different sexual values—these and a lot more can make it hard for the best parents, married or not, to provide a disciplined, healthy, orderly home with regard to communicating and encouraging biblical chastity. For example, many military families face huge challenges, even when led by adults with great marriages. I grew up in a family that lived in three countries and five houses, attending six different schools in a seven-year period in a family of seven children. That was hard for my parents to manage, no matter how one slices it.

EARLY, SERIAL, AND INTENSE DATING

One of the most critical issues parents deal with is their children dating. This includes discouraging them from dating too early, guiding children away from seriously dating too many different people, or allowing these dating relationships to become too exclusive and emotionally intense when marriage is realistically too far in the future. I interacted with a woman recently who admitted that, despite both her and her husband being involved in solid conservative churches, their dating became exclusive and intense in high school, but neither could marry until after college. To paraphrase her, "We had sex constantly until we married years later." She is now divorced and sexually active, holds to evangelical beliefs including believing fornication is wrong, but accepts it as a "need" she has to fulfill, and she is no longer involved in the church.[39]

The first sexual experience is usually within the context of a dating relationship.[40] One recent literature review pointed out consistent support for this. For example, the authors noted that in the NSFG "about three quarters of young women and over half of young men report that first sexual intercourse occurred within the context of a romantic or dating relationship."[41] In the 2013 through 2019 NSFG, among never-married evangelical Protestant females who had ever had sex asked about their partner at first intercourse, 67 percent said that they were "going out with him or going steady," and another 8 percent said they were "going out with him once in a while." Those findings are not much different than never-married non-evangelical females who have ever had sex those in the same NSFG years, which were 65 percent going out or going steady, and 9 percent going out once in awhile.

The earlier young people start dating, the younger they are when they begin having sex. This should not surprise us. First, because dating is the context in which most Americans begin having sex. Second, because younger people are less mature and a lot more vulnerable.

Data from the National Survey of Children (NSC) conducted from 1976 through 1987 showed that 56 percent of boys and 36 percent of girls who started dating by age fourteen had sex before they turned fifteen. Only 15 percent of the former and 32 percent of the latter held off on sexual intercourse until they were eighteen or older. But for those who waited until they were seventeen to date, just 7 percent of males and 6 percent of females had sex before turning fifteen, while 63 percent of males and females waited until they were eighteen or older to have intercourse. Worse, females who started dating by fourteen were twice as likely to be forcibly raped as other girls—18 percent, or almost one in five.[42]

More recent data from a controlled study strongly verifies this connection. Both early dating and "going steady" greatly increase the chances that teens will begin having sex early. Of those who began having sex by age sixteen, half began dating first. As the authors dryly put it, "Overall, the odds of sexual initiation were significantly higher for youth who reported going steady by ages 13–14 than for those who were not dating."[43] What Regnerus says about this is common sense—dating more often places one "in situations that foster sexual activity."[44] In his research using the National Study of Youth and Religion, Regnerus found that dating several people in a short period of time is associated with having more motivation and opportunity to have sex. Thus, there is more of it. In fact, simply being involved in dating at all, rather than refraining from it, is associated with more sexual activity.[45]

Having larger numbers of dating partners also increases the chance of being subject to intimate partner violence as young adults. As Manning and her coauthors reported, "Greater dating experience is a risk factor for intimate partner violence."[46]

Having numerous dating partners is also at least slightly correlated with being sexually active as teens. One set of researchers found that while the average number of dating partners for those ages eighteen to nineteen was four, for sexually active respondents the same age, the average number was five.[47]

Peer Relationships and Media

PEER RELATIONSHIPS

Singles who have many sexually active and sexually permissive friends are more likely to become so themselves. Much of this is, as the old saying goes, "birds of a feather flock together." But much of this is also causal: being friends with peers who are sexually active and liberal rubs off. This has been verified in numerous controlled studies. When people who are sexually active form strong peer groups, their behavior becomes mutually reinforcing, and their involvement in such networks is likely to increase their opportunities and social rewards (such as status and praise) for having sex.

Boislard and her coauthors note, in a recent extensive literature review of studies on adolescent sexuality, that "with regards to peer relationships, numerous studies have shown that adolescents who postpone their first intercourse until later in life are more likely to have friends who also believe in delaying sexual intercourse."[48] Girls are more likely than boys to have peers who discourage sexual activity, while boys are more likely to have peers that pressure them toward sexual activity.[49] In some peer groups social status is enhanced by being sexual active.[50] An extensive synthesis of fifty-eight studies verified a strong relationship between peer influences and sexual activity.[51] Young people who become sexually active affiliate with others who are similar. But there is also a "socialization effect," where sexually active peers influence friends toward the same conduct.[52] The authors conclude: "Adolescents who perceived their peers as (a) more sexually active, (b) more approving of having sex, and (c) exerting more pressure on them to be sexually active tended to be more sexually active themselves. Similarly, adolescents who believed that their peers engaged in more risky sexual behavior were more likely to engage in such behavior themselves."[53]

One study looked at 2,436 adolescents, connecting what was happening in 1994 and 1995 to them engaging in sexual intercourse later, in 1996. This enabled them to see if coming into contact with sexually active friends led to this in kids. They found that having more sexually active peers in the earlier period was associated with abstinent kids beginning to have sex later: "In analyses controlling for gender, family structure, and romantic relationships, the higher the proportion of a youth's friends who were sexually experienced, the greater the odds of sexual debut. ... The odds also were elevated among youth who believed that they would gain their friends' respect by having sex." They conclude that if we hope to delay teen involvement in sexual intercourse, we must address not just their own beliefs about it, but we must also understand and tackle what their close friends are believing and doing.[54]

It is important to consider that the impact of peers on youthful sexual activity is connected logically to that of parents and family and to religiosity and the church. Positive church, parental, and familial bonds will help offset negative peer influences. Also, parents have much to say about their children's friendships and can guide them toward healthier friendships in many ways, including through involvement in church and community groups. Church, provided the congregation is cultivating positive peer groups, provides a natural supportive peer network for Christian young people. Church, parents and family, and peers are all ideally connected. The kids who are the best situated will have positive friendships and solid commitments to sound churches and fellowship groups, as well as healthy parental and family ties. This describes the kind of world my wife and I, and so many of our fellow struggling parents, have sought for our children.

MASS MEDIA

We are in a media-saturated environment drenched in sexual content, much of it not even mildly supportive of biblical chastity. When something is coming in from virtually all avenues throughout the day—television, Internet, books, magazines, billboards and other advertising—we know its influence is powerful and can almost feel it. Our access to the Internet alone, over the past couple decades, and with the advent of smartphones, has become ubiquitous. This makes studying the impact of media on sexual beliefs and activities quite difficult. It is coming from everywhere and evolving constantly.

By 2002, mass media had already become heavily sexualized. Sexual intercourse was depicted in one of ten television programs. All types of sexual content in television programs increased from around half to over two-thirds of programs in just the two years prior to 2000; teenage girls' and ladies' magazines rapidly expanded their sexual content, while negative consequences such as sexually transmitted infections and unwanted pregnancies were rarely shown in conjunction with all this sex.[55] In the wildly popular sitcom *Friends*, which is still widely watched in reruns today, the six main characters are depicted having eighty-five different sexual partners in just ten seasons. The most prolific was Joey, who had sex with seventeen different women, less than a quarter of which he had any kind of long-term relationship with, without contracting STDs or impregnating anyone.[56] To name another example, *Teen Vogue* recently published a guide for teenagers on the benefits, joys, and skills of having anal sex, with many experts and media pundits applauding it and denouncing critics.[57]

Research supports the claim that mass media's widespread depiction of sexual license does lead to great acceptance and practice of it, even among adolescents.[58] The relationship between exposure to sexual media and increased sexual activity and liberalism is mutually reinforcing—each leads to the other, setting up a vicious cycle that is hard to break.[59] As one prominent group of researchers noted, citing numerous sources:

> Exposure to sexual media is one of several factors that promote risky sexual behavior. Public opinion ... as well as scientific evidence ... suggests that exposure to sexual content in media is associated with early sexual initiation or progression of sexual activity, as well as the extent and timing of sexual intercourse ... and a range of other sexual behaviors. ... Exposure to sexual content on television (e.g., sexually oriented genres or specific programs) is also associated with expectations about sex, perceptions about peer sexual behavior, and permissive attitudes about sex. ... The relationship between exposure to sexual content and sexual activity can be characterized by a feedback loop: The more sexual activity adolescents engage in, the more likely they are to be exposed to sex in media; and the more they are exposed to sex in media, the more likely they are to have progressed in their sexual activity.[60]

Young people have regularly rated the media as a major way they learn about sex, along with parents, friends, and schools.[61] Parents restricting sexual media content significantly reduced this risk.[62]

An article reviewing nine studies on the impact of social media—including apps such as Instagram and Snapchat—affirmed that the media are now among adolescents' primary teachers about sex. Parents and peers are still important, but the media now surpasses all in providing information about sexual matters. As the authors note, these are not small concerns in a world where 95 percent of teens have smartphones and most access media daily and even continuously. In fact, as this article also details, a lot of sexual activity takes place online, not just through viewing pornography but by sex chatting, sexual role playing, users sharing nude images of themselves, and a lot more. There are very real concerns, and suggestive research, that aberrant sexual behaviors viewed in Internet pornography, such as incest, can seem normal to naive users repeatedly exposed to it. The authors of this review of the literature on the relationship between exposure to sexual content and adolescent sexual attitudes and actions claim that both old and new types of media may be considered a possible "sexual super peer" for adolescents.[63]

There is much we do not know about the impact of the constantly evolving media content and interaction upon our sexual beliefs and behaviors, including that of evangelical singles. What we do know ought to concern us greatly. This goes beyond the changes sexualized media might produce in evangelical singles' values and actions, important as that is. A lot of the content of online media is interactive, illicit sexual activity, contrary to what the Scriptures teach us about maintaining purity in our whole beings, including governing our thoughts and what we take in with our eyes (Job 31:1; Matthew 5:27–30). We all must be on guard against it.

Unnecessarily Delaying Marriage

Within the space of a couple weeks, in two very different settings, I had two passionate evangelical adults direct almost identical comments to me in response to my teaching and writing on high levels of sexual activity among evangelical singles. There were two prongs to both of their claims. The first was the main reason young evangelicals are having sex out of wedlock is because they are not marrying until quite late in life compared to even the recent past. They claimed this is a one-way powerful relationship—delayed marriage causes evangelical out-of-wedlock sex. It is unrealistic, both said, to expect evangelical singles to hold off until their late twenties or longer. The second prong was that this was entirely rooted in economic and labor market realities—low wages, high taxes, crushing student debt, long education required to get the best jobs, time necessary to establish careers. The church should therefore focus on alleviating these financial and occupational barriers to marriage and stop making young people feel bad about fornicating when they really cannot get married reasonably young.

There is a lot that these two people had right. In fact, in my last book I spent some time on the problems caused by unnecessarily delaying marriage among evangelicals in which I agreed that addressing the latter is key if we are to rein in the evangelical fornication problem.[64] However, at least as it applies to the typical young adult today, the idea that this is simply thrust upon people by financial and career realities outside their control and there are no other potent causes for delayed marriage is not true. The notion that delayed marriage is the main cause of fornication among evangelicals is also inaccurate. So, what is going on?

To start, we must recognize, as these two did, that the Bible is clear that marriage is a legitimate remedy for sexual temptation, as much as we also need to "flee from sexual immorality" (1 Corinthians 6:18) whether we are married or not. Recall that the apostle Paul said that "because of the temptation to sexual immorality, each man should have his own wife and each woman her own husband" (1 Corinthians 7:2). He quickly applies this even more explicitly to singles struggling with sexual desire: "To the unmarried and the widows I say that it is good for them to remain single, as I am. But if they cannot exercise self-control, they should marry. For it is better to marry than to burn with passion" (1 Corinthians 7:8–9). Remember too that, when the apostles suggested to Jesus that it would perhaps be better not to marry, he answered that this was only for "those to whom it is given," referring to various categories of eunuchs (Matthew 19:10–12). These statements are earthy, honest, realistic, and without condemnation. Our sex drives and desires are legitimate, and marriage is a sanctified, honorable way to satisfy them (Hebrews 13:4).

This does not mean we should rush people into an ill-advised marriage or one in which believers are not yet mature enough to succeed. Regnerus and Uecker urged devout Christians struggling with fornication to stop *unnecessarily* delaying marriage but not if that means forming potentially bad marriages:

> We have no interest in dragging immature men and women into marriages for which they are unprepared. (Although, to be fair, not all such marriages turn out bad. Most married people can look back and honestly admit they were not entirely prepared for marriage, but learned how to navigate and thrive within it.) Our point is more modest than that. ... We simply wish to encourage men and women who've met someone who is "marriage material" to think twice before rejecting the notion that they're just not ready yet. Life plans seldom develop exactly as adults anticipate and on the schedule they wish for.[65]

While believers wait for the right partner at the right time, God will give them his grace to maintain chastity. There is help available through pastoral counseling, the encouragement and prayers of parents and peers, and the ongoing means of grace found in worship and the sacraments. When these believers pointed out to me that pushing marriage too far out into the future for singles otherwise ready for it and who have suitable partners is laying an unnecessary burden on young people and separating them from the very godly remedy the Scriptures offer, they were right. Paul would agree.

Delaying marriage is a huge trend in recent years. When coupled with the decreasing age in puberty, it dramatically expands the period to almost two decades when young people are sexually capable and interested but not married.

I was born in 1956. That year, the median age at first marriage was 20.1 for women and 22.5 for men. In 1982, the year I was married, these ages were 22.5 and 25.2 respectively. By 2019, the median age at first marriage was 28 for women and 29.8—almost 30—for men.[66] Meanwhile, the average age of puberty, especially for girls, keeps dropping. For females in the U.S. it is now down from sixteen or seventeen years of age in the early twentieth century to roughly twelve to thirteen; some have set it lower. Boys now begin puberty around age ten, down from perhaps about eleven.[67] The normal range in puberty onset is eight to thirteen for girls and nine to fourteen for boys.[68]

We have gone, in about a hundred years, from a place where women could have babies only a few years before they typically married to this period expanding toward two decades. This lengthy gap between sexual awakening and marriage is unprecedented. It is a major factor in promoting a lot of the problems we see among singles—high levels of sexual activity, serial cohabitation, and other consequences associated with that.[69] Figure 7–3 shows that among married evangelical women—even those whose first marriages are still intact—the older they were when they got married, the more sex partners they had and the more likely they were to cohabit and to have had more than one cohabiting partner. All this is highly statistically significant.[70]

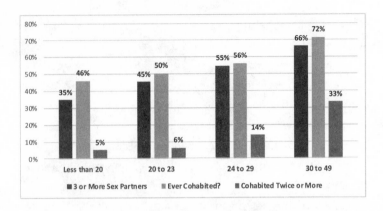

FIGURE 7–3: VARIOUS SEXUAL OUTCOMES BY AGE AT
MARRIAGE AMONG FEMALE EVANGELICALS IN
INTACT FIRST MARRIAGES (*NSFG* 2015–2017
AND 2017–2019 CYCLES COMBINED)

However, this is certainly not the sole or even main cause for
the skyrocketing acceptance and levels of fornication among
evangelicals generally and singles in particular. We have
already seen that there are many other factors. Moreover, this
explanation does little to explain or excuse the high levels of
teenage sex.

Taking it a step further, blaming all of this on financial
pressures and restricted or unstable job markets is insuffi-
cient. As I have already documented, we are seeing very high
levels of cohabitation, most not even involving partners who
are engaged or have firm marital plans. If young people have
the means to set up a household with a live-in lover and to
manage that while continuing in school, careers, and so forth,
they could do so if they were married. They simply do not wish
to make that commitment. Many couples who are engaged live
together while saving up for weddings, which now average well
over $33,000.[71] When singles cohabit to save money for lavish
weddings, it is hardly evidence that they are so burdened by

financial pressures that they cannot afford to get married before living together. When I have suggested that cohabiters saving up for a big wedding simply get married and then have a large celebration later if they wish to and can afford it, people look at me as if I were crazy.

Again, there are many young poor and working-class people who are struggling with low wages, high debt, and fragile employment that make marriage difficult. They may cohabit at least partly, and to a significant degree, because of their perceptions of future uncertainties. However, this is not a *general* reality. It is not what I am normally seeing with my college students and their post-graduation plans or actions to delay marriage but cohabit. In fact, one of my former students, a professed evangelical, just announced his new "domestic partnership" on Facebook this past week. He and his partner are well financially situated and in their forties.

Instead, many of the struggles of poor and working-class people to generate stable and sustainable lives that provide a better foundation for marriage are due to becoming sexually active, serial living together, and having children out of wedlock. It is easy to try to blame economics alone for all this, but that does not make historical sense. Things were far worse for young singles in the 1930s during the Great Depression, and yet we did not see this pattern of sexual activity, cohabitation, high illegitimacy even with high abortion, and so on. Trying to reduce everything to finances and labor markets ignores the dramatic shifts in morals and worldview we have already discussed.[72]

This argument also ignores the extent to which a culture of later marriage not only encourages sex outside of wedlock but is made possible by the widespread availability and acceptance of fornication, cohabitation, pornography, and other forms of illicit sexual gratification. For both men and women, there are alternative, less "expensive" paths to sex than marriage. Women can have sex with a man they find attractive but do not regard as "marriageable," especially now that the latter is defined to include a lot of desirable personal traits beyond the male being a steady, godly person, who loves them and is a reliable earner. Meanwhile, men can have sex without cultivating the kind of maturity, stability, and relational skills that they would need to be considered eligible and desirable marriage partners. Mark Regnerus makes this argument in *Cheap Sex*.[73] Males hooked on porn who play endless video games are not good marriage bets, even if they have high income and low debt. In short, the relationships among delayed marriage and fornication are complex.

To many young people today, marriage is something they want eventually but see as a loss of freedom, self-gratification, and autonomy.[74] Often, they have unrealistic, lavish ideas about how "financially set" they need to be to marry which, ironically, they do not see as issues preventing them from cohabiting.[75] Meanwhile, they report pressures from their parents and other authority figures to marry later given all the success they are expected to achieve before "settling down."[76] In the evangelical world, as Russell Moore has documented, this also means that many parents willfully turn a blind eye to the sexual activity of their twenty-something offspring even once they are in love with a committed, suitable partner. Provided they do not have to think about it too much, overlooking the fornication makes it easier for them to press their children to continue delaying marriage.[77] When I was teaching a mixed group of parents, pastors, and youth a few years ago, a young single person respectfully confronted his elders directly about this: "You demand that we accomplish all these things before we can marry, which means we have to wait until we are in our thirties to settle down. But you also demand that we not have sex. This is not fair."

Some of the advice from older people is rooted in a misguided interpretation about the divorce dangers of early marriage. The risk of divorce is high for those married as teens, but from about age twenty-one on, waiting longer does not dramatically improve chances of success, while it does introduce a lot of other problems.[78] This misperception actually leads many people to view two people getting married in their early twenties as irresponsible, almost immoral.[79] I have even seen well-meaning evangelical professors tell students that they need to push marriage way back in order to avoid a bad marriage or divorce.

Ultimately, sociologists say that moderns view marriage as more of a capstone than a foundation for establishing a mature and satisfying life. It is no longer viewed as necessary—one can share a household and even have children without it and will suffer no stigma. Gone is the idea of marriage as a "mutual help" within the struggles to become settled in our careers and build a nest egg together. Marriage's value is increasingly seen in terms of personal satisfaction, fulfillment, and status.[80] Access to sex and cohabitation outside marriage has made this appear viable. Delayed marriage is as much an effect as it is a cause for widespread sex outside of wedlock. When we see how Andrew Cherlin succinctly puts it, clearly this has strayed far from a biblical understanding of the purpose and place of marriage, including as the acceptable location in which sex and reproduction are to take place:

> [Marriage] has evolved from a marker of conformity (doing what every adult was required to do) to a marker of prestige (attaining a special status). Today, marriage

is a status young adults build up to, often by living with a partner beforehand, by gaining steady employment or starting a career, by putting away some savings, and even by having children. A half-century ago, marriage's place in the life course used to come before those investments were made, but now it comes afterward. It used to be the foundation of adult personal life; now it is sometimes the capstone—the last brick put into place before the foundation is complete. … Two generations ago people got married *before* they had everything they needed. But cohabiting was not an option back then, so they faced the choice of marrying or not living together. Today, with cohabitation as an option, many young adults are postponing marriage until they pass the milestones that used to occur early in marriage.[81]

Here we see another mutually reinforcing set of factors—sex outside wedlock and dramatically delayed marriage. Each promotes and enables the other. As expectations harden around these things—that marriage *ought* to come in our late twenties and that fornication and cohabitation are morally fine—this becomes hard for evangelicals to resist, despite the clear scriptural teaching that marriage is to be our sexual outlet. As David Brooks notes in a quote I used in the opening of this chapter, the period from teenage years to marriage is no longer a relatively short transition. It is a new stage of life—one that is not institutionally anchored in the way marriage has historically been—where we make up the rules as we go along.[82]

Conclusion

In this chapter and the previous two, we have gotten a comprehensive understanding of the sources of our current scandalously high levels of sexual activity among unmarried evangelicals. These illustrate, in so many ways, the accuracy of biblical teaching in many areas—religious orthodoxy and commitment, the necessity of a whole and integrated theology, the importance of aspirations and goals, and the reality of the pressures of practical, everyday factors (be it the lures and tugs of our postmodern culture or the challenges posed by basic financial, occupational, and life realities).

In the next chapter, we will look at the real-world consequences for this on the people in our churches. Moderns like to believe that they have figured out how to separate sex from marriage and escape the negative repercussions of this that are built right into creation. They are wrong, and it is important, as we prepare to enact solutions, that we know how to communicate with grace and point them back to the truth.

As much as this type of knowledge can help us practically to order our lives better and live them in ways that will enhance our enjoyment and glorification of God, there is no shortcut to godly wisdom that can bypass our need to fear God, rely on him, know him personally, and keep that relationship with him active and vital. We must pray diligently and humbly for our own efforts, for the people we love and serve, and that we attain through patient and careful study true wisdom that will enlighten us and give us confidence to persevere: "The fear of the LORD is the beginning of wisdom, and knowledge of the Holy One is insight" (Proverbs 9:10); "If any of you lacks wisdom, let him ask God, who gives generously to all without reproach, and it will be given him" (James 1:5).

THE CONSEQUENCES OF SEX DIVORCED FROM MARRIAGE

Keep your way far from her, and do not go near the
    door of her house,
lest you give your honor to others, and your years to
    the merciless,
lest strangers take their fill of your strength, and your
    labors go to the house of a foreigner,
and at the end of your life you groan, when your flesh
    and body are consumed,
and say, "How I hated discipline, and my heart
    despised reproof!
I did not listen to the voice of my teachers or incline
    my ear to my instructors!
I am at the brink of utter ruin in the assembled
    congregation."
Drink water from your own cistern, flowing water
    from your own well.
Should your springs be scattered abroad, streams of
    water in the streets?

Proverbs 5:8–16

Be killing sin, or it will be killing you.

John Owen, *The Mortification of Sin*

Some years ago, when I was a young believer, I was delighted to see a young woman repent and give her life to Christ. Unfortunately, she eventually became enamored with an exciting, "fun" guy in her church who had a charismatic personality but whose Christian walk was extremely unstable, including ongoing sexual promiscuity and substance abuse. Their relationship became serious and sexual, but none of her friends or family could dissuade her from it. This very quickly led to pregnancy, "resolved" by a hasty marriage. After several children and numerous attempts to make the marriage work, things fell apart. Her children—growing up amid chaos and without the steady presence of a godly father—have all gone on to have out-of-wedlock children, cohabitation, broken marriages, and a great deal of relational instability. At the time all this began, there was no history of this in the woman's own family.

This sister in Christ follows the Lord still. She was faithful to her marriage vows and did her best to be a good wife and mother despite the challenges. God has blessed her and her children in many ways. He has carried her through these challenges and will continue to do so. Yet the consequences of her initial foray into an extended period of unrepentant sexual activity outside of marriage, once unleashed, were awful and undeniable. Her later repentance restored her relationship with Christ but did not negate the negative effects on her and her children, and even her grandchildren. The repercussions will likely continue for many more years in multiple generations.

This story may sound dramatic, but accounts such as this are not all that unusual, as many of us have witnessed personally and as many pastors and Christian counselors have seen in their ministries. I could easily provide many more examples, some far more unsettling.

It is long past time for us to be honest about the extent of sexual unfaithfulness in evangelical churches and the consequences of it. Doing so does not need to be self-righteous, or finger-wagging, or trying to pursue some kind of "scared straight" approach. The Bible is honest about the risks we take and the prices we pay for disobeying God's commands and violating the created order. For example, consider the earthy, practical, urgent warnings about the dire risks of sleeping with married women in Proverbs (6:32–35; 7:21–23). It is not unspiritual to acknowledge and avoid the practical consequences of sin as part of our motivation for avoiding sin.

It is necessary that we face these risks and consequences fairly. The alarm must be sounded whether it is heeded or not (Ezekiel 33:1–6). As the church undertakes renewal and repentance in the area of fornication, part of our task is to redemptively address the damage caused by sexual licentiousness. That means identifying what, and how much, fallout there is. Loving God and our fellow saints requires it.

In this chapter we will consider the practical consequences of sex outside marriage. These will be elaborated in three areas—children, personal health, and future marital and family success. In the context of personal health, we will also consider condoms, comparing popular myths with facts. As we shall see, the negative effects become more likely and damaging the earlier young people begin having sex, the more partners they have, and the more often they engage in it. Cohabitation also brings some unique realities into play beyond those of fornication alone.

To be sure, there are spiritual repercussions as well. Consciously and willfully continuing in unrepentant sin leads to alienation from God (Isaiah 59:2; Ephesians 5:5), spiritual anemia (Proverbs 28:9), spiritual death (Matthew 5:27–30; 1 Corinthians 6:9–10; James 1:15; Revelation 21:8), personal defilement (Matthew 15:19–20a), spiritual depression and the absence of joy (Psalm 32:3–4; 51:8, 12), and punishment from God (1 Thessalonians 4:3–6). It eventually means going from bad to worse and beyond (Romans 1:24–32). It undermines the good we have otherwise done (Ecclesiastes 10:1). And it does so no matter what we tell ourselves, or what our culture convinces us to think, about such sins being trivial compared to "really bad" things we might do. As we have already noted, God takes *all* sin seriously and treats sexual immorality as a grave offense against him, his created order, and even our own bodies (1 Corinthians 6:18). Tolerating it in the church as a whole undermines our witness and exposes us to the legitimate charge of hypocrisy when we overlook this sin while confronting, for example, homosexuality.

In terms of what is of ultimate significance, the spiritual consequences are more to be feared than the practical ones. Separation from God is worse than an unplanned pregnancy, no matter how we calculate the seriousness of both from a temporal perspective. However, the aim of this chapter is to look at the physical, personal, and social effects.

Children

OUT-OF-WEDLOCK PREGNANCY AND BIRTH

The Scriptures are clear that God's ideal is for children to be born to married men and women. The fact that sexual intercourse—the normal path to procreation, especially when the Bible was written—is restricted to marriage implies this. We also see teaching in the Old Testament's restrictions on those born illegitimately (Deuteronomy 23:2). This discouraged sex outside of marriage and encouraged men to be responsible to marry women they had gotten pregnant. The author of Hebrews strongly implies that illegitimacy is an undesirable state, separating children from the guidance and love of their fathers (12:8). The Lord even engineered the birth of Jesus to provide for him a married mother and father (Luke 3:23). We do not find any examples in Scripture of out-of-wedlock birth treated as a positive thing (for example, Genesis 19:36–38; Judges 11:1; Zechariah 9:6).[1]

We see from social science that, on average, children born out of wedlock do worse in every area of life compared to those born to two married parents. We overviewed some of that research in the last chapter when discussing the impact of divorced and single-parent homes on children. Anything that leads to out-of-wedlock birth hurts children. This does not doom them to failure, but it certainly makes it much harder for them to be successful and healthy relative to their peers who were raised in married households.[2]

Out-of-wedlock birth creates great difficulties for the mothers as well, especially when they are young. Authors of a major government-funded study of maternity homes noted that teens who become mothers often come from difficult backgrounds, which in itself makes it harder for them to succeed. However, their lives are often made much harder, their problems more intractable, and the damage more intergenerational, by having children out of wedlock:

> The majority of teenagers who become pregnant are from disadvantaged backgrounds, and early pregnancy and childbirth create additional challenges. These teen parents and their children struggle with difficult

circumstances in the short term and throughout their lives. The problems facing pregnant and parenting teens are well-documented. Teen mothers tend to be very poor, and more are single parents. ... Pregnancy can interrupt teens' educational pursuits and early employment experiences. ... The negative outcomes associated with teen pregnancy, including lifelong poverty and lengthy spells on public assistance, can follow mothers and children for the rest of their lives. ... The daughters of teen mothers often become teen mothers themselves, with all the accompanying negative outcomes, thus perpetuating the intergenerational cycle of poverty and disadvantage.[3]

Some research has suggested that negative impacts of childbearing on teenage women are due to disadvantages that existed prior to the pregnancy, such as poverty and other dysfunctions in the home that are more common in the experience of teenagers who become pregnant. However, plenty of data show that the difficulties of teen pregnancy are still more likely even when background disadvantages are controlled for. Well-documented deficits include dropping out of high school and being less likely to marry and more likely to have more children out of wedlock. Even when young single mothers do marry, their marriages are less likely to succeed. If they marry young in response to the pregnancy, they are much more likely to end up divorced.[4] In fact, noted family sociologist Andrew Cherlin points out that, all things considered, the relative position of middle-class women is hurt more by having babies young and out of wedlock, compared to age peers who are already poor and otherwise disadvantaged.[5]

The woman I described at the beginning of this chapter was from a well-educated, middle-class home and in college;

her pregnancy and subsequent marriage to the father led her to abandon her degree. Subsequent problems led to her being on various forms of public assistance. We have all seen cases like this. These negative outcomes are not inevitable, just more likely. I have seen similar cycles repeatedly in the lives of women, including former students who had children out of wedlock. God has worked redemptively even then, and their children's lives—like those of all little ones (Matthew 19:14)—are still beautiful and of infinite value. Many women and their children in these situations do succeed by diligence, focus, extraordinary effort, and God's grace. Often, they get great support from family members, compassionate churches, and Christian ministries, as they should. Yet these are difficulties that could have been avoided if these women and the men they partnered with had practiced chastity.

The situation with out of wedlock births can be broken down into three components: fertility rates, pregnancy rates, and percentages of births that are out-of-wedlock births. We can start with fertility rates (births per one thousand) for unmarried women. As of the latest government data at this writing, this has been steadily declining, from 47.5 in 2010 to 39.9 in 2019. These declines have been particularly steep among teens.[6]

Fertility among unmarried women overall, and for teens, is highest among Hispanic and black respondents, lowest among Asians.[7] The overall birth rate has been declining for many years,[8] and unmarried births are no exception. The latter is a good thing in itself, although the overall drop in births, which is occurring throughout the developed world, does not bode well for the future.[9]

These lower fertility rates are associated with declining pregnancy rates, which combine all possible outcomes—live birth, stillbirth, abortion, and miscarriage—per one thousand females in designated age groups.[10] Pregnancy has been declining among American women ages fifteen to forty-four combined, and for every age group under the age of thirty. Teen pregnancy is especially dropping, which is, of course, great news. For example, the number of pregnancies per one thousand girls under fifteen peaked in 1988 at 17.8, but by 2016 was down to 2.5. For those fifteen to seventeen the peak was in 1989 at 74.8, down to 15 in 2016. Virtually all these girls were unmarried. And for those eighteen to nineteen, most of whom are unmarried, the peak of 202.1 in 1990 declined to 115.2 in 2016.[11] Data suggest that this is because of both increased use of contraception and, as we have already discussed, more teens delaying sexual onset—that is, waiting until they are older to begin having sex.

The third, less optimistic data set has to do with the percentage of live births outside of wedlock. Unlike the past when teens—particularly pregnant ones—were commonly married at ages eighteen and nineteen, teenage births today are overwhelmingly out of wedlock. In 2018, for those under fifteen, 99.8 percent were out of wedlock. At ages fifteen to seventeen, this was 97 percent, and for those eighteen and nineteen, 88 percent were.[12]

The percentage of births out of wedlock has skyrocketed over the past few decades. It shot up in the 1970s from 10 percent to 18 percent overall—6 percent to 11 percent for whites and 38 percent to 56 percent for African Americans.[13] It has risen sharply since then. The most recent percentages of births out of wedlock stand at 40 percent overall in 2019, with 70 percent of African American, 52 percent Hispanic, 28 percent non-Hispanic white, and 12 percent non-Hispanic Asian births being out of wedlock.[14]

How do things look for evangelical singles regarding out-of-wedlock pregnancy? Here, we turn to the last two cycles of the NSFG. We will focus on females, starting with the percentages of never-married evangelicals who have ever been pregnant in Figure 8–1. These percentages are astoundingly high. Among those ages eighteen to twenty-two almost a quarter of single evangelical females have been pregnant at least once, and for those twenty-three to twenty-eight, most have. Almost half of those twenty-three to twenty-eight have given birth, as have more than six in ten of women older than that. Digging into the data more deeply, we find among never-married evangelical women, 4 percent of those eighteen to twenty-two, 19 percent of those twenty-three to twenty-eight, 46 percent of those twenty-nine to thirty-four, and 47 percent of those thirty-five to forty-nine have been pregnant two or more times.

Looking at evangelical females who *have* been married underscores what a large issue out-of-wedlock birth is in the church. Of currently married evangelical women, 45 percent began their first pregnancy when they had never been married. Among those evangelicals who are currently divorced or separated, that figure is 55 percent. Among married evangelical women twenty-nine to thirty-four, 39 percent had at least one child born out of wedlock. That figure was 29 percent for those thirty-five to forty-nine.

What about never-married *male* evangelicals? Figure 8–2 shows the percentages who reported ever having impregnated a woman. Note that males are often less certain of being responsible for impregnating women, which helps explain why these percentages are so much lower than those in Figure 8–1. Still, the fact that over one in four single evangelical males between twenty-three and twenty-eight at least had reason to believe they impregnated a woman is discouraging.

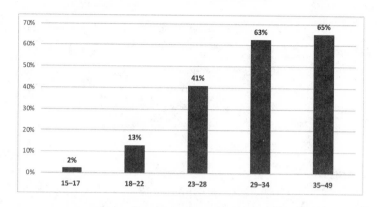

FIGURE 8–1: PERCENTAGES OF NEVER-MARRIED
EVANGELICAL FEMALES WHO HAVE EVER BEEN
PREGNANT, BY AGE GROUP (*NSFG* 2015–2017
AND 2017–2019 CYCLES COMBINED)

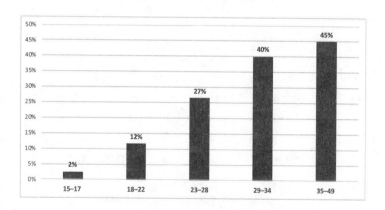

FIGURE 8–2: PERCENTAGES OF NEVER-MARRIED
EVANGELICAL MALES WHO REPORTED
IMPREGNATING A FEMALE, BY AGE GROUP
(*NSFG* 2015–2017 AND 2017–2019 CYCLES COMBINED)

ABORTION

Pregnancy only has a handful of possible outcomes—live birth, stillbirth, miscarriage, and abortion. If the child is born alive, the mother may choose to keep the child or give it up for adoption. The latter is not very common, not even among pregnant evangelical singles. For example, in the last two cycles of the NSFG, among never-married evangelical females who had ever been pregnant, only 2 percent gave a child up for adoption.

By all major forms of measurement, abortion has fallen steadily for decades—a wonderful thing. Rates per one thousand women ages fifteen to forty-four, the ratio of abortions to live births, and absolute numbers have all been dropping for many years, overall and among every age group.[15] Numbers of abortions reached a high point in 1990 at a little over 1.6 million and had fallen to a little over 874,000 in 2016; there were 862,000 abortions in 2017.[16] Abortion has fallen only partly due to pregnancy rates dropping, though that is a huge factor. We also see a decline in the ratio of abortions to live births. Fewer pregnant women are choosing abortion.[17]

Still, the numbers are tragic. When we acknowledge that each unborn child is a person made in the image of God, we should not be complacent with "only" 862,000 or whatever the exact number is now. This is, after all, equivalent to more than the combined populations of Cincinnati, Cleveland, and Dayton, Ohio. Consider the following: almost one in five pregnancies still end in abortion.[18] As of 2014, it was estimated that almost one-quarter of American women will have an abortion before they turn forty-five years of age.[19] As of 2016, among adolescents younger than fifteen, there were more than seventy abortions for every one hundred live births, for those fifteen it was about forty-six, for those sixteen about thirty-five, and for those seventeen and eighteen close to thirty abortions per every one hundred live births.[20] Pregnant unmarried women are much more likely to have abortions. In 2016, 86 percent of abortions were for unmarried women, and there were thirty-three abortions for every one hundred live births among them, compared to just about three and a half for pregnant married women.[21] A pregnant black woman is about 3.7 times more likely than a pregnant white woman to have an abortion rather than give birth, and a pregnant Hispanic woman is more likely than a non-Hispanic white woman to have an abortion rather than give birth.[22] The disparate application of abortion is perhaps the worst form of racial and ethnic discrimination in the U.S. In fact, early in the fall 2020 election season, over one hundred prominent African American pastors, officials, and attorneys called American abortion practices and Planned Parenthood forms of "systemic racism."[23]

How do evangelicals fare? Unfortunately, we have known for some time that abortion is more common among evangelicals than we would like to believe. It is one of the unspoken pathologies of the modern evangelical church.

Surveys of abortion patients found that 15 percent in 2008, and 13 percent in 2014, identified as evangelical Protestant. This was lower than the percentages of women who got abortions who were Catholics, mainline Protestants, and especially those of no religious affiliation. The evangelical percentages were half the national average, which is good news.[24] But the numbers of evangelical women obtaining abortions is still disturbingly high. For example, in the last two cycles of the NSFG combined, 24 percent of never-married evangelical women who had ever had a completed pregnancy had at least one abortion. That figure was 18 percent for those thirty-five to forty-nine.

Even in a confidential survey conducted by professionals, abortion is underreported, especially among those in conservative religious communities. The reality is likely worse and almost certainly not better than this sample estimates. In fact, solid research suggests that for the NSFG, female respondents report just a little over half of abortions that actually occurred.[25] If we take the percentages above and at least double them, as some competent scholars believe is reasonable, the reality of abortion in evangelical churches is devastating, no matter how much "better" we are doing than others. Nor does this consider those who play an ancillary role. We have women who have had abortions, others who helped them obtain abortions, and figures such as parents and boyfriends who encouraged or even pressured pregnant women to have them. All have objective guilt before God for what they have done, and many suffer psychologically as a result of their actions.

The true impact of abortion on evangelical churches is greater than most of us would like to believe. Knowing the statistics about this, I keep this in mind when speaking in college classes and churches on this issue. I assume that if there are more than a few women in the room, there is a very good chance that one or more have had abortions and that it is likely still a closely kept, painful secret.

Biological fathers are often neglected in discussions about abortion. While the legal decision and much of the emotional weight falls on women, the babies being killed are their children too, no matter what pretensions our culture advances to the contrary. We in the church need to recognize how many women in our midst are struggling with either strong temptations and pressures to have abortions or are postabortion. They need our honest counsel, based on truth and tempered by great compassion and empathy. But we also need to consider their male partners, especially when they too are under our ministry. Many men in our midst are struggling with the issue of whether to encourage pregnant sex partners to have abortions, or they have partners who have aborted their babies. They need ministry too.

Abortion always leads to the loss of innocent life. It is sometimes medically necessary, but rarely. There is much debate about the mental health effects upon women postabortion. The best assessment of the research literature suggests that women who have had an abortion have higher rates of mental illnesses of various kinds than those who did not and that, at least for some women, their abortions directly contributed to these problems. The likelihood of experiencing psychological aftermath is rooted heavily in social factors surrounding the pregnancy, the social pressures and reactions associated with her abortion, and the women's own perceptions of her abortion, pregnancy, and child.[26]

However, for Christians with orthodox beliefs on this issue, whether a woman is experiencing psychological problems rooted in her abortion or not, there is the need to address guilt based upon very real and serious sin. The abortion is often, but not always, heavily tied to her voluntary choices. However, there are quite often other guilty parties who need to be brought to a place of real repentance and healing as well—enablers and encouragers who pressured them—be they parents, peers, adult counselors, or so-called lovers.

CHILDREN RAISED IN COHABITING HOUSEHOLDS

There are numerous ways in which children being raised in cohabiting households are on average less likely to thrive and succeed. First, the relationships of the adult partners leading their households are less likely to be as healthy as those in marriages.[27] We saw indications of that in chapter 4 when we looked at cohabiting partnerships, even between professed evangelicals. On average, cohabiters are less invested in and committed to their partners.[28] They spend less time with them.[29] As we saw already, these relationships commonly break up without getting married.[30] Moreover, most cohabiters end up divorced if they do marry their partners.

There are variations that matter, of course. Children living with two biological parents who are cohabiting do better than those in the far more common situation where one of the partners is not biologically related to the children—what is commonly referred to as a "step-cohabiting family."[31] However, no cohabiting relationship is equivalent to marriage, for either the adults or their children. What are the problems?

The primary problem is instability. Where cohabiting relationships are stable and involve two biological parents, the children may have "*many* of the same ... benefits" as those in two married parent households, but that is not the norm.[32] As Isabel Sawhill notes, cohabiting relationships are "fragile."[33] Even in "progressive" European nations that have been on the frontier of normalizing cohabitation, the relationships are extremely unstable, even when they involve children. In fact, in Europe, less educated married families are more stable than highly educated cohabiting ones.[34] Here is how family scholar Wendy Manning puts it:

> Family stability is a major contributor to children's healthy development. A fundamental distinction between cohabiting and marital unions is the duration or stability of the relationship. Overall, cohabiting unions last an average of 18 months. From a child's

perspective, more children born to cohabiting parents see their parents break up by age five, compared to children born to married parents. Only one out of three children born to cohabiting parents remains in a stable family through age 12, in contrast to nearly three out of four children born to married parents. Further, children born to cohabiting parents experience nearly three times as many family transitions (entering into or dissolving a marital or cohabiting union) as those born to married parents (1.4 versus 0.5). ... The number of family transitions experienced by children in cohabiting unions has changed relatively little over the past 20 years.[35]

Family instability in turn leads to many negative outcomes for children. Even controlling for other relevant factors such as poverty and parental education, compared to those being raised in stable marriages, children in unstable homes have lower cognitive achievement and social competence, are more likely to be violent and aggressive, break rules which can include a range of actions regarded as destructive and delinquent, and are more likely to be anxious, depressed, and withdrawn.[36] The more family transitions a child experiences, the worse the impact.[37] Anna Sutherland says,

> Family instability is bad for kids. This generalization doesn't apply in every case—children stand to benefit when their mother kicks out an abusive ex-boyfriend, for example—but as a description of how the phenomena plays out on average, it is not subject to much dispute.[38]

Cohabiting households do not offer the same legal protections as married ones. The parental and related family relationships are not bound by the same institutional norms as marriage. For example, in a step-cohabiting household, are the parents of the nonbiological partner grandparents to the children? Are his or her siblings the children's uncles or aunts?

In recent decades, there has been a large expansion in the number of cohabiting households raising children. Between 1996 and 2014, the number of cohabiting couples in the United States raising children under eighteen increased by almost three times.[39] Most out-of-wedlock births are now to women cohabiting with the child's father. [40]Census data show that by 2019, about 8 percent of children under eighteen were living in a cohabiting household. That year, 34 percent of cohabiting couples were raising at least one biological child of at least one partner, compared to 38 percent of married couples. Raising children is now the norm among "middle age" cohabiters. For example, where the female cohabiting partner was thirty to thirty-four, 50 percent were raising a child, if the latter was thirty-five to thirty-nine or forty to forty-four, those percentages were 59 percent and 54 percent respectively.[41]

For children born to cohabiting parents, is this a temporary transition until their parents get married? Not usually. Not quite half will ever see their parents get married.[42]

So, what is the situation with evangelicals, cohabitation, and children? Once again, we can see by turning to the last two cycles of NSFG. Among evangelical women ages eighteen to forty-nine who have ever given birth, 31 percent have done so within a cohabiting union. That percentage is lower among those who are both younger than eighteen and older than forty-nine. For those ages twenty-three to thirty-four, it is 40 percent. Among cohabiting evangelicals ages twenty-nine to forty-nine, 57 percent of females and 53 percent of males had at least one child eighteen or under living with them.

Personal Health

SEXUALLY TRANSMITTED
INFECTIONS AND CONDOMS

The only real protection against sexually transmitted infections (STIs) is abstinence or restricting sex to a mutually exclusive relationship with one uninfected partner for life.[43] No health experts can argue differently. What liberal unbelievers object to is the idea that maintaining chastity is realistic. We as believers know that is what we are called to. We know that when those who have sinned sexually but repented move on to a faithful marriage in which both partners begin their union free of sexually transmitted infections, they should be as safe from these infections as anyone can be.

Out of all types of contraception, such as birth control pills, spermicides, intrauterine devices (IUDs) or systems (IUS), vaginal rings, diaphragms, surgical procedures such as vasectomies and female sterilization, contraceptive implants, injections, and patches—all of which help to prevent pregnancy—only condoms protect against STIs.[44] Ignorance about condoms leads people to believe that using them means that sex is "safe" from both pregnancy and STIs. With condoms, sex is "safer," but not safe, as even the most liberal sex educators admit. The more sexually active people are—in frequency and number of partners—the more the odds work against them. The Centers for Disease Control and Prevention (CDC) says condoms *reduce* risks.[45] They do not eliminate risks.

First, condoms work best on STIs that are transmitted through genital secretions such as HIV (which causes AIDS), gonorrhea, chlamydia, and trichomoniasis. They are less effective against STIs that can also be passed from skin-to-skin contact, such as syphilis, genital herpes, and human papillomavirus

(HPV). They also offer less protection against HPV-related diseases such as genital warts and cervical cancer.[46]

Second, even Planned Parenthood admits that, for preventing pregnancy, on average condoms have a 2 percent failure rate with "perfect use" and a 15 percent failure rate with "typical" use. The latter means that out of one hundred average sexually active women using only a condom to prevent pregnancy, fifteen will get pregnant in a year.[47] Of course, extend that out across several years, or increase sexual activity to higher levels, and it is not hard to see that "counting on" condoms to avoid pregnancy is risky, especially for people who have numerous sex partners. It is important to see that these failure rates are tied to risks for STIs and not just pregnancy. For example, if fifteen women in one hundred using only a condom get pregnant in a year, a lot more are being exposed to STIs.

Another myth is that oral sex is "safe" from STIs. Many young people believe that to be the case, though this claim is not true.[48] Although the risk of HIV from oral sex is very low, many other STIs can be transmitted this way. In fact, HPV transmission during oral sex is now a major cause of mouth and throat cancer.[49] The only protection—again not perfect—against this is using a condom for fellatio and a "dental dam," which is a barrier between the mouth and genitalia, when the much lower risk activity of cunnilingus is engaged in.[50] The latter is cumbersome, reduces sensation significantly, and is rarely used.[51] NSFG data suggest that using male condoms during fellatio is also not very common.[52] There are forms of oral sex involving the anus which have high potential for infection and would also need the use of a dental dam to lower the risk of infection.[53]

Anal sex is risky. Not only can other STIs, including HIV, be transmitted this way, but so can infections such as hepatitis, salmonella, and e. coli, not to mention parasites.[54] There is high potential for the skin to tear, increasing STI risk.[55] Using condoms in anal sex requires additional lubricants to reduce friction and breakage.[56]

Given the level of sexual activity, the degree to which our best preventative methods fail more than most think, and that these are often not used well or at all by singles having sex, we would expect to have serious problems with STIs among sexually active singles. At least among teenage girls, that appears to be the case. A landmark study published in 2009 based on biological data collected on females ages fourteen through nineteen in 2003 and 2004 found that 38 percent of those who had become sexually active had acquired one of five major STIs. The most common was HPV, followed by chlamydia. Many had more than one. Shockingly, 20 percent of those who had only had one sex partner had at least one STI, as did 26 percent of those whose medical information was collected the same year, or within one year, of their first sexual act. This means not only were the infection rates extremely high, but that this was true even relatively soon after sexual onset and even if these teenage girls had only one sex partner.[57]

STIs have increased in the United States in recent years. The most recent CDC data documents that rates of syphilis, gonorrhea, and chlamydia have been rising dramatically nationally as of 2018. All these were reflected in younger populations. In fact, among females ages fifteen to twenty-four, the rate of syphilis increased by a staggering 29 percent in the one year from 2017 to 2018; for males in this age group this rate increased 45 percent between 2014 and 2018. Syphilis is a serious threat to newborns—the rate of this disease out of a hundred thousand live births increased 40 percent just between 2017 and 2018, and 291 percent from 2014 to 2018. HPV appears to be down in teenage girls as a result of the increased use of effective vaccines to prevent it. Thankfully, herpes simplex (HSV) and chancroid (genital ulcers) are also down, while trichomoniasis is stable. About half of all new STI cases come from those ages fifteen to twenty-four. Condom use has decreased among teens, worsening the problems.[58]

Our current national situation with STIs, despite the bright spots mentioned above, is dire. We cannot expect evangelical singles who choose to be sexually active to be any more protected from these infections than anyone else. A quick look at the percentages who used condoms the last time they had sex—opposite-sex oral, anal, or intercourse—among those who had engaged in such sexual activity, suggests a high level of vulnerability to STIs among evangelical singles. Figure 8–3, which looks just at never-married evangelicals who are not currently in a cohabiting relationship, makes this clear.[59]

First, note that this only shows whether they used a condom the *last time*. That does not mean they do so every other time; some do, some do not. Second, this does not indicate if they used the condom properly, which, as we saw above with "typical" versus "perfect" use, makes a big difference. Third, the degree to which anal sex, when it occurs, is unprotected is appalling. Generally, the low use of condoms across the board underscores the degree to which evangelical singles are having sex, including the high-risk activities of intercourse and anal sex, with virtually no means to prevent STI transmission.

The negative impact of evangelical singles not using condoms is a subject about which many conservative evangelicals are sensitive and wary. After all, we know that these unmarried evangelicals should be abstaining, not having sex with condoms. Encouraging condom use appears to many of us to be a kind of "green light" to have sex. At the same time, once we know that so many *are* having sex, it is helpful to know the extent to which they are doing so unprotected. Single evangelicals are much more vulnerable than we like to believe to not only pregnancy and abortion, as we have seen, but also to STIs—not just because they are having sex or because condoms are not perfectly reliable in preventing STIs but because, when they engage in high-risk activities such as anal sex, they are so often not bothering with condoms. At the very least, our churches need to be prepared to minister to a lot of singles, and their families, who are dealing with STIs. In premarital counseling with couples in which one or both partners have had sex partners beyond each other, STIs also need to be openly discussed.

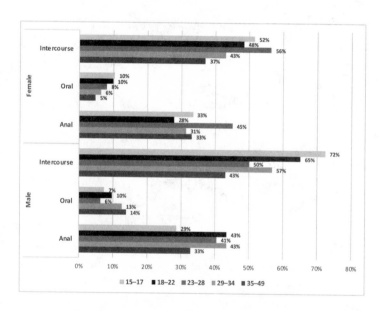

FIGURE 8–3: PERCENTAGES OF NEVER-MARRIED, NON-COHABITING EVANGELICALS WHO HAD ENGAGED IN VARIOUS OPPOSITE-SEX ACTS AND WHO SAID THEY HAD USED A CONDOM THE LAST TIME THEY DID SO, BY AGE GROUP (*NSFG* 2015–2017 AND 2017–2019 CYCLES COMBINED)

MENTAL HEALTH ISSUES

Most singles, even teens, who have engaged in sex outside marriage do not suffer from significant, measurable mental health issues. However, there is a strong and consistent relationship between early sexual onset, casual sex (not attached to a committed relationship), and sexual promiscuity, and negative psychological issues. In considering these relationships, it is difficult to disentangle cause and effect—does poor mental health lead to early, casual, and promiscuous sexual activity, or vice versa? The answer appears to be both; the relationships are reciprocal and mutually reinforcing. Regardless, these sexual activities are not associated with positive mental health.

None other than *Psychology Today* noted that the hookup culture of casual sex is leading to terrible psychological outcomes.[60] In an extensive review of scientific research on casual sex among college students and others, a team of authors led by Justin Garcia noted extensive evidence that, in addition to unwanted pregnancy and STIs, it is associated with "emotional and psychological injury … substance abuse … depressive symptoms … loneliness … lower overall self-esteem … guilt and negative feelings … regret."[61] The relationships between these emotional and psychological issues and casual sex can be complex. For example, sometimes singles use casual sex to relieve depression or loneliness, and this often kind of "works," at least temporarily. But casual sex can then increase depression and loneliness in those who started out with fewer problems to begin with.[62] A picture emerges that is similar to what one finds among drug users— the person uses drugs because they feel bad, but they end up feeling bad because they are using drugs. The picture of the emotional and psychological realities of casual sex painted by these researchers was not positive.[63]

Other research has underscored the relationship of both multiple sex partners and early sexual onset with negative mental health. Depression, substance abuse, and various types of anxiety issues are prominent. There is also the accumulated psychological fallout from people experiencing many intense physical relationships falling apart.[64] A Heritage Foundation report based on the 1996 *National Longitudinal Survey of Adolescent Health* further connected elevated risk of both depression and suicide among sexually active teenagers.[65] Later research using the same ongoing survey found depression, including severe depression, associated with teen involvement in sexual activity with nonromantic partners, especially for those under fifteen.[66]

I did a basic analysis by combining the 2015 through 2019 YRBS high school surveys conducted by the Centers for Disease Control and Prevention.[67] For both males and females, beginning to have sex before age thirteen, having intercourse with three or more sexual partners in their lifetimes, and even just ever having had sexual intercourse, were all significantly and strongly associated with seriously struggling with feelings of sadness and hopelessness, seriously considering suicide, and actually attempting suicide.[68]

Certainly, most teens who are sexually active do not suffer from these things, and it is not clear that the latter causes these effects. However, we do need to realize that among young people who are sexually active, and especially those who started early or take on multiple partners, there are going to be more serious mental health issues. Put another way, there is no evidence that abstinence makes young people miserable.

PHYSICAL HEALTH

Having lots of sexual partners is associated with poorer physical health and shorter life expectancy. This should not surprise us, given all that we have considered already regarding the association between promiscuity and STIs, as well as emotional and psychological health. Some of this is because other high-risk behaviors—such as substance abuse, smoking, inadequate sleep, and poor diet—are often part of the lives of the more promiscuous. Then there are cancers associated with STIs such as oral, cervical, and prostate. Among the sexually promiscuous, there is also a lot more skin-to-skin and other close contact with a variety of people.[69] Of course, HIV leads to AIDS, which in turn opens up the body to many serious medical conditions. As one medical doctor succinctly put it: "Despite the emphasis that society puts on sexuality, the best emotional, physical, and sexual health can be found in long-term relationships. If you find yourself jumping from relationship to relationship, you should consider the price you could be paying in both sexual health and longevity."[70]

SEXUAL VICTIMIZATION AND OTHER VIOLENCE

Casual, early, and promiscuous sex is associated with sexual victimization. The review of literature we have already considered by Garcia and his coauthors explored this quite bluntly. In casual sex, participants—typically women—often take part in forms of sex that they are uncomfortable with but fear objecting to. Particularly men tend to overestimate the degree to which their partners are comfortable with the sex acts they want to engage in.[71] "Unwanted" and "nonconsensual" sex is extremely common in the context of casual sex, much more than in committed relationships.[72]

In looking over the combined 2015 through 2019 YRBS, the statistical associations between early sexual onset and sexual promiscuity with having ever been forced to have sexual intercourse among females was dramatic. Fully 59 percent of girls who had sexual intercourse by age thirteen had been forced to have sexual intercourse compared to 9 percent of those who started sex later or not at all. Among girls who had three or more sex partners in their lifetimes, 34 percent had been forced into sexual intercourse, compared to 7 percent of those who had not been as promiscuous. Both early sexual onset and having three or more sexual partners were also significantly and strongly associated with females reporting sexual dating violence.[73]

Once again, the causal chain is not clear. We do know that being sexually assaulted can impact women's sexual behavior and lead to more promiscuity, although it can also decrease sexual activity.[74] However, getting into sex at very young ages or with lots of different men increases the risk for rape for women. The fact that, as we have seen, drug and alcohol abuse are often part of the mix makes this especially true. For example, in the 2015 through 2019 YRBS, among high school students who had ever had sexual intercourse, one in five high schoolers consumed alcohol or drugs before engaging in it.

Having lots of sex partners and casual sex is also strongly associated with other types of violent victimization.[75] Sexual promiscuity is considered one of the major risk factors for physical violence between adolescents.[76] Again, throwing substance abuse into the mix, as is often the case, this creates an especially toxic brew. In the YRBS for 2015 through 2019, reporting physical dating violence (being hit, slammed with something, or injured with an object or weapon) was strongly associated with various measurements of sexual activity. The overall percentages were higher for females, but this relationship was true for both males and females. Among females, 31 percent of those who had sex by age thirteen had experienced physical dating violence in the past twelve months, compared to 10 percent of those who were virgins or waited until after age thirteen to have sex. Among females who had sex with three or more partners, 24 percent had experienced physical dating violence in the last twelve months, compared to 8 percent of females with less than three sex partners. Among females who had ever had sexual intercourse, 16 percent had experienced physical dating violence in the past twelve months, versus only 5 percent for those who had never engaged in sexual intercourse. It is common sense that, among teens, getting involved sexually, especially at an early age and with multiple partners, carries a higher risk of becoming a victim of dating violence.

Future Marital and Family Success

SEXUAL PROMISCUITY AND HEALTHY MARRIAGE

Controlled social scientific research consistently supports a strong association between having multiple sex partners before marriage and increased risk of divorce.[77] In this way, sexual promiscuity is part of a vicious cycle. Those who are sexually promiscuous prior to marrying are more likely to divorce, and that means their children are more likely to become sexually promiscuous. It is an intergenerational legacy of sorrow that can only be broken by decisively repenting of and turning away from sexual promiscuity.

Nicholas Wolfinger has taken an in-depth look at this phenomenon among women in particular, comparing more recent marriage experiences with those of previous eras in which expectations about premarital sex were more conservative. He takes on some of the complex and counterintuitive findings, such as that, in the population as a whole in recent years, women with just two sex partners before marriage were more likely to divorce than those with, say, three or four.[78]

Especially valuable is that Wolfinger points out some of the reasons why premarital promiscuity is associated with higher divorce risk. He notes those who choose to only have sex with their spouse or eventual spouse tend to be more religiously active, particularly attending church more, and this lowers divorce risk dramatically.[79] We could add to this that monogamous people, even if they did have sex with their spouse before marriage, are almost certainly more committed to the institution of marriage. As Wolfinger notes, women who are promiscuous before marriage are more likely to have a child out of wedlock, which undermines marital happiness and increases risk of divorce.

Wolfinger also says that having sex outside marriage within committed relationships can undermine subsequent marriages more than if it were casual sex, when it ends up involving more partners than one's eventual spouse. The reason appears to be that, even in first marriages, people tend to compare sexual relationships with their spouse with sex they had with their previous, serious dating partner(s). Says Wolfinger:

> My best guess rests on the notion of *over-emphasized comparisons*. In most cases, a woman's two premarital sex partners include her future husband and one other man. That second sex partner is first-hand proof of a sexual alternative to one's husband. ... The man involved was likely to have become a partner in the course of a serious relationship ... thereby emphasizing the seriousness of the alternative.[80]

I looked at evangelical Protestants in the last two NSFG cycles to provide some picture of how sexual promiscuity is undermining marital stability in the church. My focus was on the number of sexual partners beyond respondents' legal spouses in their lifetimes.

The more sex partners evangelicals had other than their spouse prior to their first marriage, the more often their first marriage resulted in divorce or separation. Focusing only on those that were twenty-nine to forty-nine years of age, Figure 8–4 shows this highly statistically significant—indeed, stunning—difference. At the time respondents who had been married once were interviewed, only 5 percent who had only had sex with their spouse were divorced, compared to over one in five who had just one additional sex partner, almost one-third of those who had four or five partners beyond their spouse, and over four in ten of the most promiscuous respondents. This is just one of many "pictures" we could take of how sexual promiscuity has elevated marital breakdown among evangelicals, but the results are so stark that I think it makes the point.

Those who had sex with six or more partners other than their spouse obviously did the worst. But the finding that the biggest jump in divorce rates—over a fourfold increase—was between those who only had ever had sex with their spouse versus those who had just one additional partner is similar to Wolfinger's counterintuitive findings.[81] The data clearly show that those who are monogamous do best by far, and the highly promiscuous set themselves up for marital failure.

Just to be extra careful, I looked at the relationship between number of sex partners and the outcome of first marriages among evangelicals who had only ever married once using multiple regression to control for gender; whether respondents were white, black, or Hispanic; household income; and whether respondents had obtained at least a bachelor's degree. The relationship was still extremely powerful and significant.

The shame is that among evangelical Protestants, having six or more sex partners other than one's spouse is actually more common than only having sex with one's legal spouse. For example, among those twenty-nine to forty-nine married only once, there were 23 percent who had only ever had sex with their spouse, versus 34 percent who had sex with six or more sex partners other than their spouse.

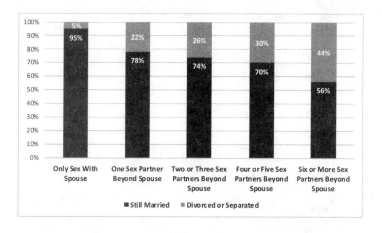

FIGURE 8–4: EVANGELICAL PROTESTANTS WHO HAVE
BEEN MARRIED ONCE, PERCENTAGES STILL
MARRIED VERSUS SEPARATED OR DIVORCED, BY
THE NUMBER OF SEX PARTNERS OTHER THAN
THEIR LEGAL SPOUSES, AGES 29 TO 49 (*NSFG*
2015–2017 AND 2017–2019 CYCLES COMBINED)

Those in the church too often turn a blind eye to sexual promiscuity among their unmarried members. Yet it undermines marriages, which in turn undermines the welfare of these consenting adults' children. People wrongly persist in looking at promiscuous sex, provided it is consensual, as "victimless." Are not the children of these broken marriages victims of decisions they had no part of, even beyond those born out of wedlock?

Our hyperindividualism has obscured the degree to which we are all part of a web of social existence that extends out from us across various people and time. Our sexual sin impacts others, including some who are innocent of what we are guilty of. On the flip side, those who are sexually faithful can be encouraged by the downstream positive benefit of the choices they have made, for themselves and their future families. Their faithfulness blesses more than just them. In short, we are affected by the choices of others, just as our choices have significant impact upon others.

Those who have sinned in these areas can know that, like the smoker who stops smoking, real repentance can recover much that has been lost by giving us a new beginning. With regard to the guilt of our sin, the blood of Jesus wipes the slate clean. I have certainly seen that in my own life. We must encourage the chaste and comfort the repentant.

COHABITATION AND HEALTHY MARRIAGE

It has been established for years that marriages preceded by cohabitation are more likely to end in divorce. Much of this is due to something called the "selection effect"—that is, cohabiters have been different, on average, in other ways that would drive up their divorce rates as a group. Examples of this include lower average education and income. However, even when controlling for these factors—comparing "apples to apples"—cohabiters who went on to marry were still more likely to divorce.[82]

Some have claimed that as cohabitation has become more mainstream, it is no longer associated with higher divorce rates for those who marry later. Some research has supported this, though with caveats and complexities.[83] This view is sometimes called the "normalization hypothesis,"[84] or the "diffusion perspective."[85] The problem is this association with higher divorce rates has been observed in countries like Sweden, where cohabitation became widely socially accepted by the end of the twentieth century.[86] A large 2003 Australian study that even looked at when couples moved in together as married or cohabiting as a possible explanation for higher divorce rates among cohabiters showed that still, all other things being equal, those who lived together first were more likely to end up divorced.[87] A study by CDC researchers found the association between cohabitation and later divorce had decreased in recent years, but it still existed and was statistically significant.[88] Stanley, Rhoades, and Markman point out similar research showing the ongoing divorce risks associated with premarital cohabitation despite these claims that the risks are disappearing as cohabitation becomes more common.[89] A major 2018 study verifies the same thing.[90]

Research does suggest that couples who were formally engaged or otherwise clearly planning on marriage at the time they moved in together no longer have a higher divorce risk than those who lived separately during engagements, as shown in controlled studies.[91] However, as we have seen, most cohabitation does not begin with formal engagement or even firm marital plans. The NSFG data we already looked at in chapter 4 clearly shows, for example, that most first cohabitations do not result in stable marriages and that most people are not engaged or clearly planning marriage when they move in together.[92]

Additionally, the idea that an engaged couple is no more likely to get divorced if they live together than if they remain apart until they are married is not verified by every recent research study that looks at this issue. The CDC research mentioned above found divorce was higher among cohabiters even if they were engaged when they moved in together.[93] Meanwhile,

a study of over 32,000 engaged couples using a highly stan-
dardized premarital inventory found that 51 percent of couples
who were engaged and living together had the best available
relationship score, compared to 60 percent who were engaged
but living apart. Of the engaged cohabiters, 13 percent had the
worst relationship score—indicating that they were at exceptionally high risk of divorce—compared to 5 percent of those
who were engaged but living apart.[94]

We can certainly say two things about the risk of divorce
for couples who cohabit first. First, contrary to what many
people today believe, a couple does not *reduce* their risk of getting divorced by "test-driving" their marriage by living together.[95] There is some evidence that cohabitation eliminates the
adjustment to living together for the first time, and thus reduces
dissolution a little bit in the first year of marriage, but this is
temporary, and after that initial period the effects are mainly
negative.[96] Second, for those seeking to establish a Christian
marriage, beginning by open rebellion against God's clear teachings on marriage and sex is not an ideal starting point, to say
the least.

Beyond the problems with cohabitation itself, we can categorically warn against the negative effects of multiple cohabitations upon the health of future marriages. As we have already
seen, cohabiting more than once before settling down in marriage has become pretty common in our culture as a whole and
even among professed evangelical Protestants. Among evangelicals ages thirty to forty-four in the 2013 through 2017 NSFG,
42 percent of males and 35 percent of females have engaged in at
least one nonmarital cohabitation—that is, a live-in partnership
that did not lead to marriage eventually. In fact, among evangelicals in that age group, 23 percent of males and 12 percent
of females had done so two or more times.[97]

I analyzed the relationship between having cohabited prior to the first marriage (regardless of how many times and whether it culminated in that first marriage) and whether that marriage ended in divorce, focusing on evangelical Protestants between thirty and forty-four.[98] Sixty percent had cohabited prior to their first marriage. The differences between "not before first marriage" and "yes, before first marriage" are significant for both males and females, though it is much stronger for males. Among males, 15 percent of those who had never cohabited had seen their first marriage dissolve, compared to 44 percent of those who had cohabited prior to their first marriage. For females, those percentages were 25 percent and 49 percent respectively. I performed a multiple regression controlling for race, Hispanic status, church attendance, college education, and income. The relationship between cohabiting before first marriage and eventual divorce or separation was still quite powerful for both genders.

Overall, at least among evangelicals, it is safe to say that cohabiting prior to first marriage is a big risk factor for divorce. One reason that cohabiters probably do so much worse is because non-cohabiters are more committed to marriage as a foundation for sexually living together. It is also safe to say that the biggest risks are marriages in which the male partner has already cohabited before marriage. Whether in our simple tables or in the multiple regression analysis, cohabiting prior to first marriage hurt more when males did it.

This kind of information can be incredibly useful in premarital counseling. For example, when a couple is serious about marriage but not cohabiting, female singles need to look at not only their cohabiting history but also their fiancé's.

Church leaders can use this research to talk about cohabiting and its consequences with singles in their congregations.

First, cohabitation is sin and is not a great foundation for a Christian marriage. Second, it will not prepare them for marriage or serve as an effective "screening" mechanism for potential spouses. Third, the preponderance of the evidence suggests that it increases the risk of divorce. Fourth, a pattern of multiple cohabitations makes later divorce not just likely by comparison but likely in general. Fifth, at the end of the day, most cohabitations do not eventually lead to stable marriages. The outcomes of cohabitation are tragic. It is time for the church to get a serious wake-up call on this issue and embrace what generations in the past widely accepted—a man and a woman should commence sexually living together after they are married and not before. This honors God and guards the welfare of God's people.

Conclusion

We find warnings about the spiritual and natural consequences of sin throughout the Bible. This is the principle of reaping what we sow. Natural consequences are not the doings of an unjust or cruel deity, an impersonal universe, or karma. Rather, they are acts of grace from the hands of a loving God who uses these negative results as one mechanism to lead us back to him, in repentance and faith, when we sin.

Many evangelicals, including singles, are deceived, fooling themselves about the dangers they face by disobeying God in how they use their bodies sexually. They rely not on biblical obedience but on human assurances and modern technology to protect themselves from the consequences of sin. Too often they have embraced the individualist lie that if anyone is going to be hurt, it will just be them. But this hurt extends to their partner's future spouse, their children, and more. There are a lot of innocent children suffering, at this moment, because of the willful sexual sin of their parents.

Throughout this book we have looked at some very difficult things in great detail. Now, in the final chapter, we will move in a positive direction. First, I want to set before you a vision for what a sexually faithful church would look like. Second, I offer some concrete steps for getting there, rooted in the facts that we have already considered. You will not find "cool" programs or cutting-edge innovation to provide a shortcut to sexual purity. Rather, I will be urging believers to consistently and faithfully apply what the Scriptures define as Christianity—living our lives as flawed but faithful believers in our private worlds, our families, and our churches guided by God's word, strengthened by his Spirit, and supporting one another.

9

A FRAMEWORK AND PRINCIPLES FOR CHURCHES TO PROMOTE SEXUAL PURITY

As the church in our culture, we must make sure not to preach a gospel that merely imagines Christ as the means to a casual, conservative, comfortable Christian spin on the traditional American dream. ... The gospel is a call for every one of us to die—to die to sin and to die to self—and to live with unshakeable trust in Christ, choosing to follow his Word even when it brings us into clear confrontation with our culture (and our own values for that matter). ... Moreover, in the culture, God beckons us to proclaim this gospel. To care enough for one another to call each other to rest in God's design for sexual identity and to flee from every form of sexual immorality.

David Platt, *Counter-Culture*

The more I engage these issues, the more I'm convinced that the church's best opportunity to encourage a biblical ethic of sex and marriage is by living out a biblical ethic of sex and marriage. As Madeleine L'Engle reminds us, we draw people to Christ by showing them a light so lovely that they want with all their hearts to know its source. In other words, in the eyes of a watching world, showing the light makes the telling about the light palpable and credible. The Christian witness cannot be in word alone. It must also be in deed.

Scott Sauls, "Toward a Graciously Historical
Sexual Ethic," *The Gospel Coalition*

Birling is a little-known lumberjack sport. The object is to maintain one's balance on a spinning log floating in the water longer than one's opponent who is trying to do the same thing on the same log. It is frightfully difficult. Funambulism, or walking on a tightrope, is similar. In both birling and funambulism, special gear is used to assist the person, including the right footwear and balancing poles. Imagery from these sports has found its way into popular speech. We might make a comment such as, "He constantly has to walk a tightrope." Or we might say that someone is trying to avoid falling off one side of the log or the other. When we point out that doing something is as "easy as falling off a log," we are stating a truth by declaring its opposite—staying on that log is extremely tricky while falling off is unbelievably easy.

Maintaining balance is a real problem when we are dealing with sin issues in the church. Christian history attests that some of our biggest doctrinal and practical errors in confronting sexual immorality have involved falling off the log. We see this today in the division between evangelicals who pitch more to the "left" or "right" on moral issues. The Bible keeps us centered on that log, balanced on the tightrope. Our mastery of appropriate doctrinal funambulism is critical to how we approach the problem of rampant fornication among professing evangelicals.

For example, we do not look to the law for salvation; we are under grace. But grace is not a license to sin (Romans 6:15). We are saved from sin by grace through faith and not our own works (Ephesians 2:8–9), but we *are* "under the law of Christ" (1 Corinthians 9:21). Having died to sin by the grace of God, we should not continue to live in sin (Romans 6:2) and, if we truly love Christ, we will strive to keep his commandments (John 14:15; 1 John 5:2–3). So, sexual purity does not save us, but those who are saved should desire and pursue sexual purity.

Are we free human beings or slaves? Both. We are set free from sin in order to become "slaves of righteousness" (Romans 6:18–20). What many people claim is sexual freedom is actually bondage to sin and death, but we are set free through repentant faith and radical obedience to Christ.

What is more important: telling someone the truth or making them feel loved? Both. In fact, one is impossible without the other. Part of the truth about anyone is that they are loved by God and should also be loved by us, not sentimentally but in action. Truly loving people means being honest about their sin, though not in a manner that is unloving and graceless. Speaking the truth, but in love, is the gospel way, and it is how we grow together in the church (Ephesians 4:15). It is an indispensable part of all true friendship: "Let the righteous man strike me—it is a kindness" (Psalm 141:5).

Likewise, should we confront someone with their sin or be gentle and humble, remembering how bad we are (Galatians 6:1)? Both. Should we pay attention to the sins of our brethren, or focus on repenting for our own trespasses (Matthew 7:3–5)? Both.

The point is this: when churches try to deal with fornication among professing believers—either to prevent what might happen or deal with what has happened—we must not emphasize one side over the other. Doing so—whether in the "leftist" way of toning down God's moral commands, or in the "rightist" way of blasting hapless sinners with them—has created a lot of harm. The degree of our problem, and the discouragement we often feel, increases the chances that we will lose our balance, falling off to the left or to the right of the log. To avoid legalism, we can easily fall into cheap grace and ignore holiness. To emphasize love and unity, we can avoid hard truth. To extol purity, we might shame and discourage repentant sinners. Or conversely, we might tone down talk of holiness to avoid making people feel bad, or to accommodate modern culture, we might minimize the tension between the church and our contemporary world. Hating division, we may avoid confrontation. Like that birling lumberjack or that high-wire performer, we will constantly need to make little corrections, sometimes even falling off and then, by God's grace, climbing back on and trying again. We will sometimes need special aids to help us along, such as verses reminding us to be more courageous or gentle or the admonishment of wise counselors. Each time, we will improve, though it is not easy.

In this final chapter, I want to look at practical things that churches can do to promote premarital sexual purity without embracing gimmicks, fads, or legalism. My approach is rooted in Scripture, an appreciation for the need to live out plain, faithful, normal Christianity, the experience and teaching of successful practices from Christian and social science sources, and an understanding of the causes of sexual promiscuity. This chapter applies what we have learned so far to help evangelical churches do better in addressing our huge problem with fornication and related issues. My aim here is not to address every possible question or to lay out a detailed, "surefire" purity program. Rather, my goal is to provide a larger framework within which our various educational and discipleship efforts can better succeed and to provide some basic principles. This is not about "sex-proofing" singles, but about helping all of us to live out lives of integrity before the Lord within which sexual chastity is woven into a larger, harmonious Christian tapestry. To do this, we must constantly maintain hard but lovely balances between biblical virtues and admonitions that sometimes seem contradictory but are actually necessary and complementary.

In preparing for a hard journey, it helps to envision the beauty of the place to which we are going, like westward-bound travelers encouraging themselves through that long drive across Kansas with pictures of the Rocky Mountains. We see it in the Bible often, especially when God encourages persecuted saints with the powerful picture of the heavenly Jerusalem he granted to John in the book of Revelation. So, let us start with a picture of the beauty and wholeness of a sexually faithful church.

Brief Vision of a Church That Upholds a High and Biblical View of Sex

Churches that do well in upholding God's moral standards for sex outside of marriage are not legalistic and perfectionist. They often have members who have been guilty of sexual failings, even serious ones, not just before but after coming to know Christ. Churches that promote chastity are congregations where sexual sin is resisted and, when people do succumb to sexual temptation, their sin is acknowledged, confessed, repented of, forgiven, addressed with firm discipleship and biblical counsel, and ultimately, forsaken. Sinners draw alongside each other in pursuit of God's holiness, watching over one another not in censoriousness or invidious judgment but in holy care for one another and passion for the glory of God. Leaders encourage faithful members to pursue holiness sincerely but are still realistic and kind. They are not shocked or discouraged when they repeatedly see Christians sin, including young people sometimes falling into fornication and even trying to excuse it. They are guided by humility and a healthy realization of the power of indwelling sin—their own first and then that of others. In dealing with members who sin sexually or in any other area, healthy members of such churches are quick to rejoice in true repentance, then forgive and move on, while offering whatever help is needed. Holding sin over people is an alien concept; they remember their own sin all too well.

Churches that are on the best path to seeing members embrace the difficult call to sexual chastity reject trendy shortcuts as a replacement for the steady diet of the basic food and drink of Christianity. Their spiritual sustenance consists of the sacraments, gathering together, prayer, worship, preaching the word, promoting sound parenting, godly marriage and family life, mutual confession of sin and mutual support, reasonable accountability, forgiveness and repentance, and Christian encouragement.

The leaders in these churches, including the pastors, are ferociously committed to caring for the flocks they have been charged to nurture, guide, and guard. They are willing to take on unpopular subjects, tackling what needs to be said, guided by Scripture, depending on prayer and the comfort and guidance of the Holy Spirit. Offending people is never their aim, but they are not going to pass over sin to avoid offense. They would rather lose members than keep them by withholding God's truth. There is no special treatment in these churches—the pastor's son and the wealthy elder's daughter are handled the same way as the children of housekeepers and auto mechanics. At the same time, their pastors address these matters with wisdom and discretion, knowing what to handle publicly and what to deal with privately and confidentially. Members struggling with sexual sin can approach such leaders knowing that they will hear the truth and get excellent guidance and ongoing support in their struggles with sin. These leaders will help them reconcile with whomever they need to make peace with. Those who fall and confess will feel safe in their vulnerability and never be demeaned. The same will be true of anyone coming to them for help with a loved one—an errant spouse or child.

These congregations have a good understanding of what needs to be left to parents to teach their children. Their goal is to equip and help parents understand what they need to know about instructing and guiding their children in age-appropriate ways. This is far superior to pushing parents aside to do all the teaching themselves. These churches will be willing and able to teach a consistent biblical sexual ethic to everyone, including youth and adult singles. However, they will leave critical decisions about many delicate and sensitive issues to parents, such as how to talk about various forms of sex or contraception or specific "policies" about dating. On sexual matters, as in so much else touching family matters, the relationship between church and parents will be, wherever possible, more of a partnership than a competition or substitute.

In dealing with believers without godly parents, many of whom come to Christ at an older age, or to singles living independently, church leaders will be able to step up and provide proper sexual teaching and guidance. This sensitive guidance will mean being willing to encourage hard questions and answer them honestly, biblically, and with sound practical knowledge.

Churches that are effectively promoting chastity are places where members are active. They are regularly in attendance, serve in practical ways, take advantage of Bible study groups and Sunday school classes, and take seriously their obligations to others in their church. When members drop off in their practical commitments, the church leaders seek them out and encourage them to renew their involvement, even if it means losing those members to other churches that they would be more willing to be committed to. The leaders all model that kind of day-in-and-day-out dedication as well. Meanwhile, they work hard to make sure that the time believers spend in fellowship is fruitful and give members the opportunity and resources to grow.

In these kinds of churches, promoting healthy marriage understanding and practice is known to be the key to sound family life, which in turn is critical to sound sexual formation and instruction. Most of the marriages and families in these churches are growing in their life together, functioning as "little churches" within the larger church. The sexual ethic is inextricably tied to the church's understanding of marriage and family as they keep in mind the centrality of a healthy and wholesome sexual life as part of marriage and the role of married parents in the nurture of godly offspring. In churches that have sustained a relatively successful approach to promoting chastity over extended periods of time, the fact that so many marriages and families are healthy leaves the church bandwidth to help those who are struggling. More households are in a position to help single parents striving to raise their children and to provide support for single-parent households to offset the deficits associated with absentee parenting, ongoing conflict between ex-spouses, financial pressures, and other challenges.

The churches I am thinking about here do not artificially divide truth but rather help members to see the harmonious, intricate web of biblical revelation. Marriage is seen as designed by God and as being at its best when it fulfills his purposes for it, including pointing to Christ and the church. Nonmarital sex is not just a "rule violation" but a counterfeit of sacred and holy things—destructive to the bodies and spiritual welfare of believers.

Churches that effectively promote chastity are grounded in a sound theology. They want members to know about God accurately so that they can know and love God. Their members are taught about right understanding of themselves as human persons, having a healthy mistrust of their own understanding and feelings and recognizing that God is greater than they are and they are dependent on him for all good. They know that "he is God, and I am not." They understand the integrated nature of the Christian moral framework—that sexual integrity is a piece of sound speech, honesty, respecting the property of others, and loving one's neighbor.

The Bible is held in high regard and is the ultimate source of church teaching and practice. Members see that pastors and other church leaders can point to the Scriptures, in sound and honest ways, to support their positions, even as they may acknowledge and draw upon solid confessions, catechisms, and other doctrinal works. This accountability to God's word, even when it indicts those who preach it, is continuously evident.

The kind of churches I am envisioning are places that know sorrow, pain, and failure, but are ultimately joy-filled places where people are happy together and know how to laugh. Their view of sex is not dour or fearful or marked by furtiveness or inordinate shame. They understand and celebrate God's good gift of sex for married men and women. They want singles moving toward marriage to be anticipating marital sex with delight, realistically and without selfish desire or lust. Frank dialogue on sexual matters is not unusual. Teaching the sexual "rules" is not about hand-slapping or scaring anyone but about honoring God while constantly pointing people to something better. To paraphrase C. S. Lewis, these churches want to warn people away from the lure of sin's pleasure not only because they are zealous to pursue holiness, glorify God, and see their members do likewise, but because they hate seeing the people that they love making mudpies in a slum when they could be having a holiday by the sea.[1]

Now, let us look at some practical steps evangelical churches can take to promote biblical chastity among singles. Some of these are directly tied to dealing with sex and fornication; others provide a context and framework conducive to doing so.

A Sexually Faithful Church

Tim Geiger defines a sexually faithful church as "a church that disciples its members in a gospel worldview of sexuality through education and redemptive ministry."[2] This is a concept that should become known and practiced by every evangelical church. Let us unpack and expand on this in detail.

1. GOSPEL WORLDVIEW EDUCATION

As I have stressed in this book, most particularly in chapters 1 and 6, biblical teaching and practice is rooted in a sound Christian worldview with the gospel at its center, one that is "biblically grounded."[3] We should not start with rules about sex. We should begin with a proper understanding of the attributes of God. We should begin by appreciating him as the only perfectly wise, all-knowing, all-powerful, and absolute ruler over all of creation. A biblical worldview embraces God's rightful demand for all who call themselves Christians to submit to his lordship, understanding that therein lies the key to true happiness and success. In this worldview, sex is inextricably tied to marriage and is sacred. It reflects, in deep ways, the relationship of Christ and the church, and the Holy Trinity. This worldview recognizes the critical importance of holiness, which God is perfectly, and calls us to pursue it fervently. There is solid teaching on creation, on covenant, on the body and the material world, and on human identity and what it means that our identity is found ultimately in Christ—not in sex, race, politics, family, or anything else. A vibrant doctrine of God is attached to an honest, biblical anthropology, which engages our understanding of human nature. This includes what it means, and does not mean, when we say that we are fallen creatures being dead in sin without Christ, totally dependent on him for all good. But it also means, as image-bearers of God, that we are called to exercise dominion over the earth in subjection to God and for his glory. It is only in light of all of this that biblical "rules" about sex and sexual sin have any meaning.

Many Christians today make a critical error. They see Christian love as having nothing to do with addressing wrong thinking or actions but as unconditional acceptance. That is humanism, not Christianity. Unlike the feel-good god and counterfeit love of humanism, the biblical worldview teaches a contradictory but far more wonderful reality—a God of holiness and perfection expresses his perfect love for us by desiring passionately that we move toward the purity he loves and knows will make us truly happy. Brothers and sisters who love us do the same thing; they do not ignore our sin in their acceptance of us but call us to true repentance and faith. Tim Geiger says this well: "A sexually faithful church educates its members to know how to discern the distortions and falsehoods that increasingly deceive Christians into thinking that to love others means to never challenge their worldviews or their behavior."[4] Challenges from our true friends are faithful (Proverbs 27:6) when they help to steer us away from death and toward life.

Intentional instruction in a holistic, biblical worldview is essential to ground believers in every aspect of Christian morality, including the sexual. There are great tools and programs churches can use to help accomplish this, such as the PEERS and American Worldview Inventory, and numerous worldview training materials directed to young people and those teaching them.[5] The *Christian Worldview Handbook* is an excellent resource for providing teachers a comprehensive background, containing over one hundred focused articles.[6] Herman Bavinck's short but powerful classic, *Christian Worldview,* is a marvelous resource for serious students of biblical worldview.[7]

Teaching a gospel worldview means pressing upon people the need to repent of their sin and turning them to Christ in faith for salvation—to a life as God's servant by the power of the Holy Spirit. Having singles refrain from sex but not have a relationship with Christ is of fleeting value. We do nothing this way but make the dead presentable. Preaching and living out the implications of the pure, unvarnished gospel of Jesus Christ—not sexual purity—must be at the heart of all evangelical ministry. Believing parents should pray and seek earnestly for the salvation of their children. Our ultimate answer should be nothing less than the message Peter gave to chastened Jews on the day of Pentecost:

> Now when they heard this they were cut to the heart, and said to Peter and the rest of the apostles, "Brothers, what shall we do?" And Peter said to them, "Repent and be baptized every one of you in the name of Jesus Christ

for the forgiveness of your sins, and you will receive the gift of the Holy Spirit. For the promise is for you and for your children and for all who are far off, everyone whom the Lord our God calls to himself." And with many other words he bore witness and continued to exhort them, saying, "Save yourselves from this crooked generation." (Acts 2:37–40)

2. BIBLICAL TEACHING ON SEXUALITY

Tim Geiger notes that we must impart a "gospel worldview of sexuality." How does this extend a general gospel worldview? I would like to answer this by quoting him at length:

> We use the word *sexuality* here as a blanket term to refer to sex, sexuality, and gender. God's people learn that these attributes of created existence and image-bearing are theirs precisely because, through the right exercise and enjoyment of them, we not only honor God, but we reveal his wisdom and glory to each other and the world. In a culture that says we are nothing more than the collection of feelings and desires that drive us, to understand and rest in God's design for sex, sexuality, and gender bestows an uncommon dignity and glory on men and women as God's image bearers and his servant-kings over his creation.[8]

I went over these biblical teachings about sex in chapter 1, but let me summarize some main points here. Biblical teaching about sex unfolds its true nature theologically in how it points us to God, what it means that sex is a sacred and exclusive form of intimate knowing, and that sex is inextricably bonded to marriage as a one-flesh, lifelong union between one man and one woman. This is for a host of spiritual and practical reasons connected to the design of marriage itself. It means seeing how and why sexual immorality is a grave sin not only against God and others but also against our very bodies he has us bear in honor and he will someday resurrect in glory. In teaching about fornication, we must help believers see it is a mockery of what sex is supposed to be and a refusal to trust God for our care and good, including the fulfillment of ourselves as sexual beings. Sex is good and beautiful but conditionally so. Outside of God's perfect design, no matter how we feel about it or how it is presented as wonderful and liberating, it is not for our good. We must unfold these truths about sex repeatedly, in age-appropriate ways.

Effectively teaching a biblical view of sex also means addressing theological, worldview, and moral "distortions and falsehoods that increasingly deceive Christians."[9] We must address the larger apologetic for orthodox Christianity against modern deceptions that is essential when laying out historic Christian doctrine and theology in general and specific lies about the nature and morality of sex. These are the beliefs we unpacked in chapters 2 and 6. It is vital to discover the seductive falsehoods enticing those in our churches, uncovering and refuting those directly—with kindness and gentleness but also clarity and boldness.

Anti-terrorism experts tell us that a common mistake is preparing for yesterday's terrorist strategy rather than what is hitting today and likely to come tomorrow. Preparing for yesterday's challenges today catches us flat-footed. For those trying to promote sexual purity—parents and religious leaders alike—we often make the mistake of thinking that young people are being seduced with what we confronted in the past, or even what was happening a few years ago, rather than knowing the form our enemy has assumed now and is likely to morph into in the near future. Teaching about biblical sexuality and against seductive error requires staying in tune with what is happening in our larger culture. We must confront not just what is being indulged in and offered—which we know is evolving constantly—but also the various theological deceptions and moral justifications that are being used to grease our single members' slides into sexual sin.

At the beginning of chapter 4, I quoted an evangelical teen who claimed to have discovered that, regardless of what the Bible clearly taught about sex, God wanted her and her boyfriend to be happy. Sex made them happy, ergo it made God happy for them to have sex. Her idea is rooted in assumptions about truth, authority, autonomy, and the place of reason, emotion, and personal experience. "God is happy if you are happy and no one is hurt" is hostile to Christianity at the core, but it is the cultural water she swims in. Trying to correct reasoning like this from people who claim to take Christ and the Bible seriously can seem impossible. Add to our challenges virtual reality sex, sex robots, "sexts" that disappear before adults can see them—in a world of radical doubt that even our own bodies are real in the ordinary sense—and we can see that we need to rely on the Spirit for guidance in this nebulous cloud we are walking into.

There is a wealth of solid materials for evangelicals that communicate a biblical view of sexuality over against error, pitched to different age levels, that present a biblical understanding of sex in the context of promoting chastity and identifying sexual sin. Space precludes me from listing them all here. Here are just a few excellent examples: David White's *God, You, and Sex: A Profound Mystery*; Dennis P. Hollinger, *The Meaning of Sex: Christian Ethics and the Moral Life*; O. Palmer Robertson *The Genesis of Sex: Sexual Relationships in the First Book of the Bible*;[10]

John Piper and Justin Taylor (editors), *Sex and the Supremacy of Christ*;[11] Beth Felker Jones, *Faithful: A Theology of Sex*;[12] Lewis B. Smedes, *Sex for Christians: The Limits and Liabilities of Sexual Living*;[13] Luke Gilkerson, *The Talk: 7 Lessons to Introduce Your Children to Biblical Sexuality*[14] and *Relationships: 11 Lessons to Give Kids a Better Understanding of Biblical Sexuality*.[15] My wife and I have found the *Passport2Purity* materials, written and produced by Dennis and Barbara Rainey, to be extremely helpful in educating all of our six children about the biblical theology and morality of sex, as well as tackling a lot of factual issues and questions.[16]

Finally, the Center for Parent/Youth Understanding (CPYU), in partnership with Project Six19, maintains an amazing, comprehensive clearinghouse for first-rate materials focused on youth sexuality called the *Sexual Integrity Initiative*. Its mission is described as, "Providing information and resources for parents, youth workers and educators to help kids navigate their sexuality." The site includes seminars, research, news, media, and a blog by Walt Mueller, who is the founder and president of CPYU. Another helpful CPYU site with vital information and materials for parents, youth workers and educators, is their *Digital Kids Initiative*, designed "to help kids navigate their digital world."[17]

3. PASTORS NEED TO BE SUPPORTED WHEN THEY TACKLE THE TOUGH ISSUES

Teaching about and promoting a biblical sexual ethic is not easy for pastors. Many are going to be lambasted no matter what they do. If they ignore the issue, some will claim that they are cowardly or capitulating to liberalism, but if they address sexual sin, they are depicted by some as mean-spirited, judgmental legalists. A 2019 report by the Barna Group showed how many

pastors simultaneously experience pressure from their congregants both to tackle and avoid sensitive sexual issues, the
classic catch-22.[18] I recently spoke to a pastor who was being
attacked by numerous people in his congregation for dismissing
a church employee in a high visibility position who was openly
cohabiting and refusing to repent. The church's doctrinal position clearly identified all sex outside of marriage as sin, and in
every respect, the pastor's approach had been incredibly kind
and low-key. Moreover, there is little doubt that had he ignored
the situation a different set of congregants would have pilloried
him. If we want our pastors to lead in promoting biblical sexual
ethics in belief and action, we must be prepared to stand with
and support them when they do the right thing.

Church discipline is a sensitive but necessary topic. It is
almost nonexistent in many evangelical churches today, even
though the Reformers generally agreed that discipline was—
along with biblical preaching and the sacraments—one of the
three marks of a true church. The purpose of discipline is restor-
ative and positive as well as negative. As Daniel Hyde notes,
"Discipline promotes God's holiness ... protects the church from
infection ... and restores the rebellious, making clear the seriousness of their resistance to Christ's word and church."[19]

It is a responsibility of pastors and elders to apply church
discipline when necessary. If they fail to do so, they are not
being faithful shepherds of the flock of Christ, just as they
would be wrong to apply discipline frivolously or in any spirit
but one of humility and love. It is in applying discipline, even
when it is clearly called for, that many of our pastors and elders
find themselves subject to great attack, like the pastor in the last
paragraph. We will never be a sexually faithful church unless we
not only support our pastors in appropriately applying church
discipline for unrepentant sexual sin, but insist that they do so.[20]

4. REDEMPTIVE MINISTRY

Every church should make theologically sound, effective, focused ministry and discipleship in sexual areas available to their members. Churches can partner with other congregations or with dedicated ministries to provide what they do not have the personnel or expertise to handle on their own. For example, *Harvest USA* provides first-rate resources for hands-on discipleship, education, and training across the entire spectrum of issues related to sex, sexual orientation, and identity. *Pródigals International* offers a range of programs dealing with various types of sexual addiction rooted in a kind of twelve-step approach and is theologically conservative. Other ministries are more focused. For example, *Restored Hope Network* deals with a range of sexual issues but is known especially for their work with homosexuality. *Dirty Girls Ministries* and *Beggar's Daughter* are dedicated to helping women who struggle with pornography, while *XXXChurch* is an online ministry to help both men and women with pornography and other forms of sexual addiction. *Harvest USA* and *Pure Desire Ministries* train church leaders in establishing sound ministries focused on sexual areas, in addition to providing direct help to believers struggling with sexual issues. While I could easily expand the list, the point is that there are a lot of resources out there to come alongside believers and churches as we battle the scourge of sexual immorality in our midst.

However, where possible, churches should offer support on their own or in partnership with local congregations. Pastoral counseling should be part of this, but small group and discipleship ministries, sometimes supported, equipped, and guided by larger organizations, are essential. One church I was part of provided training and oversight for mature younger Christian singles to set up accountability groups for young men struggling with sexual temptations of various kinds that met in local college dormitories.

Jim Weidenaar of *Harvest USA* provides some solid, common-sense principles churches need to honor in establishing such ministries. First, they need to involve leadership and commitment that goes beyond one person. Too often, a ministry fails when the one person who led it loses their passion, burns out or moves on, leaving those who depended on it orphaned. Second, ministries need to be designed to address the needs of people within their various "roles and stations"—children, parents, singles, married people, those crushed by their sin and those complacent about it, and so on. One size does not fit all. Third, the leadership must be well equipped and both transparent and humble, openly modeling "gospel repentance and faith in their own lives." They also need to depend on God to deal with sexual temptations in their own lives. Weidenaar puts this well: "Preach and teach on sexuality not as generals in a culture war but as shepherds mending a ravaged flock."[21]

5. ENCOURAGE COMMITMENT

We must be willing to encourage real commitment to Christ, his people, and Christian growth while addressing sexual sin. If there is anything we have seen from the statistics in this book, it is how much things as simple as attending church regularly and believing that our faith matters affect how we live each day. Moreover, being faithful in these areas is *necessary* to sanctification in every sin area. We can add more to this beyond what I have covered statistically too. Confession of sin, prayer, regular Bible reading, and taking in sound Christian books addressing the areas we are struggling with are essential.

I have been told that I should not emphasize these basic aspects of normal Christianity when talking about sexual sin because pastors, Christian parents, and leaders already know this and address it. However, first, there are some things we need to hear repeatedly. How often does John repeat himself, in his first letter alone, about fellowship, about obeying God and not sinning, about loving one another? In fact, Peter strongly emphasized the need for repeating to disciples what they already know: "Therefore I intend always to remind you of these qualities, though you know them and are established in the truth that you have" (2 Peter 1:12; see also 3:1–2). Second, most pastors and elders I have known in my Christian walk have found it challenging to get large swaths of their voting and communicant members to attend church weekly. In some churches even some elders and deacons are sporadic in these basic disciplines. If a church is dealing with a single person who is cohabiting or sexually active, there is a good chance that he or she is not faithful in other aspects of commitment. Part of ministering to people effectively must include addressing those deficiencies.

6. SOUND LEADERSHIP WITH HIGH MORAL STANDARDS

As I was working on the initial draft of this chapter, celebrity pastor Carl Lentz of Hillsong Church was removed for adultery, which appears, at this writing, to have been with several women over numerous years.[22] It is not hard to recall spectacular sexual failures of nationally known Christian leaders. Confirmed charges of sexual harassment against the late apologist Ravi Zacharias began surfacing in the summer and fall of 2020 and, like the Hillsong revelations, continue to appear in the national media.[23] More dated perhaps are the highly publicized sexual downfalls of Ted Haggard, Jimmy Swaggart, James Bakker, and Tullian Tchividjian, to name a few.[24] It is easy to focus on the famous and forget how often similar stories play out in churches and ministries across the country, and often include—like many of these—discoveries of "enabling" church elders and others whose neglect ranged from being inattentive to active complicity and cover-up.

We cannot expect the people in our congregations to take sexual sin seriously if Christian leaders engage in it themselves or overlook it among each other. Confession, repentance, and even discipline is not just for the rank and file. On the contrary, the Scriptures teach us by precept and example that those who teach the flock face greater judgment (James 3:1). We have numerous Scriptures urging pastors and elders to, as Peter put it, be "examples for the flock" (1 Peter 5:3; see 1 Timothy 4:12; 1 Corinthians 11:1; Philippians 3:17).

Yet evangelical pastors and other church leaders are fallen, sinful creatures, like the rest of us. Here is another balance we must maintain, another tightrope to walk—high expectations for spiritual leaders while acknowledging and empathizing with their weaknesses.

Pastors often have an acute need for deep friendship and accountability within which they can proactively address their struggles with sexual temptation. Churches, especially elders and those supporting and overseeing pastors, need to be honest about their vulnerability and make sure that their pastors, and each other, have access to honest and compassionate ministry that addresses sexual challenges, among other potentially challenging areas. Our pastors are under a lot of pressure. Many suffer from long hours, low pay, social isolation, being elevated on unrealistic pedestals, and family pressures, coupled with intense scrutiny. As we ask our pastors for leadership in promoting sexual purity in our churches in their teaching, counseling, programmatic ministries, and personal example, we have to work to ensure that they are also being protected and cared for.

A bombshell survey conducted by Barna Research in cooperation with the Josh McDowell Ministry helped uncover at least one dimension of this problem—pornography. Given that even on anonymous surveys respondents underreport behavior of which they are ashamed, the realities are almost certainly worse than this report found.

This project found that among American Protestants, at least 21 percent of youth pastors and 14 percent of pastors admitted to currently using pornography, and 43 percent of both indicated that they had struggled with it in the past. The overwhelming majority of both groups stated they face as much temptation in this area as anyone else. About a quarter of youth pastors and a third of pastors went further, indicating that they were at *greater* risk of succumbing to pornography than people in other professions.[25]

Among clergy who are struggling with pornography use, senior pastors especially fear discovery and suffer shame. While in most cases their spouses and a few trusted friends know, 80 percent say that they have kept this from their elders and deacons. Many, particularly pastors, say that their jobs give them a lot of opportunity to secretly indulge and pornography helps them to temporarily escape the pressures of their pastoral work.[26]

Other data on pastoral sexual sin and struggle are sparse. A survey commissioned in 1988 by *Christianity Today* found that of three hundred pastors who responded out of the one thousand contacted, 23 percent admitted to some kind of sexual indiscretion, 12 percent admitted to having sexual intercourse, and 18 percent admitted to engaging in some other form of mutual intimate sexual contact with someone other than their spouse while in the ministry. A large group, 66 percent, admitted to fantasizing about sex with someone other than their spouse; 26 percent did so daily to weekly.[27] A 1991 survey of 186 male Protestant ministers found that 6 percent had immoral sexual intercourse, and another 10 percent had engaged in intimate sexual contact outside their marriages.[28]

Given the low response rate and known underreporting on these sensitive survey questions, the percentages were probably higher. Perhaps, if the surveys were restricted to pastors in more conservative denominations, they may have yielded better results, for no other reason than their ministers may have been more likely to be removed over serious sexual sin. Although these studies are dated, we have no reason to believe the current reality would be much different; it is certainly not better.[29]

In addition to helping pastors avoid burnout, there are things churches can do and the rest of us can encourage. These include pastors participating in accountability groups that are discreet but truthful, avoiding being put in compromising positions (such as lunches and office time alone with women), and putting safeguards on their computers such as filtering and accountability software. We should also encourage other church leaders, such as elders and deacons, to ask our pastors—and one another—purposeful and personal questions on sexual matters on a regular basis, for our good and theirs. These preventative and corrective steps can help pastors with a host of other sexual temptations, often allowing for intervention before a temptation blossoms into action. They also demonstrate to believers that their leaders are humble, transparent, and take chastity seriously.[30]

My father was a covert officer with the Central Intelligence Agency (CIA) for decades. Years after he retired, he told me that after an operation in the field he and others were often given intense polygraph tests that addressed, among other things, sexual infidelity. This was not done out of the agency's moral or personal concern but to be sure that intelligence officers were not being compromised and rendered vulnerable to blackmail. They believed that *anyone* was at risk from sexual temptation, especially when they were isolated from their families and under pressure.

I see this as real wisdom. The CIA took for granted that anyone can mess up badly, that certain pressures and opportunities raise the risk, and that the results could be harmful not just to their personnel but to all who rely upon them. Jesus pointed out that the "the sons of this world are more shrewd in dealing with their own generation than the sons of light" (Luke 16:8). Although we do not need to be rude, suspicious, or as brutal as CIA investigators—and we do not typically need lie detectors—we should not be afraid of our leaders being asked honest questions about sexual sin by those we designate to oversee them. And we should not be shocked that they suffer temptations as much as the rest of us and sometimes slip. Their vulnerability is one of the things that enables them to understand our struggles and to identify and empathize with us.

When pastors commit egregious sexual sin, there should be an emphasis on Christian restoration but no delay in removing them from the gospel ministry if the situation calls for it. Cover-ups and looking the other way harms churches and wrecks people's souls, denying them what all of us need when we sin. I have witnessed churches being unbelievably lax in dealing with pastoral infidelity—including one married minister with several children having an affair with a married woman who also had children and then marrying *her*, all without missing a day in the pulpit. What did that communicate to their congregants about the importance of sexual purity?

The response of church leaders when those in leadership (pastors, elders, deacons, vestry members, and so on) fall into sexual sin can vary, and here is neither the right place nor space to address such a complex or sensitive issue in detail across the variations of church polities, circumstances, and specific sins.[31] Yet the church should see that sexual faithfulness is strongly expected of its leaders. At the same time, along with this strictness, sexual sins in pastors and other church leaders should be addressed with the same biblical balance, compassion, and humility with which we would all hope to be treated. Our response to fallen pastors ought to include after-care—not abandonment—for ministers who are removed and, when true repentance is evident, every attempt should be made to help them establish themselves in a position where they can financially care for themselves and their family. Churches ought to have clear plans in place to deal with fallen pastors should this tragedy occur, just as we have so many other contingency plans for things we hope will never happen.[32]

Paul expected elders to be "above reproach," "sober-minded, self-controlled," "not open to the charge of debauchery," and "upright" (1 Timothy 3:2; Titus 1:6–8). This includes more than chastity but not less than it. Such leaders—honorable though transparent and humble as they, like us, struggle against sin—will be "able to give instruction in sound doctrine and also to rebuke those who contradict it" (Titus 1:9), in biblical sexual ethics as in so much else.

7. GUARDING AGAINST DESTRUCTIVE SOCIAL INFLUENCES

As we saw in chapter 7, churches and parents need to be aware of the potentially destructive pull of negative influences from the media. It is impossible to completely insulate ourselves or others from the barrage of sexual messaging in the mass media, but we can avoid the worst of it and teach believers to be critical, discerning consumers of it.

We also need to be cautious about negative peer relationships, especially friendships. Church leaders cannot demand that evangelical singles and youth completely avoid relationships with peers involved in illicit sex. After all, like all believers, they need to interact with unbelievers to function in this world, and it is necessary if they are to share the gospel. However, these relationships should be offset by stronger ties to positive peers, parents, family, and church, and should be accompanied with open dialogue about their sexual activities and temptations. They should also be taught to guard relationships with sexually immoral unbelievers against excessive entanglement—reaching out to the lost requires guardrails and distance. As Paul said, "Do not be unequally yoked with unbelievers" (2 Corinthians 6:14a), meaning we should not be partnered with them as two oxen pulling a plow, potentially being pulled in the direction of your partner. This is another balancing act, as discussed above. Additionally, parents and church leaders need to be especially concerned about singles' relationships with peers who profess to be fellow believers but are not honoring the biblical sexual ethic in their beliefs or conduct. Wayward professed believers can pull them away from faithfulness in powerful ways. Paul explains this succinctly in 1 Corinthians 5:9–11, reminding believers "not to associate with sexually immoral people" (5:9), by which he did not mean those in the world (5:10), but rather "not to associate with anyone who bears the name of a brother if he is guilty of sexual immorality" (5:11).

8. PARENTAL PRACTICES

Parents need to be encouraged to have strong and positive bonds with their children. They ought to be proactive in teaching their children about sex and given every resource, teaching, and support possible from the church. Parents should be transparent about supervising their children's relationships with the opposite sex and unafraid to ask tough questions. Youth pastoring, ministering, and accountability can be a big help in raising godly children, but it is not a replacement for effective parenting.

For church leaders to help parents guide their children, they need to offer solid, practical teaching on dating. Serial and romantically intense dating that is too early and totally recreational, and disconnected from marriage possibility and intentions, ought to be discouraged. Most evangelical singles begin having sex as teenagers, still under their parents' roofs, and in the context of dating relationships. Churches should provide real encouragement, education, and support for parents in guiding dating activities.[33]

Finally—and this is as much for couples and the church as for parents—unnecessarily delaying marriage is a bad idea. Pushing the average age of marriage back to the late twenties or later is not compatible with reducing fornication among singles. That does not mean rushing into marriage with unsuitable partners to beat a ticking clock or neglecting hard practical realities. However, when two suitable Christians love each other, pressuring them to push back their marriages until every other aspect of their lives is settled—great job, fat bank account, advanced degrees, and so on—is inviting trouble.

I recall some years ago a young woman my wife and I were close to introduced us to the fine Christian man she was engaged to. They were deeply in love. But his parents, though they supported them getting married, kept pressuring them to delay marriage until they had more money in the bank and more education; the new demands went on and on. We were not surprised when the wedding had to be moved up abruptly after this young lady got pregnant. Is this how we want our young people starting out their marriages, when it is so often avoidable?

9. WHAT ABOUT VIRGINITY PLEDGES?

Various forms of abstinence pledges are popular among evangelicals and conservative Catholics. These are public vows to resist having sex until marriage, often accompanied by ceremonies, signing of written promises, and physical symbols such as rings. Prominent examples include the Southern Baptists' True Love Waits sponsored by LifeWay Christian Resources and the Silver Ring Thing. There are various pledges used. Here is one for students from a True Love Waits covenant card: "Believing that true love waits, I make a commitment to God, myself, my family, my friends, my future mate, and my future children to a lifetime of purity including sexual abstinence from this day until the day I enter a biblical marriage relationship." In this version, the signed pledge from an adult witness accompanies the student's: "Believing that true love is pure, I join (insert student's name) in committing to a lifestyle of purity. I make a commitment to God, myself, my family, and my community of faith to abstain from pornography, impure touching and conversations, and sex outside a biblical marriage relationship from this day forward."[34]

Research on the impact of virginity pledges is difficult, given that those who participate in them are, on average, very different from those who do not in ways that are directly relevant to their risk of being involved in sex outside marriage.[35] These factors influence abstinence among believers whether they use virginity pledges or not. Still, researchers have been able to do studies on large samples that control for such factors and have shed light on the impact of virginity pledges. So far, results have been mixed. For example, in a highly regarded 2008 study controlling for just about all the factors I cited above, Jeremy Uecker found that both religious commitment and pledging increased the likelihood of abstaining from sex until marriage among those who married early, which was a little over one-quarter of pledgers.[36] However, a more recent study in the same top-ranked journal found that pledgers were much more likely to get pregnant out of wedlock. Meanwhile, at least among younger teens, they were not more likely to delay sexual onset.[37]

On this last point, other research (but by no means all controlled studies) suggests that private, but not public, pledging is associated with waiting longer to have sex. The power of private pledging may be because it is evidence of personal conviction more than of succumbing to group pressure.[38] Most research suggests that pledgers have fewer sex partners,[39] which is in turn tied to marrying earlier.[40] All research agrees that the majority of virginity pledgers do end up having sex before marriage; in other words, most break their vow.

Overall, I see no reason, rooted in research or personal experience, to recommend churches to encourage and sponsor virginity pledge programs or to avoid them. If churches are engaging in all the other practices I am suggesting here, these programs will not hurt, but they may add little. I am also leery of having young people make vows before God and others when they are young, impressionable, highly subject to group pressure, and the keeping of them will typically require years to bear out. The Scriptures are clear that the Lord takes these vows seriously and that "it is better that you should not vow than that you should vow and not pay" (Ecclesiastes 5:5).[41]

10. PREMARITAL COUNSELING AND MARRIAGE

No evangelical church should conduct wedding ceremonies for couples who have not participated in systematic, thorough premarital counseling for at least six to eight weeks. Given the quality of premarital counseling resources and training today, the known positive results, and the availability of excellent programs to train pastoral staff members in doing it, there is no excuse for using the often haphazard, hit-or-miss approach to preparing for marriage that the church has used in the past.[42]

A vital part of premarital counseling is exploring the sexual *pasts* of future mates. As someone who has done premarital preparation with numerous engaged couples, I know this can be difficult. Without becoming overly graphic or tawdry, it is critical to get these things out on the table—pornography usage, past partners, sex in the current partners' own relationships, STIs, abortions, and babies given up for adoption. Difficult disclosures such as these allow partners to begin their marriage from a place of honesty, even removing potential causes of future divorce. It also helps us to ensure that true repentance has taken place, that healing and accountability have substantially occurred, and that any residual challenges have been thought about and planned for. Taking on these topics usually occurs later in premarital counseling, after couples have gotten accustomed to tackling tough, but less sensitive, issues with each other and the pastor or counselor. By doing so, churches establish the importance of purity and the reality of sin, but redemptively and with grace, which is so important as the couple moves forward into married life, which will carry its own temptations.

Next, premarital counseling must address the sexual *present* of the spouses-to-be. Where there is ongoing sin—from various forms of illicit sexual activity together to the use of porn and other concerns—*now* is the time to apply the pure word of God to those issues and encourage repenting and turning from those sins. God's forgiveness is sure; his mercy is boundless. How wonderful it will be to begin marriage by making a clean break from besetting sexual sins and carrying forward those commitments to chastity into married life, by God's grace.

The elephant in the room, as I have amply documented, may be cohabitation. I recommend couples who are cohabiting show fruits of repentance by separating and ceasing all sexual activity until premarital counseling is completed and they have become man and wife before God and witnesses. With great respect for many pastors who differ from me in this regard, I think anything less diminishes our witness and our public adherence to Christian theology and morals, and it stops short of pressing upon couples the seriousness of the sin they are engaging in.

Insisting on this kind of repentance will often spawn serious challenges. For example, a cohabiting couple may have tight finances and children that make this very difficult. Discussions I have had with numerous pastors have helped me to see that such challenges are common. Flexibility may be called for; for example, partners can sleep in separate rooms and refrain from sex, under conditions of accountability. Sometimes churches will need to provide housing, finances, or both. The period of time need not be excessive, but repentance is vital and never involves continuing unbroken in the sins we claim to deeply regret before God.

Finally, we must deal with the sexual *futures* of our engaged couples. Premarital counseling is a good time to gauge and discuss each of the partner's expectations, including their comfort levels. Many times, these are distorted. Males have commonly indulged in pornography, which has given them perverse notions of the sexual needs and desires of women in general, and their future wife in particular. Many couples are not prepared for the valleys and challenges they will experience in their sexual lives over a lifetime—age, sickness, boredom, pregnancy, childbirth and children, the impact of medication, injuries, and many more. Poor pastoring can encourage young Christians to refrain from sex by lurid, unrealistic ideas about marital sex, often revolving around self-gratification rather than true, godly marital love and intimacy. Couples often need to make decisions about contraception. Others need help understanding the physical reality of having sex. It is a good idea for pastors and churches to keep libraries of wholesome materials about sex in marriage, especially for those who are newly married. My mother-in-law presented my wife and I with an excellent book about this when we were married almost forty years ago.[43]

There is an error floating around the church that ought to be addressed right up front in premarital counseling. It is that wives are somehow responsible to meet their husband's sexual "needs," whatever their preferences or compunctions. Some are even led to believe that failure to do so can "cause" their husbands to look to illicit avenues for sexual gratification, such as pornography or even adultery. I have had women tell me that women leaders of study groups they have been in have communicated this. Paul admonished Ephesian husbands to love their wives as Christ loved the church, to be concerned with their care, provision, and holiness (Ephesians 5:25–30). The high calling of husband is not even remotely consistent with men viewing their wives as mechanisms of sexual gratification, demanding sex however and whenever they want. Marital love must be kind, mutual, and first and foremost a sacred expression of love. Being married does not relieve any of us, men or women, from the need to be self-controlled, even in marital sex.

Another common mistake couples make in thinking about their future sex lives is to view things like orgasms and powerful experiences as the goal and measure of good sex. There will be such times, but in a healthy marriage, sex will also often be, for want of a better term, somewhat routine—nourishing and pleasurable but not always explosive. I like to use the analogy of food and drink. These are legitimate things to desire, and it is good to have times of feasting and of consuming particularly gourmet delights. Yet a steady diet of rich and exquisite food and drink is neither realistic nor healthy. That does not make each meal anything less than a gift of God which should satisfy us and for which we should thank him.

Church leaders must expect that often, if not normally, premarital couples will come to them with various types of sexual baggage in their moral beliefs, expectations, and prior actions, not to mention ongoing consequences they may be suffering for past sin. We owe it to these dear souls to address such matters forthrightly and in love.

11. HONESTLY AND THOROUGHLY HANDLING THE FACTS

I have encountered many Christians, including church leaders and parents, who believe that, when it comes to sex, what believers need to know is just what the Scriptures teach. As I have noted, too often this is separated from the rich tapestry of Christian theology, doctrine, anthropology, history, symbolism, and identity. But even if it is not, it is also vitally important to make sure that believers know the relevant facts about things like fornication, pornography, and cohabitation, and their consequences. To argue that they should be able to obey God regardless of this knowledge is a bit unrealistic. In fact, with the Scriptures to guide us, as John Calvin taught, we are called to consider the world as it is and seek to understand it more accurately.[44] Understanding the practical realities and risks is an additional layer of knowledge and protection. It helps to confront and defeat harmful urban myths that have infiltrated the church, and the facts help to illustrate that God's creation reflects and upholds his word—that in human affairs we see what the Bible would lead us to expect. There is protection in obeying God, and there are terrible pitfalls associated with rebelling against him.

The facts that believers need to know have been addressed throughout this book. Most importantly for singles are the consequences covered in chapter 8. How many believers think that condoms provide strong protection against virtually all STIs? That's false. How many believe that they can engage in oral sex without fear of STIs? Another widely accepted falsehood. Over 60 percent of Americans under thirty, and over 50 percent of those thirty to forty-nine believe living together reduces the risk of divorce. Less than 20 percent are aware that the opposite appears to be the case, at least for cohabitation overall.[45] I deal with this notion when speaking with relatives, with friends, and virtually every time I teach a college class on marriage. It is a destructive myth. How many evangelicals know that having sex before marriage, especially with someone other than your future spouse, increases one's risk of divorce? Would it help them to "just say no" if they knew, even if they already know that the Bible says that fornication is wrong?

I am a strong proponent of arming people with facts. When the other pieces—our commitment to God and our theology—are correct, the facts can only help us further. They also establish our credibility with young people who are, understandably, often a bit suspicious of what we tell them, perhaps believing that we are out of touch with the real world. In Christ—in all he is and all he teaches and all he has done for us—we can tackle reality with honesty and the utmost confidence. We can plant our feet on real earth, not merely floating on spiritual abstractions and platitudes and detached moral rules.

12. PROVIDE A POSITIVE VISION FOR CHRISTIAN SINGLES

Being a single Christian is meant to be filled with opportunity and purpose. Church life can focus too much on married people and families, unintentionally communicating the notion that singleness is just a way station between childhood and marriage. Many churched singles feel like second-class Christians.

Marriage has been a delight for me, but my years as a Christian single were busy, satisfying, and provided unique opportunities for ministry that would have been difficult if I had been married. It was not just about abstaining from sex and preparing for marriage. This is not the same as the world's view of singleness, which is often focused on fun and the self, reveling in the lack of commitments and entanglements.

Churches should provide solid biblical teaching on singleness, including encouraging Christian singles to use their freedom to serve Christ. This does not mean that being free from the obligations of marriage requires they work constantly, become drudges, and cannot enjoy this precious time of their life. There is no reason not to enjoy the company of friends and recreation, including getting to know potential mates. But they, like married people, need to have meaningful purpose and direction tied to their commitment to Christ and to his people in their present moment. Their single life should not just be gritting their teeth, abstaining until marriage, and praying and looking for a spouse, but using their energies for the kingdom in that stage of their Christian walk.[46]

13. PRAY

My final recommendation is we must pray for the sexual purity of our churches, for all those—not just singles—struggling with sexual temptation. The praying should be in private and in public, by parents and congregations, lifted up by dating and engaged couples recognizing their need for strength and wisdom in exercising sexual self-control. Praying these things communicates clearly to ourselves and others that chastity is something that is important to God and to us. Far more importantly, however, it is tapping into that bottomless reservoir of comfort, encouragement, and power that only God can give us. We are not in this struggle alone. In fact, these challenges against our sinful desires are designed, at least partly, like so many other earthly challenges, to draw us nearer to God, to enforce our dependence upon God, and to enable him to be our ultimate provision and sufficiency in our weakness (see 1 Corinthians 12:7–10). Consider what Jesus said, recorded in John 15:4–5: "Abide in me, and I in you. As the branch cannot bear fruit by itself, unless it abides in the vine, neither can you, unless you abide in me. I am the vine; you are the branches. Whoever abides in me and I in him, he it is that bears much fruit, for apart from me you can do nothing."

Conclusion

These basic, common-sense calls for us to rest our efforts at pursuing sexual faithfulness on the biblical, time-tested foundation of normal Christianity flow naturally out of the chapters in this book that preceded this one, and only make sense in light of the whole. I would like to conclude by looking again at what Christ is aiming at and what we should be pursuing, yearning for, and looking forward to: the glorious church, pure and spotless, presented as a bride to the Groom at the completion of all things. In this vision, sexual purity is a piece of the larger tapestry of holiness, of spotlessness, and of perfection toward which God is guiding us through the blessings and trials of this world:

> Then I saw a new heaven and a new earth, for the first heaven and the first earth had passed away, and the sea was no more. And I saw the holy city, new Jerusalem, coming down out of heaven from God, prepared as a bride adorned for her husband. And I heard a loud voice from the throne saying, "Behold, the dwelling place of God is with man. He will dwell with them, and they will be his people, and God himself will be with them as their God. He will wipe away every tear from their eyes, and death shall be no more, neither shall there be mourning, nor crying, nor pain anymore, for the former things have passed away. … The one who conquers will have this heritage, and I will be his God and he will be my son. But as for the cowardly, the faithless, the detestable, as for murderers, the sexually immoral, sorcerers, idolaters, and all liars, their portion will be in the lake that burns with fire and sulfur, which is the second death." (Revelation 21:1–4, 7–8)

METHODOLOGY APPENDIX

Major Survey Data Sources

GENERAL SOCIAL SURVEY

The General Social Survey (GSS) is a national survey of the United States population that started in 1972. It used to be done every year but switched to only even-numbered years in 1994. It is conducted by the National Opinion Research Center at the University of Chicago and is funded by the National Science Foundation. The survey covers adults starting at age eighteen with no fixed upper age limit. Most of the survey is conducted through face-to-face interviews, though in some cases telephone interviews may be used. Total sample sizes in the years from 1972 through 1993 ranged from a low of 1,372 to a high of 1,860 but fall generally closer to the 1,500 to 1,600 range. With the switch to every other year in 1994, the sample sizes were increased. Except for the year 2006, where a third sample was added, bringing the sample size up to 4,510, these samples ranged from a low of 1,974 to a high of 2,992—most substantially exceeding 2,500.[1] Data for 2020 was scheduled to be released sometime in fall 2021, which was too late to be used in this book.

In chapters 3 and following, I typically combined surveys across multiple years. This enabled me to work with samples large enough to meaningfully compare subgroups, while looking at more recent realities. In the GSS, especially when focusing only on evangelicals, dividing the samples into further subgroups (such as in examining those who attend church regularly versus those who do not, those having different views of the Bible, and so on) often creates groups that are too small to meaningfully compare. Normally, I combined all five GSS surveys from 2010 through 2018. My GSS data typically combines genders, though I do provide comparisons of men and women where it is feasible, appropriate, or necessary. Here are the sample sizes for the religious affiliations I compare in the combined data set: evangelical Protestants (2,782), mainline Protestants (1,421), black Protestants (844), Catholics (2,674), and "nones" (no religious affiliation, 2,434), for a total of 10,155: 4,521 men and 5,634 women.

In this combined GSS for 2010 through 2018, there were more women than men (55.4 percent versus 44.6 percent). Thus, except when comparing males and females directly, I weight the data by gender to correct for this statistically, making things as they would be if the sample size was fifty-fifty women and men.

NATIONAL SURVEY OF FAMILY GROWTH

The National Survey of Family Growth (NSFG) is conducted by the Centers for Disease Control and Prevention on large national samples. It began in 1973 with only women who had ever been married ages fifteen to forty-four, then expanded to include all women in this age group regardless of marital status in 1982. A comparable survey of men of all marital statuses ages fifteen to forty-four was added in 2002. The men surveyed are not related to the women surveyed. In 2015, the age range was expanded to include those forty-five to forty-nine. Thus, to be strictly comparable, if later years are compared to surveys before 2015, those ages need to be excluded. The survey is conducted through face-to-face interviews, though very sensitive questions are addressed through an anonymous self-administered questionnaire to encourage honest answers.

Since 2006, the NSFG has been conducted through a "continuous field work" approach that has survey administration taking place over extended periods of time, wrapping up at a given point. This began with cycle 6, which included data collected from 2006 through 2010. Since then, there has been cycle 7 conducted from 2011 into 2013 (5,601 women and 4,815 men), cycle 8 conducted from 2013 into 2015 (5,699 women and 4,506 men), cycle 9 conducted from 2015 into 2017 (5,455 women and 4,540 men), and cycle 10—the most recent release as of this writing—conducted from 2017 into 2019 (6,141 women and 5,206 men). I was fortunate to obtain this most recent data set in time for this book—the next cycle of interviewing is not scheduled to commence until January 2022, assuming funding is available. It will likely be several years before we see more recent data from this valuable survey than what is covered in this book.[2]

When I compare religious affiliations using NSFG data, I only use the last survey cycle and report the data for each gender separately. The samples for both the male and female surveys are large enough to allow for this. It is simpler to analyze the data files independently, and reporting percentages for men and women separately provides added detail.

However, when I focus on evangelicals exclusively, I compare them internally on many factors, dividing evangelicals further into subgroups. This is hard to do with only a sample of evangelicals for one survey cycle divided further by gender.[3] Therefore, when I focus my analysis just on evangelicals, I combine the 2015–2017 and 2017–2019 cycles *and* I usually combine males and females—separating genders when appropriate, of course. Because my combined file is 54.5 percent females and 45.5 percent males, when I am not comparing males and females directly, as with the 2010–2018 GSS, I weight the data by gender to correct for this statistically, making things as they would be if the sample was fifty-fifty.

In the 2017–2019 (cycle 10) combined file that I use for comparing religious affiliations, sample sizes are as follows: evangelical Protestants (1,867), mainline Protestants (1,289), black Protestants (1,460), Catholics (2,436), and "nones" (no religious affiliations, 3,265). In the file combining the last two cycles (2015–2019) that I use to look at subgroups of evangelicals, there are 3,799 evangelicals.

YOUTH RISK BEHAVIOR SURVEY

The national Youth Risk Behavior Survey (YRBS) is conducted on public- and private-school students, ninth through twelfth grades, across the United States. It has been completed every odd-numbered year since 1991 and is overseen by the Centers for Disease Control and Prevention. It is a premier part of a large collection of data sources entitled the Youth Risk Behavior Surveillance System. The YRBS is completed by students in a single class period using a self-administered, anonymous questionnaire. The sample size is huge—for example, in 2019 there were 13,677 completed questionnaires.[4] Surveys are administered between February and May. The 2021 survey will not be released until the summer of 2022, and thus could not be included in this book.

Brief Note on Statistical Significance

In this book, I often compare different groups of survey respondents on some measure. For example, are those who attend church regularly more likely than those who do not to believe that sex between unmarried adults is morally wrong? Contrasts such as these are critical to understanding just about everything social science studies.

When comparing groups, outcomes and percentages are bound to fluctuate. The question is, are the differences large enough that we can be certain that they were not just a fluke? The standard way social scientists answer that is by a measure called "statistical significance" or "probability of error." It tells us what the probability is that the differences we are seeing between groups on some measures are nothing more than normal, random fluctuation. It is based on how big the variations are and how many cases are involved. The standard rule of thumb is that if the "probability of error" is 5 percent or less, the observed difference is "significant."

I am not asking readers to wallow in these kinds of details. However, I do check all my findings this way, as I should. So, if I say that a difference is "not significant," it means that the chance of error is too high to be confident that the difference is meaningful and can be applied to the general population. On the other hand, if I note that a difference, or I could say an "association" or "relationship," is "significant," that means that there are enough cases and a big enough variation that we can confidently accept this as an accurate description of the real world. Sometimes I do this in the text itself; often I will get it out of the reader's way by putting that information in a brief note. Most of the time, the differences I talk about have much lower than a 5 percent probability of error. Often, that probability of error is effectively zero. When that happens, I may say that the differences are "very significant."[5]

ACKNOWLEDGMENTS

Writing a book means many hours spent alone doing research and writing endless drafts. But it is not a solo task. Good writing, like living well, requires wise counsel and timely, constructive critical input. I am grateful to those who gave me that through the many months I labored on this. These include my editor at Lexham Press, Elliot Ritzema, as well as pastors Robert Hall, Nathan Devlin, and Joe Tyrpak, each of whom read over every line and gave me excellent and honest feedback and direction. Carl Trueman was kind enough to review my early chapters. I also received excellent input from Victor Kuligin on several chapters. My wife Kathy took on a lot and exercised endless patience to liberate me enough that I could sneak away for many hours undisturbed, despite an active household with lots of coming and going. She also showed grace in being willing to listen to me talk through sometimes distressing and embarrassing topics and facts. She also never batted an eye at me stepping away from administrative responsibilities, and pay, at my college so I could devote my remaining professional years to teaching and writing, despite the belt-tightening this created. Finally, I have several colleagues at Grove City College who encouraged my efforts in many ways. Paul Kengor and the college's Institute for Faith and Freedom (IFF) agreed to take me on as a fellow, giving me a bit of course relief to facilitate my writing. And the college itself granted me a one-semester sabbatical to focus my attention on completing this project. To all, a sincere thank you, and may our Lord bless you richly.

ENDNOTES

CHAPTER 1. GOD'S DESIGN FOR SEX AND MARRIAGE

1. See my interviews with a spectrum of evangelical pastors, David J. Ayers, "First Comes Love, Then Comes House Keys," *Christianity Today* (April 2021): 36–41.

2. See Question 1 in the Westminster Shorter Catechism: "Q: What is the chief end of man? A. Man's chief end is to glorify God and enjoy him forever." *The Westminster Confession of Faith, Together with the Larger Catechism and Shorter Catechism, with Scripture Proofs*, 3rd ed. (Atlanta: Committee for Christian Education & Publication, 1990), 3.

3. Thomas Adams, *An Exposition Upon the Second Epistle General of St. Peter*, rev. and corrected by James Sherman (repr., London: Henry G. Bohn, 1848), 84.

4. "Wedding Song (There Is Love)," Noel Paul Stookey, Hal Leonard Music, 2008. It appeared on the solo album *Paul and* (1971).

5. Rev. Nathan Devlin, in private communication.

6. René Gehring, *The Biblical "One Flesh" Theology as Constituted in Genesis 2:24: An Exegetical Study of This Human-Divine Covenant Pattern, Its New Testament Echoes, and Its Reception History throughout Scripture Focusing on the Spiritual Impact of Sexuality* (Eugene, OR: Wipf & Stock, 2013), 230.

7. Sherif Girgis, Ryan T. Anderson, and Robert P. George, *What Is Marriage? Man and Woman: A Defense* (New York: Encounter, 2012), 24.

8. Including intimate knowledge, perception, comprehension, to have knowledge of, to be revealed (see Genesis 18:19; Proverbs 1:2; Jeremiah 1:5–6). See Francis Brown, S. R. Driver, and Charles A. Briggs, *The Enhanced Brown-Driver-Briggs Hebrew and English Lexicon* (Oak Harbor, WA: Logos, 2000). Here, I benefited from the search and translitera- tion tools provided by Bible Study Tools at https://www.biblestudytools .com/lexicons/hebrew/kjv/yada.html.

9. Greg Smalley, "Does 'Yada, Yada, Yada' In Your Marriage Means Its 'Blah, Blah, Blah'?," *Focus on the Family*, March 29, 2017, https://

www.focusonthefamily.com/marriage/does-yada-yada-yada-in-your -marriage-mean-its-blah-blah-blah.

10. See, for example, "consummation of marriage," in William J. Stewart, *Collins Dictionary of Law* (London: Collins, 2006).

11. Edmund S. Morgan, *The Puritan Family: Religion and Domestic Relations in Seventeenth-Century New England* (New York: Harper & Row, 1966), 31, 34.

12. Diane V. Bowers, "To Spite the Devil: Martin Luther and Katharina von Bora's Wedding as Reform and Resistance," *Religions* 11.3 (March 2020): 116, 127.

13. *The Book of Common Prayer*, introduction by James Wood (New York: Penguin, 2012), 311. Emphasis added.

14. See John Calvin, *Commentary on the Epistles of Paul the Apostle to the Corinthians,* vol. 1, trans. John Pringle (Edinburgh: Calvin Translation Society, 1848), 218–19. Originally published in English in 1578.

15. For a Protestant expression of this, see Richard Coekin, "Marriage Is a Mirror," *The Gospel Coalition*, November 9, 2015, https://www. thegospelcoalition.org/article/marriage-is-a-mirror/. For a Roman Catholic statement, see Pope Benedict XVI, "Angelus: Feast of the Holy Family," *Vatican.va,* December 27, 2009, http://w2.vatican.va/ content/benedict-xvi/en/angelus/2009/documents/hf_ben-xvi_ ang_20091227.html.

16. David White, *God, You, and Sex: A Profound Mystery* (Greensboro, NC: New Growth Press, 2019), 20.

17. See also my book *Christian Marriage: A Comprehensive Introduction* (Bellingham, WA: Lexham Press, 2018), 84, 365.

18. S. M. Baugh, *Ephesians: Evangelical Exegetical Commentary* (Bellingham, WA: Lexham Press, 2015), 493–94.

19. *The Book of Common Prayer*, 311.

20. See White, *God, You, and Sex*, 3–4.

21. Francis Schaeffer, *The Church before the Watching World: A Practical Ecclesiology* (Downers Grove, IL: InterVarsity Press, 1971), 45. I am also grateful for the excellent list of biblical references on spiritual adultery and "whoredom" Schaeffer provides on pages 47–50. In addition, see Peter Jones, *The God of Sex* (Escondido, CA: Main Entry Editions, 2006), 135–36.

22. Jones, *The God of Sex*, 135–36. Emphasis original.

23. C. S. Lewis, *Mere Christianity* (New York: Harper Collins, 2001), 98.

24. Stanley J. Grenz, *Sexual Ethics: An Evangelical Perspective* (Louisville: Westminster John Knox, 1997), 112.

25. *Merriam-Webster*, s.v. "fornicate," https://www.merriam-webster.com/ dictionary/fornication.

26. Ernest Best, *First and Second Epistles to the Thessalonians,* Black's New Testament Commentary (Peabody, MA: Hendrickson, 1972), 160.

27. See Ayers, *Christian Marriage*, 46–47. There is also an excellent overview of this in Grenz, *Sexual Ethics*, 99–100. On the last point, Paul assumed the men to whom he was writing were monogamous. On the "one-woman man" implications of the Timothy and Titus passages, see Philip Towner, *1–2 Timothy and Titus,* IVP New Testament Commentary Series (Downers

Grove, IL: InterVarsity Press, 1994), 84, 225. Although these passages refer to elders, it is clear that the latter were to be examples to those under their care—modeling qualities all men should seek to emulate.

28. Richard Baxter, *Baxter's Practical Works,* vol. 1 of *A Christian Directory: or, A Sum of Practical Theology, and Cases of Conscience* (1673; repr., Ligonier, PA: Soli Deo Gloria, 1990), 333.

29. *Merriam-Webster,* s.v. "chastity," https://www.merriam-web-ster.com/dictionary/chastity. See Leland Ryken, *Worldly Saints: The Puritans as They Really Were* (Grand Rapids: Zondervan, 1986), 46, on Protestant understandings of chastity, and the entry on "Chastity" for the United States Conference of Catholic Bishops for the current Roman Catholic view on it, http://www.usccb.org/issues-and-action/marriage-and-family/natural-family-planning/catholic-teaching/upload/Chastity.pdf. The Catholics came to this understanding of chastity as more than just virginity a bit later than the Protestants did.

30. R. C. Sproul, *The Intimate Marriage: A Practical Guide to Building a Great Marriage* (Phillipsburg, NJ: P & R, 1975), 117.

31. J. I. Packer, *A Quest for Godliness: The Puritan Vision for the Christian Life* (Wheaton, IL: Crossway Books, 1990), 261; Ryken, *Worldly Saints,* 40–42.

32. On this Catholic view of marital purposes as being only mutual help, procreation, and child-rearing, see the *Catechism of the Catholic Church,* 2nd ed. (Washington, DC: The United States Catholic Conference, 2000), 400. Catholics today do tend to have a more positive, affirming view of marital sex than was true in the medieval times and even the era of the Reformation.

33. Packer, *Quest for Godliness,* 265–66; Edmund Leites, *The Puritan Conscience and Modern Sexuality* (New Haven: Yale University Press, 1986), 12–13; Ryken, *Worldly Saints,* 43–45.

34. Ryken, *Worldly Saints,* 45.

35. Sproul, *Intimate Marriage,* 120.

36. A. A. Hodge, *The Westminster Confession: A Commentary* (1869; repr., Carlisle, PA: Banner of Truth Trust, 2002), 302.

37. Joshua Harris, *I Kissed Dating Goodbye: A New Attitude Toward Relationships and Romance* (Colorado Springs: Multnomah Books, 1997); *Boy Meets Girl: Say Hello to Courtship* (Colorado Springs: Multnomah Books, 2000); and *Sex Is Not Wrong (Lust Is): Sexual Purity in a Lust-Saturated World* (Colorado Springs: Multnomah Books, 2003).

38. Larry Tomczak, "Miley Cyrus: From Purity Ring to Perversion," *The Christian Post,* August 31, 2015, https://www.christianpost.com/news/miley-cyrus-from-purity-ring-to-perversion.html.

39. *I Survived I Kissed Dating Goodbye,* directed by Jessica Van Der Wyngaard, written by Joshua Harris and Jessica Van Der Wyngaard, 2018, DOCSology Productions, https://www.isurvivedikdg.com/.

40. Mike Allen, "Josh Harris, Fallen Evangelical Mega-Pastor: 'I Excommunicated Myself,'" *Axios,* November 3, 2019, https://www.axios.com/josh-harris-evangelical-pastor-excommunicated-64674ffd-4e09–458a-8697–3d207100e11e.html. On criticisms that reject core Christian teachings on sex outside marriage, see Joe Carter, "The FAQs: What You Should

Know About Purity Culture," *The Gospel Coalition*, July 24, 2019, https://www. thegospelcoalition.org/article/faqs-know-purity-culture/.

41. I address this in detail in *Christian Marriage*, 136–47.

42. Rachel Joy Welcher, who was a pastor's daughter in high school during the height of the influence of Joshua Harris's and other so-called "sexual purity" teaching on dating, courtship, and sexual purity, has written a fine critique of the movement that honors biblical teaching on chastity while rejecting what many now recognize as its distortions, imbalances, and errors: *Talking Back to Purity Culture: Rediscovering Faithful Christian Sexuality* (Downers Grove, IL: InterVarsity Press, 2020). See also the excellent review by Jen Pollock Michel, "Don't Overstate the Rewards of Sexual Faithfulness. Don't Understate Them Either," *Christianity Today*, November 16, 2020, https://www. christianitytoday.com/ct/2020/november-web-only/talking-back-purity -culture-rachel-joy-welcher.html.

43. Leah MarieAnn Klett, "Purity Culture Harmed Thousands of Evangelical Teens; What Did the Church Get Wrong About Sex?," *The Christian Post*, May 20, 2019, https://www.christianpost.com/news/purity-culture-harmed-thousands-of-evangelical-teens-what-did-the-church-get-wrong-about-sex.html?page=2.

44. Cited in David French, "Whither Evangelical Purity Culture? Thoughts on the Legacy of a Lost Pastor," *National Review*, July 29, 2019, https://www.nationalreview.com/2019/07/ whither-evangelical-purity-culture-thoughts-on-the-legacy-of-a-lost-pastor/.

45. Lewis, *Mere Christianity*, 134. Lewis was reacting directly to those who were making "health one of your main, direct objects." I owe my dear friend and former pastor, the Rev. Robert Hall, for reminding me of the relevance of this quote here.

46. French, "Whither Evangelical Purity Culture?"

47. Klett, "Purity Culture Harmed Thousands."

CHAPTER 2. FROM AN ETHIC OF COVENANT TO AN ETHIC OF CONSENT

1. Dennis Hollinger, *The Meaning of Sex: Christian Ethics and the Moral Life* (Grand Rapids: Baker Academic, 2009), 43.

2. For a thorough, compelling account of Philip Rieff's ideas on this issue, and the rise of the therapeutic mindset and "expressive individualism" in general—its manifestations and consequences—drawing on literature, philosophy, and a lot more, see Carl Trueman's recent masterpiece, *The Rise and Triumph of the Modern Self: Cultural Amnesia, Expressive Individualism, and the Road to the Sexual Revolution* (Wheaton, IL: Crossway, 2020).

3. Philip Rieff, *The Triumph of the Therapeutic: Uses of Faith after Freud* (New York: Harper & Row, 1966). See especially the final chapter starting on page 232; also 48–78.

4. Rieff, *Triumph of the Therapeutic*, 62.

5. Rieff, *Triumph of the Therapeutic*, 61.

6. Michael Lewis, "My Life Among the Deathworks by Philip Rieff," *Commentary*, April 2006, https://www.commentarymagazine.com/articles/ michael-lewis/my-life-among-the-deathworks-by-philip-rieff/.

7. Lewis, "My Life Among the Deathworks by Philip Rieff."

8. Robert Bellah, Richard Madsen, William M. Sullivan, Ann Swidler, and Steven M. Tipton, *Habits of the Heart: Individualism and Commitment in American Life* (New York: Harper & Row, 1985). See especially pages 85–112.

9. Bellah et al., *Habits of the Heart*, 109–10 (emphases added).

10. Barbara Dafoe Whitehead, *The Divorce Culture* (New York: Alfred A. Knopf, 1996), 45–48, 53–54, 56. See my discussion in Ayers, *Christian Marriage*, 199–200.

11. Andrew Cherlin, *Public and Private Families: An Introduction*, 9th ed. (New York: McGraw-Hill, 2020), 194.

12. Rev. Nathan Devlin, private communication.

13. Pitirim Sorokin, *The Crisis of Our Age* (New York: E. P. Dutton & Company, 1941). In 1957, Sorokin also released an abridged version of the original four volumes in one large book of about 750 pages, which is still intimidating. I use the former.

14. Sorokin, *Crisis of Our Age*, 17.

15. Sorokin, *Crisis of Our Age*, 17–20.

16. Sorokin, *Crisis of Our Age*, 20–21.

17. Sorokin, *Crisis of Our Age*, 87, 97, 99.

18. Sorokin, *Crisis of Our Age*, see, for example, 158–64, but the idea permeates his analysis of sensate culture.

19. Sorokin, *Crisis of Our Age*, 43, 51, 293.

20. Pitirim Sorokin, *The American Sex Revolution* (Boston: Porter Sargent, 1957), 4.

21. Sorokin, *American Sex Revolution*, 19.

22. Russell Nieli, "Critic of the Sensate Culture: Rediscovering the Genius of Pitirim Sorokin," *The Political Science Reviewer* 35 (July 2006): 264–379. This lengthy piece is an excellent introduction to Sorokin and to the continued relevance and validity of his work.

23. Hollinger, *The Meaning of Sex*, 18.

24. Lisa Wade, *American Hookup: The New Culture of Sex on Campus* (New York: W.W. Norton, 2017), 241–48.

25. Cherlin, *Public and Private Families*, 171. Cherlin also agrees with Wade that one problem with hookup culture is the lack of gender equality.

26. In fact, Sorokin's accurate grasp of the modern mindset on many things, including sex and marriage, was recognized in detail by the late, eminent evangelical theologian Harold O. J. Brown in his book *The Sensate Culture: Western Civilization Between Chaos and Transformation* (Nashville: Word, 1996).

27. David Riesman, with Nathan Glazer and Reuel Denney, *The Lonely Crowd: A Study of the Changing American Character* (New Haven, CT: Yale University Press, 1963; orig. 1950).

28. Riesman, *The Lonely Crowd*, 16, 24.

29. Archer Wallace, *Boys of Grit Who Became Men of Honor,* rare collector's edition (1925; repr., Mount Morris, NY: Lamplighter Press, 2001).

30. Riesman, *The Lonely Crowd*, 25, 21–22.

31. Riesman, *The Lonely Crowd*, xxvii.

32. See Abigail Shrier, *Irreversible Damage: The Transgender Craze Seducing Our Daughters* (Washington, DC: Regnery, 2020).

33. Rupert Wilkinson, " 'The Lonely Crowd,' at 60, Is Still Timely," *The Chronicle of Higher Education*, September 12, 2010, https://www.chronicle.com/article/the-lonely-crowd-at-60-is-still-timely/.

34. Ronald Inglehart, *The Silent Revolution: Changing Values and Political Styles Among Western Publics* (Princeton, NJ: Princeton University Press, 1977).

35. Christopher Lasch, *The Culture of Narcissism: American Life in an Age of Diminishing Expectations* (New York: W. W. Norton, 1979). See especially pages 21–23, 27–70, and 326–30.

36. James Davison Hunter, *The Death of Character: Moral Education in an Age Without Good or Evil* (New York: Basic Books, 2000), xv.

37. Kristin Luker, *Abortion and the Politics of Motherhood* (Berkeley: University of California Press, 1984). Here I draw on content in the second half of her book, and particularly the chapter "World Views of the Activists" on pages 158–91. Luker describes her activist interviewees on pages 249–56.

38. Luker, *Abortion and the Politics of Motherhood*, 163–65.

39. Luker, *Abortion and the Politics of Motherhood*, 176–78.

40. Teo Armus, "A Virginia Teacher Was Fired for Refusing to Use a Trans Student's Pronouns. Now, He's Suing His School District," *The Washington Post*, October 1, 2019, https://www.washingtonpost.com/nation/2019/10/01/virginia-teacher-fired-not-using-transgender-pronouns-sues-school/; Lambda Legal, September 17, 2018, "Changing Birth Certificate Sex Designations: State-by-State Guidelines," *Know Your Rights,* https://www.lambdalegal.org/know-your-rights/article/trans-changing-birth-certificate-sex-designations.

41. Sian Ferguson, "What Does It Mean to Be Gender-Fluid?," *Healthline*, June 11, 2020, https://www.healthline.com/health/gender-fluid.

42. Even this has changed, at least in how "treatment" for unwanted same-sex attraction is now only considered appropriate if it involves changing the "unwantedness" or "social impairment" rather than trying to change the attraction itself.

43. "The A.P.A Ruling on Homosexuality: The Issue Is Subtle, the Debate Still On," *The New York Times*, December 23, 1973, 109, emphases added.

44. David Glenn, "Prophet of the 'Anti-Culture,' " *The Chronicle of Higher Education*, November 11, 2005, A14-A17.

45. Wilfred M. McClay, *The Masterless: Self and Society in Modern America* (Chapel Hill, NC: North Carolina University Press, 1994), 6.

46. Carl Trueman, "Queer Times," *First Things*, May 21, 2020, https://www.firstthings.com/web-exclusives/2020/05/queer-times, emphases added.

47. Tellingly, a recent American Institute of Stress report held that three-quarters of college students had experienced "overwhelming anxiety," with almost 30 percent reporting it in the last two weeks ("Anxiety in College Students: Causes, Statistics & How Universities Can Help," October 21, 2019, https://www.stress.org/anxiety-in-college-students-causes-statistics-how-universities-can-help). Depression and relationship problems are also at epidemic levels among this demographic (American Psychological Association, "College students' mental health is a growing concern, survey

finds," *Monitor on Psychology* 44, no. 6 (June 2013): 13. At least 80 percent of colleges and universities are reporting alarming increases in mental health issues among students (Hollie Chessman and Morgan Taylor, "College Student Mental Health and Well-Being: A Survey of Presidents," *Higher Education Today*, August 12, 2019, https://www.higheredtoday.org/2019/08/12/college-student-mental-health-well-survey-college-presidents/).

48. Dale Kuehne, *Sex and the iWorld: Rethinking Relationship beyond an Age of Individualism* (Grand Rapids: Baker, 2009).

49. Kuehne, *Sex and the iWorld*, 21.

50. Stanley Grenz, *Sexual Ethics: An Evangelical Perspective* (Louisville, KY: Westminster John Knox), 94–96.

51. Kuehne, *Sex and the iWorld*, 44.

52. Combining 2010 through 2018 data, the views about the morality of having sex with someone other than one's spouse while married are: 77 percent say it is "always wrong" and 13 percent say it is "almost always wrong." Only 2 percent say it is "not wrong at all." The rest say it is only "sometimes wrong." On divorce, 38 percent want it to be easier and another 22 percent like things as they are. For more information about the General Social Survey, see the Methodology Appendix.

53. Bromleigh McCleneghan, *Good Christian Sex: Why Chastity Isn't the Only Option—And Other Things the Bible Says about Sex* (San Francisco: HarperOne, 2016).

54. Jonathan Merritt, "Sex Outside of Marriage Can be Holy, According to this Christian Minister," *Religion News Service*, July 21, 2016, https://religionnews.com/2016/07/21/sex-outside-of-marriage-can-be-holy-according-to-this-minister/.

55. Merritt, "Sex Outside of Marriage."

56. Jeff Elder, "AI-powered Sex Robots Are Selling Well During Lockdown—Which Worries Some Experts, Who Say That They Can Introduce Some Surprising Regulatory Problem," *Business Insider*, June 13, 2020, https://www.businessinsider.com/ai-sex-robots-are-selling-well-realdoll-regulated-2020-6.

57. Richard Weaver, *Ideas Have Consequences* (Chicago: University of Chicago Press, 1948).

58. Cherlin, *Public and Private Families*, 168, 210; Sinikka Elliott, *Not My Kid: What Parents Believe about the Sex Lives of Their Teenagers* (New York: New York University Press, 2012), 14; Michael Wiederman, "Premarital Sex," in *Sex and Society*, vol. 3 (New York: Marshall Cavendish, 2010), 664–65.

59. Edward O. Laumann, John H. Gagnon, Robert T. Michael, and Stuart Michaels, *The Social Organization of Sexuality: Sexual Practices in the United States* (Chicago: University of Chicago Press, 1994).

60. Laumann et al., *Social Organization of Sexuality*, 201–2.

61. See U.S. Census, 2019, "Figure MS-2 Median Age at First Marriage: 1890 to Present," Source: U.S. Census Bureau, Decennial Censuses, 1890 to 1940, and Current Population Survey, Annual Social and Economic Supplements, 1947 to 2019, https://www.census.gov/content/dam/Census/library/visualizations/time-series/demo/families-and-households/ms-2.pdf. Note that due to rounding, all percentages do not add up to 100 percent. In all

figures in this book, where numbers add up to 99 percent or 101 that "should" be 100 percent, it is due to rounding issues.

62. Laumann et al., *Social Organization of Sexuality*. Calculated by the author from Table 5.7.

63. Nicholas L. Syrett, *American Child Bride: A History of Minors and Marriage in the United States* (Chapel Hill, NC: University of North Carolina Press, 2016), 232. For example, in 1950, a high year for youth marriage, only 7.6 percent of girls were married before age eighteen, almost all of those between ages fifteen and seventeen. For boys, it was tiny—1.6 percent. By 1970, those figures were down to 5.3 percent and 2.2 percent, respectively.

64. For more information on the YRBS, see the Methodology Appendix.

65. Note that by not including those who dropped out of high school prior to the twelfth grade, this probably underestimates the percent who have sex by, say, seventeen to eighteen years of age. We have reason to believe that those who drop out would be more sexually active. Also, given that the survey is conducted February through May, this won't pick up student sexual behavior milestones reached *after* they are surveyed. Thus, these percentages are a bit lower than the totals would be by the finish of their senior year of high school.

66. Details about the National Survey of Family Growth are provided in the Methodology Appendix.

67. To give some idea—although adultery is not measured directly in the NSFG, it is in the GSS. In the combined GSS for 2008–2018, among respondents who had married and never been divorced or separated, between the ages of eighteen and thirty-two, only 6 percent of both males and females had ever committed adultery. See the Methodology Appendix for more information about the General Social Survey.

68. In the next chapter, we will get into a lot more detail on this vital item.

69. Each number represents a couple—two people—not one individual.

70. On changes in measurement, see Benjamin Gurrentz, April 12, 2019, "Cohabitation Over the Last 20 Years: Measuring and Understanding the Changing Demographics of Unmarried Partners, 1996–2017," see also the Supplemental Tables, https://www.census.gov/library/working-papers/2019/demo/SEHSD-WP2019–10.html. Data from 1996 through 2019 taken from each year's Table UC1 based on the Current Population Survey. Summarized at the table UC1 collection spreadsheet available at https://www.census.gov/data/tables/time-series/demo/families/adults.html?#.

71. Wendy D. Manning, Kara Joyner, Paul Hemez, and Cassandra Cupka, "Measuring Cohabitation in National Surveys," *Demography* 56, no. 4 (June 2019): 1196.

72. Laumann et al., *Social Organization of Sexuality*, 206–7.

73. Scott Stanley and Galena Rhoades, July 19, 2016, "Testing a Relationship Is Probably the Worst Reason to Cohabit," *Institute for Family Studies*, https://ifstudies.org/ifs-admin/resources/testing-a-relationship-is-probably-the-worst-reason-to-cohabit-family-studiesfamily-studies.pdf.

74. These estimates were calculated by comparing Table UC-3 "Opposite-Sex Unmarried Couples by Presence of Biological Children Under 18, and Age, Earnings, Education, and Race and Hispanic Origin of Both Partners:

2019" to Table FG3, "Married Couple Family Groups, by Presence of Own Children Under 18, and Age, Earnings, Education, and Race and Hispanic Origin of Both Spouses: 2018." Both available at https://www.census.gov/data/tables/2019/demo/families/cps-2019.html.

75. For one example of stories covering this, see Gaby Galvin, April 29, 2020, "U.S. Marriage Rate Hits Historic Low," *U.S. News and World Report*, https://www.usnews.com/news/healthiest-communities/articles/2020-04-29/us-marriage-rate-drops-to-record-low.

76. Galvin, "U.S. Marriage Hits Historic Low."

77. 2020, "Marriage," *Gallup News*, https://news.gallup.com/poll/117328/marriage.aspx.

78. Percentages do not add up to 100 percent as there were tiny percentages who refused or answered "don't know."

79. Katharina Buchholz, "How Much of the Internet Consists of Porn?," Statista, February 11, 2019, https://www.statista.com/chart/16959/share-of-the-internet-that-is-porn/.

80. Curtis Silver, "Pornhub 2019 Year In Review Report: More Porn, More Often," *Forbes*, December 11, 2019, https://www.forbes.com/sites/curtissilver/2019/12/11/pornhub-2019-year-in-review-report-more-porn-more-often/#7880f34e4671.

CHAPTER 3. FROM COVENANT TO CONSENT IN THE PEWS (PART 1): WHAT AMERICAN EVANGELICALS BELIEVE ABOUT SEX OUTSIDE MARRIAGE

1. See Michael J. Kruger, "One of the Main Ways that the Earliest Christians Distinguished Themselves from the Surrounding Culture," *Canon Fodder*, September 10, 2014, https://www.michaeljkruger.com/one-trait-that-set-the-earliest-christians-apart-from-the-surrounding-culture. For a thorough and more secular treatment of the sexual differences of and impact by early Christians on the ancient Roman Empire, see Kyle Harper, *From Shame to Sin: The Christian Transformation of Sexual Morality in Late Antiquity* (Cambridge: Harvard University Press, 2013).

2. Morgan, *The Puritan Family*, 33. See also Hollinger, *The Meaning of Sex*, 18.

3. Sproul, *Intimate Marriage*, 17.

4. Quoted in Ryken, *Worldly Saints*, 40.

5. Information about both of these surveys as I use them here, including all relevant sample sizes, are provided in the Methodological Appendix.

6. See, for example, Stephen V. Monsma, "What Is an Evangelical? And Does It Matter?," *Christian Scholar's Review* 46, no. 4 (summer 2017): 323–40; Robert D. Woodberry, Jerry Z. Park, Lyman A. Kellstedt, Mark D. Regnerus, and Brian Steensland, "The Measure of American Religious Traditions: Theoretical and Measurement Considerations," *Social Forces* 91, no. 1 (September 2012): 65–73.

7. RELTRAD is laid out and defended in: Brian Steensland, Jerry Z. Park, Mark D. Regnerus, Lynn D. Robinson, W. Bradford Wilcox, and Robert D. Woodberry, "The Measure of American Religion: Toward Improving the State of the Art," *Social Forces* 79, no. 1 (September 2000): 291–318. The seven

black Protestant denominations are listed on page 311. The NSFG has the RELTRAD variable in it already. To create the RELTRAD classifications in GSS I used the SPSS syntax authored by Jerry Park, released August 6, 2018 and downloaded from http://www.thearda.com/code/park.asp.

8. See Monsma, "What Is an Evangelical?"

9. Woodberry et al., "The Measure of American Religious Traditions," 67.

10. As RELTRAD critic Monsma suggests in "What Is an Evangelical?," 339.

11. A tiny proportion indicated "Other," "Don't Know," or "No Answer." Those cases were excluded from the analysis. This is how I have handled survey items throughout this book, unless I indicate otherwise.

12. Statistical significance is very important when looking at group differences. I explain it in detail in the Methodological Appendix.

13. "Divorced" here includes legally separated, which is usually permanent or a divorce-in-process. Widowed people constitute too small a group to measure here, and there are other issues with including them such as their high average age.

14. Dividing each marital status by age group divides evangelicals into six different groups, which is too small to do truly valid comparisons in the GSS at this level of detail, especially for married and divorced who are less than thirty years old. Hence, why I included more years to check this.

15. Percentages were similar for the past ten years of the GSS but, again, too few cases in some categories to be sure.

16. Looking at prayer as a factor was considered. Only the GSS has an item on prayer, and it does not provide information beyond frequency (once per day and so on), such that saying grace every day and an hour-long daily prayer session plus corporate prayer several times a week would be scored exactly the same. In 2010 to 2018, 79% of evangelicals—77% of those 23 to 44—said they prayed daily. So, this does not differentiate very well among evangelicals anyway.

17. The importance of church attendance has been clear for a long time and appears in other surveys. For example, see Mark Regnerus, *Forbidden Fruit: Sex and Religion in the Lives of American Teenagers* (New York: Oxford University Press, 2007), 87.

18. Jeff Diamant, August 31, 2020, "Half of U.S. Christians Say Casual Sex between Consenting Adults Is Sometimes or Always Acceptable," *Fact Tank, Pew Research Center*, https://www.pewresearch.org/fact-tank/2020/08/31/half-of-u-s-christians-say-casual-sex-between-consenting-adults-is-sometimes-or-always-acceptable/. This data also showed regular church attenders were more conservative on these issues but did not break that out separately for different religious groups.

19. Anna Lewis, "Is This the Reason Chris Pratt and Katherine Schwarzenegger Only Just Moved in Together?," *Cosmopolitan*, January 6, 2019, https://www.cosmopolitan.com/uk/entertainment/a25915094/chris-pratt-katherine-schwarzenegger-only-just-moved-in-together-real-reason-engaged/; Ruth Graham, "Newly Engaged Chris Pratt Has Been Getting Super Evangelical and Maybe You Didn't Even Notice," *Slate*, January 14, 2019, https://slate.com/human-interest/2019/01/chris-pratt-engaged-evangelical-christian-katherine-schwarzenegger.html; Leah MarieAnne Klett,

"Chris Pratt Engaged; Actor Vows To 'Live Boldly in Faith' With Katherine Schwarzenegger," *The Christian Post*, January 14, 2019, https://www.christianpost.com/news/chris-pratt-engaged-actor-vows-to-live-boldly-in-faith-with-katherine-schwarzenegger.html; Trilby Beresford, February 7, 2019, "Fresh From Fasting, Chris Pratt Talks About His Spiritual Side on 'The Late Show,' " *The Hollywood Reporter*, https://www.hollywoodreporter.com/live-feed/chris-pratt-talks-his-spiritual-side-late-show-1184160; Martha Ross, "Is Chris Pratt's Evangelical Church Really Welcoming to LGBTQ People?: Actor has Denied Ellen Page's Claim That His Church Is Anti-Gay," *The Mercury News*, February 12, 2019, https://www.mercurynews.com/2019/02/12/is-chris-pratts-evangelical-church-really-welcoming-to-lgbtq-people/.

20. Pew Research Center, "Marriage and Cohabitation in the U.S.," November 2019, https://www.pewresearch.org/social-trends/2019/11/06/marriage-and-cohabitation-in-the-u-s. Select the "Complete Report PDF" option to obtain the full report.

21. The additional results were graciously pulled together for me by Juliana Horowitz. Pew does not release their datasets until two years after they have released a report. For example, this dataset wasn't released until fall 2021, which was after this manuscript was completed. Thus, I was unable to provide as much detail in this section of the chapter as I would normally like.

22. Pew Research Center, "Marriage and Cohabitation in the U.S.," 22–23.

23. Pew Research Center, "Marriage and Cohabitation in the U.S.," 23–24.

24. The only alternative was "Doesn't Matter." So the latter is 100 percent minus the percentage shown.

25. Pew Research Center, "Marriage and Cohabitation in the U.S.," 23.

26. Researchers did not provide breakdowns for age by religious groups.

27. Like church attendance, the power of self-identified religious importance in promoting more conservative views on sex has been clear for a long time and appears in other surveys. For example, see Regnerus, *Forbidden Fruit*, 87.

28. To keep things simple here, I simply distinguished between bachelor's and higher versus less education.

29. Among those who were asked the question about the chance of cohabiting in the future—that is, not currently married or living together—younger ages are significantly *more* likely to attend church weekly. So to play it safe, I checked the relationship between church attendance and consideration of future cohabitation separately for each of the age groups shown in Figure 3–9. Within each age group, this relationship was still very statistically significant. We can be sure that the impact of church attendance here is quite robust.

30. Ayers, "First Comes Love, Then Comes House Keys," 36–41.

31. Samuel Perry's 2018 research showed that evangelical Protestants are much more likely than others to morally oppose pornography use. He also affirmed that higher levels of church attendance and prayer, as well as more conservative views on the Bible, were associated with stronger moral opposition to it. However, he relied on a dataset collected in 2006. See Samuel Perry, "Not Practicing What You Preach: Religion and Incongruence between Pornography Beliefs and Usage," *Journal of Sex Research* 55, no. 3 (2018): 373.

32. Andrew Dugan, "More Americans Say Pornography Is Morally Acceptable," Gallup, June 5, 2018, https://news.gallup.com/poll/235280/americans-say-pornography-morally-acceptable.aspx. All percentages 50 percent or higher are italicized.

33. Barna Group and Josh McDowell Ministry, *The Porn Phenomenon: The Impact of Pornography in the Digital Age* (Plano, TX: Barna Group, 2016).

34. Barna Research, "Methodology," https://www.barna.com/methodology.

35. Gleaned from Barna Group, *The Porn Phenomenon*, 141–56.

36. Barna Group, *The Porn Phenomenon*, 69, 142–43, 146–47.

CHAPTER 4. FROM COVENANT TO CONSENT IN THE PEWS (PART 2): HOW SEX AMONG UNMARRIED EVANGELICALS COMPARES TO OTHER RELIGIOUS GROUPS

1. Jason D. Hans, Martie Gillen, and Katrina Akande, "Sex Redefined: The Reclassification of Oral-Genital Contact," *Perspectives on Sexual and Reproductive Health* 42, no. 2 (June 2010): 74–78, 76. Males were more likely to view *receiving* manual genital stimulation and *giving* oral or manual breast stimulation as being sex. Otherwise, there were not notable gender differences in perception. There were no breakdowns by religious affiliations or beliefs.

2. Regnerus, *Forbidden Fruit*, 163–66; Hollinger, *The Meaning of Sex*, 137–39.

3. White, *God, You, and Sex*, 5.

4. Hollinger, *The Meaning of Sex*, 137.

5. Hollinger, *The Meaning of Sex*, 137–38.

6. I summarize this, citing medical research, in Ayers, *Christian Marriage*, 128 and in this book in chapter 8. The risk of STDs and numerous other dangerous health problems associated with oral and anal sex are extremely high.

7. I am deeply grateful to reviewer Victor Kuligin for pointing this out.

8. This makes almost no difference in measurable outcomes. In the NSFG for example, in a sample of well over thirty thousand, there were only two seventeen-year-old respondents who had ever married, and none younger than that. In fact, there were only fifteen aged eighteen, and twenty-one aged nineteen.

9. See Charles Fain Lehman, "Fewer American High Schoolers Having Sex Than Ever Before," *Institute for Family Studies*, September 1, 2020, https://ifstudies.org/blog/fewer-american-high-schoolers-having-sex-than-ever-before.

10. To keep things less cluttered, in Figures 4–1A and 4–1B I have not identified those who have had sex with only one partner separately. That percentage is what is left after subtracting each of the others from one hundred.

11. This is an important point that we will be exploring later in the book—that many young evangelicals wishing to avoid these types of sexual patterns simply get married earlier.

12. In each case, the later age includes those in the younger ages. For example, those who have had sex at age fifteen or younger *include* those who had sex at fourteen or younger, at thirteen or younger, and so on.

13. We will be looking at the differences associated with being "born again" in chapter 5. However, these still do not allow us to determine with precision *when* that happened in the life of a respondent, and to what extent particular sexual outcomes preceded this conversion. Many believers cannot even state with precision exactly when their full conversion took place—they know they have been "born again" but the process unfolded over time. That was my experience, actually.

14. One religious classification the GSS used for years is a "fundamentalist-moderate-liberal" (FML) dimension. See Tom Smith, "Classifying Protestant Denomination," *Review of Religious Research* 31, no. 3 (March 1990): 225–45. The other breaks down into very specific groups, including non-Christian, no religious affiliation, and so on.

15. For example, I broke down the number of sexual partners that GSS respondents said they had after turning age eighteen, for never-married evangelicals between the ages of eighteen and forty-four. To give me a sample large enough to meaningfully analyze, I combined the last twenty-five years of GSS (1993 through 2018). When I compared the number of sex partners of never-married respondents, those from conservative Protestant backgrounds actually did worse than "moderate Protestants," and no better than those of other religious backgrounds. For example, while 20 percent of those who were fundamentalist Protestant at age sixteen were virgins, compared to 15 percent of all others, 24 percent of moderate Protestants were. Meanwhile, 45 percent of those who were fundamentalist Protestants said they had four or more sex partners, compared to 39 percent of moderate Protestants and 46 percent of all others.

16. Among males, overall differences among the groups are significant for eighteen to twenty-two in oral sex and for eighteen to twenty-two, and twenty-three to thirty-two, for anal sex. Among females, overall differences among the groups are significant for the latter two age groups for oral sex, and for twenty-three to thirty-two for anal sex.

17. Which is different than "working up to" intercourse by starting with fondling and oral sex play.

18. Regnerus, *Forbidden Fruit*, 167–69.

19. See my book *Christian Marriage*, 146–48, for a detailed discussion of this tendency, which has remained stable across centuries.

20. These are percentages from all evangelicals, *not* just those who have ever cohabited.

21. These differences were not statistically significant, mainly because the total numbers of currently cohabiting were not that large. For example, among females, 46 percent of Catholic and 38 percent of "None"s said "definitely yes" compared to the 56 percent for evangelicals. See the Methodological Appendix on statistical significance.

22. See an excellent overview of this by Scott M. Stanley, Galena Kline Rhoades, and Howard J. Markman, "Sliding Versus Deciding: Inertia and the Premarital Cohabitation Effect," *Family Relations* 55, no. 4 (October 2006): 499–509.

23. In the NSFG, for males, the outcome of first cohabitation *only* pertains to situations where this cohabitation occurred before the respondent had ever

been married. For females, the outcome of first cohabitation pertains to *any* cohabitation, even if it occurred, say, following a divorce or in widowhood. In practice, both still give us a good idea how well the first cohabitation fared. Also, in the last cycle of the NSFG, only 6 percent of both males and females who had ever cohabited had their first cohabitation after their first marriage.

24. Practicing Christians are Christians who go to church at least monthly and consider their faith to be important to their daily life. Many generic evangelicals do neither of these things, as we have seen.

25. Barna Group, *The Porn Phenomenon*, 32–33.

26. Barna Group, *The Porn Phenomenon*, 108–9.

27. Barna Group, *The Porn Phenomenon*, 74.

28. C. S. Lewis, *The Great Divorce* (New York: Macmillan, 1946), 99–106.

29. For example, in the GSS grouped by decade, among evangelical Protestants, the percentages of people considering consensual sexual activity between adults of the same sex to be always wrong went from 82 percent to 57 percent between the 1970s and the most recent decade among those eighteen to thirty-nine, and from 87 percent to 74 percent among those forty to fifty-nine, during that time. Over that period, among those eighteen to thirty-nine the percentages saying that such activity was "not wrong at all" increased from 8 percent to 33 percent, and from 5 percent to 20 percent among those forty to fifty-nine.

CHAPTER 5. FROM COVENANT TO CONSENT IN THE PEWS (PART 3): HOW DEMOGRAPHIC FACTORS AND RELIGIOUS DISCIPLINES AFFECT THE SEX LIVES OF UNMARRIED EVANGELICALS

1. To be fair, let me point out that associations that matter for evangelicals typically do so for other religious groups as well, and in the same directions. What is associated with lower sexual activity among evangelicals is usually tied to less sex in other religious groups. There are also instances in which "ideal" evangelicals do not do better than comparable respondents from other religious groups.

2. This would include those who have never had sex—that is, "0 Sex Partners."

3. Note that black believers often attend black Protestant churches. Here only those within evangelical Protestant denominations are addressed.

4. The reader may recall that in considering the impact of religious factors on *beliefs* about sex outside wedlock in chapter 3, we also considered—using the GSS—views on the Bible and whether the respondent had a born-again experience. Here, however, we are looking at singles up to age thirty-two only, and in the GSS, even with combining the last five surveys, there are not enough never-married evangelicals in this age group to do valid comparisons within them on sexual activity by which view of the Bible they have or whether they are born-again. Also, the GSS does not address cohabitation behavior—which I will address below—sufficiently, so we would not be able to tackle the role of views of the Bible and being born-again there either. Hence, we will not be addressing these religious factors in this chapter.

5. Even big differences are not statistically significant when the number of respondents is very low. See the discussion of the statistical significance in the Methodological Appendix.

6. Though on this last measure, there was not a real difference between monthly and weekly attenders.

7. Except for higher education, where I only included those twenty-three to forty-four to restrict our analysis to those who could have finished college.

8. Ayers, "First Comes Love, Then Come House Keys," 38.

CHAPTER 6. THE THEOLOGICAL AND PHILOSOPHICAL ROOTS OF SEXUAL LIBERALISM AMONG EVANGELICAL SINGLES

1. Gresham M. Sykes and David Matza, "Techniques of Neutralization: A Theory of Delinquency," *American Sociological Review* 22.6 (December 1957): 668.

2. Though as we saw, the older generations are not *that* much better off in their beliefs or actions regarding fornication.

3. Recall this from the discussion of Pitirim Sorokin in chapter 2.

4. Dietrich Bonhoeffer, *The Cost of Discipleship* (1937; repr., New York: Simon & Schuster, 1995), 44–45.

5. Jerry Bridges, *The Pursuit of Holiness* (Colorado Springs: NavPress, 1978), 20–21.

6. Bridges, *Pursuit of Holiness*, 22.

7. Sorokin, *Crisis of Our Age*, 143.

8. Bridges, *Pursuit of Holiness*, 23.

9. The combined 2015–2017 and 2017–2019 cycles.

10. I am making reasonable assumptions that the non-virgins would be less likely to choose the right moral reasons for at least *trying* to abstain, if they had indeed made a real effort to remain chaste.

11. Christian Smith and Melinda Lundquist Denton, *Soul Searching: The Religious and Spiritual Lives of Teenagers* (New York: Oxford University Press, 2005), 118.

12. See the discussion of these ideas and thinkers in chapter 2.

13. Smith and Denton, *Soul Searching*, 162–63.

14. Smith and Denton, *Soul Searching*, 163.

15. Smith and Denton, *Soul Searching*, 164–65.

16. Smith and Denton, *Soul Searching*, 163 (emphasis added).

17. Smith and Denton, *Soul Searching*, 163–64.

18. Smith and Denton, *Soul Searching*, 147.

19. Smith and Denton, *Soul Searching*, 144.

20. Famous as the refrain in the song "Everyday People" by Sly and the Family Stone, later shortened into the title of a well-known 1970s sitcom, *Diff'rent Strokes*.

21. Smith and Denton, *Soul Searching*, 166.

22. Smith and Denton, *Soul Searching*, 166.

23. Smith and Denton, *Soul Searching*, 149–50.

24. Smith and Denton, *Soul Searching*, 167.

25. I say this based on the 2006–2010 NSFG, with respondents fifteen to eighteen years of age, assuming their interviewees were a good cross-section. Smith and Denton did their interviews in 2003 on a cross-section of teens thirteen to eighteen. So, I am estimating here. Smith and Denton note that forty-one of their interviewees were Baptist and another ten were in churches that were clearly evangelical. However, some other categories (for example, Presbyterian or Methodist) were too broad to be sure. See Smith and Denton, *Soul Searching*, 302–3.

26. Smith and Denton, *Soul Searching*, 164–65.

27. Smith and Denton, *Soul Searching*, 166. Even if adults hadn't already begun living out MTD at the time—and my experience as a social researcher is that they certainly were—as the book was written in 2005, these teens are now well into adulthood and raising children of their own, even pastoring churches.

28. Kenda Creasy Dean, *Almost Christian: What the Faith of Our Teenagers Is Telling the American Church* (New York: Oxford University Press, 2010).

29. Brian Cosby, *The Gospel Coalition*, April 9, 2012, https://www.thegospelcoalition.org/article/mtd-not-just-a-problem-with-youth-ministry.

30. Leroy Huizenga, "What Is Moral Therapeutic Deism and Why Does It Fail?," *St. Paul Center*, November 21, 2019, https://stpaulcenter.com/what-is-moral-therapeutic-deism-and-why-does-it-fail. Generally, gnosticism was a religious movement that flourished during the era of the early church, interacting with and often corrupting true Christianity. Gnostics saw salvation as more about possessing certain kinds of special knowledge rather than submitting one's will and belief to God and his divine, perfect revelation. The gnostic view of God was more pantheistic—God in everything—than viewing God as truly personal. Gnosticism also denigrated the material world and believed the aim was to transcend it rather than live well, according to God's commandments, within it. This warred against a biblical idea of the importance of the body and what we do with it. Thus, gnosticism was also associated with a prideful elitism, based on the idea that the special knowledge held by truly spiritual people relieved them of, and set them above, the concerns and constraints of ordinary people. This latter attitude is evident in modern evangelicals who see those who hold to established beliefs about fornication, sexual orientation and identity, and the like as legalistic and backward given their greater knowledge derived from a better understanding of God than those held by the historic church or than is revealed in the plain text of the Scriptures.

31. Judith Balswick and Jack Balswick, *Authentic Human Sexuality: An Integrated Christian Approach*, 3rd ed. (Downers Grove, IL: InterVarsity Press, 2019), 116.

32. Balswick and Balswick, *Authentic Human Sexuality*, 129 (emphases added).

33. Balswick and Balswick, *Authentic Human Sexuality*, 117.

34. Balswick and Balswick, *Authentic Human Sexuality*, 117–24; see also what follows on pages 124–29.

35. Balswick and Balswick, *Authentic Human Sexuality*, 143. See whole chapter on cohabitation, pages 130–45. Note that this is *not* the same as

churches that might marry a couple but not require that they obtain a marriage license from the state.

36. Balswick and Balswick, *Authentic Human Sexuality*, 84.

37. Barna Research, "Competing Worldviews Influence Today's Christians," *Barna Access*, May 9, 2017, https://www.barna.com/research/competing-worldviews-influence-todays-christians.

38. Barna Research, "Competing Worldviews Influence Today's Christians."

39. Barna Research, "Competing Worldviews Influence Today's Christians."

40. See definition in chapter 3, n. 34: Christian, attend church at least monthly, and say faith is very important in their lives.

41. Barna Research, "Competing Worldviews Influence Today's Christians." Marxism has been evident in the attraction many on the evangelical left have to socialist economics.

42. George Barna, "CRC Survey Shows Dangerously Low Percentage of Americans Hold Biblical Worldview," in *American Worldview Inventory 2020—At a Glance* (Glendale, AZ: Cultural Research Center of Arizona Christian University, March 24, 2020), 5. Please note that the survey has not been released for analysis by outside researchers. It is common for institutes not to do so for several years while they do their own initial reporting. Thus, my discussion here is limited to breakdowns they chose to report. However, they have been quite thorough and clear, so we are able to get a clear picture of the current status of critical worldview beliefs among evangelicals at this time.

43. George Barna, "Salvation through Christ Attracts Just One in Three Adults; More Believe It Can Be Earned," in *American Worldview Inventory 2020—At a Glance: Perceptions of Sin and Salvation* (Glendale, AZ: Cultural Research Center of Arizona Christian University, August 4, 2020), 3.

44. They distinguish charismatics and Pentecostals as a separate category. Both categories overlap heavily with evangelical Protestants as I have been defining them in this book, so I will include both where possible. From here forward I will refer to these as simply "Pentecostals."

45. George Barna, "Is the Bible True? CRC Study Finds America's Distrust of the Bible Undermines Its Worldview," in *American Worldview Inventory 2020—At a Glance: Faith and Worldview* (Glendale, AZ: Cultural Research Center of Arizona Christian University, April 7, 2020), 3.

46. Elements of Table 6–1 are distilled from a summary report released by George Barna, "American Christians Are Redefining the Faith: Adherents Creating New Worldviews Loosely Tied to Biblical Teaching," in *American Worldview Inventory 2020—FULL Release #11: Churches and Worldview* (Glendale, AZ: Cultural Research Center of Arizona Christian University, October 6, 2020), 5.

47. George Barna, "Surveys Find America's Moral Pillars Are Fading Away," in *American Worldview Inventory 2020—At a Glance: Perceptions of Morality and Life Choices* (Glendale, AZ: Cultural Research Center of Arizona Christian University, June 2, 2020), 5.

48. Barna, "American Christians Are Redefining the Faith," 2.

49. R. C. Sproul, "What Is Imputed Righteousness?," *Ligonier Ministries*, https://www.ligonier.org/learn/qas/what-is-imputed-righteousness/.

50. Barna, "American Christians Are Redefining the Faith," 2.

51. George Barna, "God Is Absent from Most People's Views of Purpose and Success," in *American Worldview Inventory 2020—At a Glance: Seeking Purpose and Success* (Glendale, AZ: Cultural Research Center of Arizona Christian University, May 6, 2020), 2.

52. Barna, "God Is Absent from Most People's Views," 3.

53. For example, if 58 percent of evangelicals believe that people can earn their salvation by good works, but 72 percent (100 percent minus 28 percent that reject the idea) believe that they are saved *only* by confessing their sins and claiming Christ as Savior, then some substantial portion of those who believe the former must also believe the latter at the same time. I cannot determine just how many without access to the raw data.

54. Barna, "Salvation Attracts One in Three Adults," 4.

55. George Barna, "Millennials Have Radically Different Beliefs About Respect, Faith, and America," in *American Worldview Inventory 2020—At a Glance: Millennials and Worldview* (Glendale, AZ: Cultural Research Center of Arizona Christian University, September 22, 2020), 2–3.

56. Barna, "Millennials Have Radically Different Beliefs," 4.

57. Note that "human life is sacred" compares millennials to baby boomers. The report did not provide specific percentages on that item for "other adults" as a whole, but I thought it was important to include as it shows how few millennials hold this critical view compared to those of older generations.

58. See information at https://www.nehemiahinstitute.com/. Full disclosure: I serve on the Nehemiah Advisory Committee but do not get any income, directly or indirectly, from Nehemiah.

59. There is the standard "pre-test" that measures worldview, then organizations are encouraged to use a separate PEERS "post-test" following educational programs to measure improvement in the biblical worldview. I am only using pre-tests here—that is, the straight measurement before any PEERS-oriented education.

60. "Agree" includes Strongly Agree, "Disagree" includes Strongly Disagree. "Neutral" is the remaining percentage. For example, 43 percent Agree and 46 percent Disagree means 11 percent Neutral (100 percent minus 89 percent).

61. Shorter time frames would not have given us a large enough sample to adequately test the relationships. The more recent years (for example, 2010 through 2018) combined show the same relationships—but with more sexual activity and more liberalism—but the sample sizes are too small to adequately test significance while dividing respondents into four groups based on views on premarital sex.

CHAPTER 7. SOCIAL INFLUENCES ON SEXUAL ACTIVITY AMONG EVANGELICAL SINGLES

1. Mark Regnerus, *Cheap Sex: The Transformation of Men, Marriage, and Monogamy* (New York: Oxford University Press, 2017), 10–11.

2. Dennis Hollinger, *The Meaning of Sex*, 223.

3. This approach is heavily associated with Travis Hirschi. See his classic statement in *The Causes of Delinquency* (Berkeley: University of California Press, 1969) and, with Michael R. Gottfredson, *A General Theory of Crime* (Redwood City, CA: Stanford University Press, 1990).

4. Hirschi and Gottfredson, *A General Theory of Crime*. The book emphasized self-control so much that some even call it "self-control theory."

5. See, for example, a reprint of Walter Reckless's 1961 essay, "A New Theory of Delinquency and Crime," in *Social Control and Self-Control Theories of Crime and Deviance*, ed. Joseph H. Rankin and L. Edward Wells (1961; repr., New York: Routledge, 2016), 29–33.

6. The focus on the role of "deviant associations" in drawing people into norm violations, and positive relationships in helping to prevent them, is most associated with Edwin Sutherland, who addresses this in a very detailed, systematic way, and whom Reckless refers to. See Edwin H. Sutherland and Donald R. Cressey, *The Principles of Criminology,* 6th ed. (Chicago: J. B. Lippincott, 1960), 77–79. Differential association theory is not considered a control theory, but rather a type of "social learning" theory. Understood properly, it is compatible with control theory, however.

7. These types of approaches, and my discussion in this chapter, are not useful for conceptualizing rarer causes of deviation, including sexual licentiousness, such as serious mental illnesses of various kinds, organic damage (such as physical conditions and injuries that destroy inhibition), or people who are raised by parents who prostitute their children, use drugs with them, and so forth. For example, I worked with a man in a state hospital many years ago who had suffered damaged impulse control after surviving massive head injuries in a car accident. Before that he was a respectable person with moral boundaries. Afterward he had to be kept institutionalized for his own and others' safety. I know pastors serving in challenging areas where they deal with those who come to faith in Christ and join their churches who, for example, were young people raised by prostitutes, drug addicts, or gang members and taught to behave in deviant ways, which were the "norm" in their households. Those types of situations will not be tackled here.

8. Sharon Scales Rostosky, Brian Wilcox, Margaret Laurie Comer Wright, and Brandy A. Randall, "The Impact of Religiosity on Adolescent Sexual Behavior: A Review of the Evidence," *Journal of Adolescent Research* 19, no. 6 (November 2004): 677–97, see especially 688–92.

9. Regnerus, *Forbidden Fruit*, 120–26, 127–28, 130–36, 155, 164–66, 170–73, 175–76, 231, 235–36, 238. Regnerus also cites many other studies in his analysis.

10. Focusing on never-married evangelical Protestants for the years 2000–2018, I analyzed the impact of church attendance, being born-again, and holding literalist views of the Bible, upon the number of sex partners and frequency of sex within the past year, looking at these three variables together while "controlling" for age, gender, education, race, Hispanic identification, and income. I employed a powerful statistical analysis called "multiple linear regression." Multiple linear regression is a statistical tool for examining the independent association of numerous factors upon one outcome we are trying to explain, while simultaneously holding the others "constant." For example, I can use it to examine the impact of church attendance on the number of

sexual partners as if all the church attenders were the same race, income, gender, held the same views on the Bible, and so on.

Among single evangelicals, both church attendance and literalist views of the Bible were associated with both the number of sex partners and the frequency of sex within the past year. Church attendance was the most powerful. Being born-again mattered because it, like having a more conservative view of the Bible, was in turn associated with higher church attendance, which then lowered the risk of sexual activity. The relationship almost certainly works the other way as well. That is, among evangelicals, church attendance encourages more literalist views of the Bible and encourages people to become born-again.

I also looked at evangelicals using the same multiple linear regression model and controls to see how church attendance, view of the Bible, and being reborn were tied to holding more conservative beliefs about sex between unmarried adults, using the same item we looked at so closely in chapter 3. The answer is a resounding "very powerfully." All three were independently and highly significantly associated with holding more conservative view about sex outside wedlock when controlling for each other and for age, gender, education, race, Hispanic identification, and income. Recall that biblical sexual beliefs are also strongly associated with less sexual immorality. So again, church attendance, a high view of Scripture, and the born-again experiences reduce illicit sexual activity indirectly as well, that is, by strengthening biblical moral beliefs.

11. Regnerus, *Forbidden Fruit*, 159. Peter Berger's book was *The Sacred Canopy: Elements of a Sociology of Religion* (New York: Anchor, 1967).

12. Regnerus, *Forbidden Fruit*, 159, 161–62.

13. See, for example, the general discussion of Andrew Cherlin, *Public and Private Families: An Introduction*, 9th ed. (New York: McGraw Hill, 2021), 329–37. Even though he tries to minimize it, the disruptive impact of divorce and single parenting comes through clearly, representing the most conservative take of the best research.

14. See my discussion of this in *Christian Marriage*, 100–101, 194–95, 332–37.

15. See, for example, the general statements on the deficits of step- and cohabiting parents versus married ones in Ayers, *Christian Marriage*, 102–3, 338–39; Cherlin, *Public and Private Families*, 340–41; Robert A. Johnson, John P. Hoffman, Dean R. Gerstein, *The Relationship between Family Structure and Adolescent Substance Abuse* (Rockville, MD: U.S. Department of Health and Human Services, 1996), 5–6.

16. Ayers, *Christian Marriage*, 53.

17. Cherlin, *Public and Private Families*, 341.

18. Ayers, *Christian Marriage*, 326.

19. For example, Megan Steele, Leslie Gordon Simons, Tara E. Sutton, and Frederick X. Gibbons, "Family Context and Adolescent Risky Sexual Behavior: An Examination of the Influence of Family Structure, Family Transitions and Parenting," *Journal of Youth and Adolescence* 49, no. 4 (June 2020): 1179–194

20. Valerie Senkowski, Shristi Bhochhibhoya, Rhonda Bernard, Taylor Zingg, and Sarah B. Maness, "Assessing the Variation of Measurement of Family Structure in Studies of Adolescent Risk Behaviors: A Systematic Review," *Vulnerable Children and Youth Studies* 14, no. 4 (May 2019): 287–311.

21. Kristin Mmari, Amanda M. Kalamar, Heena Brahmbhatt, and Emilie Venables, "The Influence of the Family on Adolescent Sexual Experience: A Comparison between Baltimore and Johannesburg," *PLOS One* 11.11, November 7, 2016, https://www.ncbi.nlm.nih.gov/pmc/articles/PMC5098750/.

22. Ayers, *Christian Marriage*, 330.

23. Ayers, *Christian Marriage*, 319–20. See also, for example, Paul R. Amato and Alan Booth, *A Generation at Risk: Growing Up in an Era of Family Upheaval* (Cambridge, MA: Harvard University Press, 1997), 220; Donna Ruane Morrison and Mary Jo Coiro, "Parental Conflict and Marital Disruption," *The Journal of Marriage and Family* 61, no. 3 (August 1999): 626–37, 631; Joan B. Kelly and Robert E. Emery, "Children's Adjustment Following Divorce: Risk and Resilience Perspectives," *Family Relations* 52, no. 4 (October 2003): 352–62.

24. Cherlin, *Public and Private Families*, 329.

25. Ayers, *Christian Marriage*, 326, 331–32; Cherlin, *Public and Private Families*, 247, 334.

26. Cherlin, *Public and Private Families*, 247.

27. J. D. Vance, *Hillbilly Elegy: A Memoir of a Family and Culture in Crisis* (New York: Harper, 2016).

28. I avoided outcomes that had tiny samples in some conditions for stepparents, such as anal sex or having three or more sex partners at such young ages. I think it is important to separate out stepparents from single parents, as the outcomes are clearly different for both.

29. That is, they supplied an answer other than "definitely no." To increase my confidence in this conclusion, I also looked at each relationship using regression to control for income, education level, and race. Even with these controls, these outcomes were still highly significant—those living with two biological or adoptive parents did much better.

30. Using regression, as described in the previous note.

31. Again, using regression.

32. This can be described as not only maintaining an angry demeanor but being very controlling without a lot of affection. See Geri R. Donenberg, Fred B. Bryant, Erin Emerson, Helen W. Wilson, and Keryn E. Pasch, "Tracing the Roots of Early Sexual Debut Among Adolescents in Psychiatric Care," *Journal of the American Academy of Child and Adolescent Psychiatry* 42, no. 5 (May 2003): 594–608. Parental hostility described on pages 602–3.

33. In addition to our discussion in the last section, consider sources such as these: Donenberg et al., "Tracing the Roots of Early Sexual Debut"; Alison Parkes, Marion Henderson, Daniel Wright, and Catherine Nixon, "Is Parenting Associated with Teenagers' Early Sexual Risk-Taking, Autonomy and Relationship with Sexual Partners?," *Perspectives on Sexual and Reproductive Health* 43, no. 1 (March 2011): 30–40; Patricia J. Dittus, Shannon L. Michael, Jeffrey S. Becasen, Kari M. Gloppen, Katharine McCarthy, and

Vincent Guilamo-Ramos, "Parental Monitoring and Its Associations with Adolescent Sexual Risk Behavior: A Meta-analysis," *Pediatrics* 136, no. 6 (December 2015): 1587–599. A very helpful review of the best research on this into 2008 is Christine Kim, "Teen Sex: The Parent Factor," *Backgrounder*, The Heritage Foundation, October 7, 2008, https://www.heritage.org/education/report/teen-sex-the-parent-factor. This includes a separate, excellent discussion of the research to date on family structure and teen sex.

34. Marie-Aude Boislard, Daphne van de Bongardt, and Martin Blais, "Sexuality (and Lack Thereof) in Adolescence and Early Adulthood: A Review of the Literature," *Behavioral Sciences* 6, no. 1 (March 2016): 1–24, https://www.ncbi.nlm.nih.gov/pmc/articles/PMC4810042/pdf/behavsci-06-00008.pdf.

35. Boislard et al., "Sexuality (and Lack Thereof) in Adolescence," 3.

36. Boislard et al., "Sexuality (and Lack Thereof) in Adolescence," 2. In the next chapter we will focus on consequences.

37. Boislard et al., "Sexuality (and Lack Thereof) in Adolescence," 5–6; see also Cheryl L. Somers and Claudia Anagurthi, "Parents' Attitudes About Adolescents' Premarital Sexual Activity: The Role of Inter-Parent Consistency/Inconsistency in Sexual Outcomes," *Health Education Journal* 73, no. 5 (September 2014): 545–53.

38. Somers and Anagurthi, "Parents' Attitudes About Adolescents' Premarital Sexual Activity," 550–51.

39. Details have been altered to protect identities.

40. Boislard et al., "Sexuality (and Lack Thereof) in Adolescence," 7.

41. Wendy D. Manning, Monica A. Longmore, Jennifer Copp, and Peggy C. Giordano, "The Complexities of Adolescent Dating and Sexual Relationship: Fluidity, Meaning(s), and Implications for Young Adults' Well-Being," *New Directions for Child and Adolescent Development*, no. 144 (June 2014): 53–69, 56.

42. Ayers, *Christian Marriage*, 198.

43. Elizabeth C. Cooksey, Frank L. Mott, and Stefanie A. Neubauer, "Friendships and Early Relationships: Links to Sexual Initiation Among American Adolescents Born to Young Mothers," *Perspectives on Sexual and Reproductive Health* 34, no. 3 (May/June 2002): 118–26, 122–23. They point out that the adolescents in their study were not typical since they were born to young mothers, but the results closely mirror more general findings from the NSC.

44. Regnerus, *Forbidden Fruit*, 123.

45. Regnerus, *Forbidden Fruit*, 126.

46. Manning et al., "The Complexities of Adolescent Dating," 63.

47. Manning et al., "The Complexities of Adolescent Dating," 7.

48. Boislard et al., "Sexuality (and Lack Thereof) in Adolescence," 3. See also Donenberg et al., "Tracing the Roots of Early Sexual Debut," whose literature review and research demonstrated a powerful role that pro-sex peers and dating partners play in early sexual onset among adolescents.

49. Donenberg et al., "Tracing the Roots of Early Sexual Debut," 4.

50. Donenberg et al, "Tracing the Roots of Early Sexual Debut," 11.

51. The technique used is called "meta-analysis," which basically pools data from many studies, integrating the findings of many different studies. Daphne van de Bongardt et al., "A Meta-Analysis of the Relations between Three Types of Peer Norms and Adolescent Sexual Behavior," *Personality and Social Psychology Review* 19, no. 3 (August 2015): 203–34.

52. Van de Bongardt et al., "Meta-Analysis of the Relations," 227.

53. Van de Bongardt et al., "A Meta-Analysis of the Relations," 225.

54. Renee E. Sieving, Marla E. Eisenberg, Sandra Pettingell, and Carol Skay, "Friends' Influence on Adolescents' First Intercourse," *Perspectives on Sexual and Reproductive Health* 38, no. 1 (March 2006): 13–19, 13, 17.

55. Jane D. Brown, "Mass Media Influences on Sexuality," *The Journal of Sex Research* 39, no. 1 (February 2002): 42–45.

56. Lindsay Powers, "'Friends' Sex Lives by the Numbers," *Hollywood Reporter*, July 28, 2011, https://www.hollywoodreporter.com/live-feed/friends-sex -lives-by-numbers-216527.

57. For example, John Paul Brammer, "Teen Vogue's 'Guide to Anal Sex' Spawns Backlash," *NBC News*, July 20, 2017, https://www.nbcnews.com/ feature/nbc-out/teen-vogue-s-guide-anal-sex-spawns-backlash-n784411.

58. Rebecca L. Collins, Victor C. Strasburger, Jane D. Brown, Edward Donnerstein, Amanda Lenhart, and L. Monique Ward, "Sexual Media and Childhood Well-being and Health," *Pediatrics* 140, Supplement 2 (November 2017): s162–s166, https://doi.org/10.1542/peds.2016-1758X; Alison Parkes, Daniel Wight, Kate Hunt, Marion Henderson, and James Sargent, "Are Sexual Media Exposure, Parental Restrictions On Media Use and Co-viewing TV and DVDs With Parents and Friends Associated With Teenagers' Early Sexual Behaviour?," *Journal of Adolescence* 36, no. 6 (December 2013): 1121–132. See, for example, Anita Chandra, Steven C. Martino, Rebecca L. Collins, Marc N. Elliott, Sandra H. Berry, David E. Kanouse, and Angela Miu, "Does Watching Sex on Television Predict Teen Pregnancy? Findings From a National Longitudinal Survey of Youth," *Pediatrics* 122, no. 5 (November 2008): 1047–54; Rebecca L. Collins, Marc N. Elliott, Sandra H. Berry, David E. Kanouse, Dale Kunkel, Sarah B. Hunter, and Angela Miu, "Watching Sex on Television Predicts Adolescent Initiation of Sexual Behavior," *Pediatrics* 114, no. 3 (September 2004): e280–e289, https://doi.org/10.1542/peds.2003-1065-L; Steven C. Martino, Rebecca L. Collins, Marc N. Elliott, Amy Strachman, David E. Kanouse, and Sandra H. Berry, "Exposure to Degrading Versus Nondegrading Music Lyrics and Sexual Behavior Among Youth," *Pediatrics* 118, no. 2 (August 2006): e430–e441, https://doi.org/10.1542/peds.2006-0131.

59. Amy Bleakley, Michael Hennessy, Martin Fishbein, and Amy Jordan, "It Works Both Ways: The Relationship between Exposure to Sexual Content in the Media and Adolescent Sexual Behavior," *Media Psychology* 11, no. 4 (October 2008): 443–61.

60. Amy Bleakley, Michael Hennessy, and Martin Fishbein, "A Model of Adolescents' Seeking of Sexual Content in Their Media Choices," *The Journal of Sex Research* 48, no. 4 (July 2011): 309–15, 309.

61. Brown, "Mass Media Influences on Sexuality," 43–45.

62. Parkes et al., "Sexual Media Exposure, Parental Restrictions," 1130.

63. Jordyn Randall and Michael Langlais, "Social Media and Adolescent Sexual Socialization," *Encyclopedia of Sexuality and Gender* (September 2019):1–10, https://doi.org/10.1007/978-3-319-59531-3.

64. Ayers, *Christian Marriage*, 147, 158–61, 198–99.

65. Regnerus and Uecker, *Premarital Sex in America*, 249.

66. U.S. Census, "Table MS-2. Estimated Median Age at First Marriage: 1890 to present," November 2019, https://www.census.gov/data/tables/time-series/demo/families/marital.html.

67. Dominic Hernandez, "The Decreasing Age of Puberty: Puberty Is Happening Younger and Younger; Here's What to Know," *Vital Record: News from Texas A&M Health*, January 10, 2018, https://vitalrecord.tamhsc.edu/decreasing-age-puberty/.

68. Dr. Robert Benjamin, interview, "When Is Puberty Too Early?," *Duke Health*, July 2, 2020, https://www.dukehealth.org/blog/when-puberty-too-early.

69. Regnerus and Uecker, *Premarital Sex in America*, 2, 111, 169, 200, 232.

70. For male respondents, age at first marriage was not directly coded; thus, there are females only here. There is no reason to expect that the situation would be better with males however.

71. Marissa Hermanson, "How to Save for a House and a Wedding at the Same Time," *RIS Media's Housecall*, April 20, 2018, http://blog.rismedia.com/2018/save-wedding-house-same-time/.

72. These remarks reflect and distill this excellent, data-intensive piece: W. Bradford Wilcox, "The Marriage Divide: How and Why Working-Class Families Are More Fragile Today," *Institute for Family Studies*, September 25, 2017, https://ifstudies.org/blog/the-marriage-divide-how-and-why-working-class-families-are-more-fragile-today.

73. Regnerus, *Cheap Sex*, 148–53.

74. For example, Regnerus and Uecker, *Premarital Sex in America*, 175.

75. Regnerus and Uecker, *Premarital Sex in America*, 182–84.

76. Regnerus and Uecker, *Premarital Sex in America*, 188–89.

77. Russell Moore, *Onward: Engaging the Culture without Losing the Gospel* (Nashville: B&H Publishing, 2015), 174–75.

78. Regnerus and Uecker, *Premarital Sex in America*, 179–82.

79. Regnerus and Uecker, *Premarital Sex in America*, 179–80.

80. See Ayers, *Christian Marriage*, 22, 47–48.

81. Cherlin, *Public and Private Families*, 196–97.

82. David Brooks, "The New Lone Rangers," *The New York Times*, July 10, 2007, https://www.nytimes.com/2007/07/10/opinion/10brooks.html.

CHAPTER 8. THE CONSEQUENCES OF SEX
DIVORCED FROM MARRIAGE

1. Ayers, *Christian Marriage*, 83–84. Despite this we celebrate every birth and love every child as a gift of God, whether they are born to married people or not.

2. For a sobering, brief summary of the main findings, which as we have already seen are abundant, on the harm this causes, see "Effects of

Out-of-Wedlock Birth on Children," *Marripedia*, August 21, 2019, http://marripedia.org/effects_of_out-of-wedlock_births_on_children. Also, Isabel V. Sawhill, Quentin Karpilow, and Joanna Venator, "The Impact of Unintended Childbearing on Future Generations," *Center on Children and Families at Brookings* (Washington D.C.: The Brookings Institute, 2014), 1–30.

3. Lara K. Hulsey, Robert G. Wood, Anu Rangarajan, *The Implementation of Maternity Group Home Programs: Serving Pregnant and Parenting Teens in a Residential Setting,* (Princeton: Mathematica Policy Research for Department of Health and Human Services, 2005), 1–2.

4. Isabel V. Sawhill, "Report: What Can Be Done to Reduce Teen Pregnancy and Out-of-Wedlock Births," *Brookings Institute*, October 1, 2001, https://www.brookings.edu/research/what-can-be-done-to-reduce-teen-pregnancy-and-out-of-wedlock-births/; Sawhill et al., "The Impact of Unintended Childbearing," 7–9; Cherlin, *Public and Private Families*, 170–71.

5. Cherlin, *Public and Private Families*, 171.

6. Joyce A. Martin, Brady E. Hamilton, Michelle J. K. Osterman, and Anne K. Driscoll, "Births: Final Data for 2019," *National Vital Statistics Reports* 70.2 (March 2021): 26.

7. Martin et al., "Birth: Final Data for 2019," 14.

8. Martin et al., "Birth: Final Data for 2019," 14.

9. Getting into the issue of declining fertility/birth rates, of which lower unmarried births is just a part, would take us away from the focus of this book and this chapter. Interested readers can easily find good overviews of this issue, which the majority of policy makers in developing countries view as a serious problem. In summary, this means that we will have growing numbers of elderly compared to younger people, and this disparity will increase over time, leading to crises in retirement, healthcare, tax funding, availability of labor, and radical disruptions in family systems as increasing numbers of people live devoid of siblings and cousins and experience loneliness and neglect as childless elderly people.

10. While fertility rates narrowly focus on births, pregnancy deals with all these outcomes. In discussing things like abortion, for example, it has to do with pregnancy but sadly not birth. It is technically possible that pregnancy can increase while fertility decreases if the population has high levels of still-born births, miscarriages, and abortions. In the past, false claims have been made about certain kinds of sex education leading to decreasing pregnancy rates when actually the latter stayed the same or increased, but birth fell due to very high abortion rates. This is why social scientists are careful to discuss these as distinct though related phenomena.

11. Isaac Maddow-Zimet, Kathryn Kost, and Sean Finn, *Pregnancies, Births and Abortions in the United States, 1973–2016: National and State Trends by Age: Appendix Tables*, Guttmacher Institute, Table 1, October 2020, https://www.guttmacher.org/sites/default/files/report_downloads/pregnancies-births-abortions-us-1973-2016-appendix-tables.pdf.

12. Joyce A. Martin, Brady E. Hamilton, Michelle J. K. Osterman, and Anne K. Driscoll, "Births: Final Data for 2018," *National Vital Statistics Reports* 68.13 (November 2019): 25.

13. National Center for Health Statistics, *Health, United States, 2016: With Chartbook on Long-term Trends in Health*, (Hyattsville, MD: National Center for Health Statistics, 2017), 94. The categories used for racial and ethnic groups changed a lot from 1970 through 1980, making comparisons that include data before and after 1980 difficult. The comparisons between 1970 and 1980 do not separate out Hispanics, nor include Asians or Pacific Islanders.

14. Martin et al., "Births: Final Data for 2019," 6.

15. For example, Zimet et al., *Pregnancies, Births and Abortions*, Tables 2, 4, and 6; *Health United States, 2016*, 99; Tara Jatlaoui et al., "Abortion Surveillance—United States, 2016," *Morbidity and Mortality Weekly Report Surveillance Summaries* 68.SS-11 (2019); Katherine Kortsmit et al., "Abortion Surveillance—United States, 2018," *Morbidity and Mortality Weekly Report Surveillance Summaries* 69.7 (2020).

16. Rachel K. Jones, Elizabeth Witwer, and Jenna Jerman, "Abortion Incidence and Service Availability in the United States, 2017," *Guttmacher Institute*, September 2019, https://www.guttmacher.org/report/abortion-incidence-service-availability-us-2017.

17. This complex and politicized issue would lead us into a lengthy side discussion. However, a big part of the answer is the work of pro-life pregnancy clinics, which have become effective, and the continuing commitment of dedicated pro-lifers to get out the message of life and the humanity of the preborn.

18. Jones et al., "Abortion Incidence and Service Availability."

19. "Induced Abortion in the United States," *Guttmacher Institute Fact Sheet*, September 2019, https://www.guttmacher.org/fact-sheet/induced-abortion-united-states.

20. Jatlaoui et al., "Abortion Surveillance—United States, 2016," 25.

21. Jatlaoui et al., "Abortion Surveillance—United States, 2016," 9.

22. Compare 156 for Hispanics to 109 for non-Hispanic whites per 1,000 live births.

23. Matthew Hadro, "Black Leaders Blast 'Systemic Racism' of Abortion in Letter to Planned Parenthood," *Catholic News Agency*, September 1, 2020, https://www.catholicnewsagency.com/news/black-leaders-blast-systemic-racism-of-abortion-in-letter-to-planned-parenthood-89007.

24. Jenna Jerman, Rachel K. Jones, and Tsuyoshi Onda, *Characteristics of U.S. Abortion Patients in 2014 and Changes Since 2008* (New York: Guttmacher Institute, 2016), 6–7. Interestingly, the proportion of abortion patients that were religiously identified dropped from 2008 through 2014—more for mainline Protestants (down 24 percent), and Catholics (down 15 percent) than for evangelicals (down 13 percent), while rising steeply for "others" (up 17 percent) and "none" (up 38 percent).

25. The National Academies of Sciences, Engineering, and Medicine, *The Safety and Quality of Abortion Care in the United States* (Washington D.C.: National Academies Press, 2018), 130–31. A common term used for this problem is "selective recall bias."

26. See David C. Reardon, "The Abortion and Mental Health Controversy: A Comprehensive Literature Review of Common Ground

Agreements, Disagreements, Actionable Recommendations, and Research," *Sage Open Medicine,* 6 (2018): 1–38, https://journals.sagepub.com/doi/10.1177/2050312118807624. I *highly* recommend this review article to those ministering to women postabortion. The list of factors that render women postabortion more or less vulnerable to psychological distress is extensive and beyond what I can cover here.

27. Rebecca Felsenthal Stewart, "Does a Better Relationship Mean Better Health? The Perks of Marriage and Long-Term Relationships," *WebMD,* January 26, 2012, http://www.webmd.com/sex-relationships/guide/relationships-marriage-and-health?page=1; Gene H. Starbuck and Karen Saucier Lundy, *Families in Context: Sociological Perspectives,* 3rd ed. (Boulder, CO: Paradigm Publishers, 2015), 249; David Popenoe and Barbara Dafoe Whitehead, *Should We Live Together? What Young Adults Need to Know about Cohabitation and Marriage: A Comprehensive Review of Recent Research,* 2nd ed. (Piscataway, NJ: The National Marriage Project, 2002), 7; Linda J. Waite and Maggie Gallagher, *The Case for Marriage: Why Married People Are Happier, Healthier, and Better Off Financially* (New York: Broadway Books, 2000), 63–64, 67–68, 73–74, 111, 113–14, 116–18.

28. Waite and Gallagher, *The Case for Marriage,* 63, 73; James Q. Wilson, *The Marriage Problem: How Our Culture Has Weakened Families* (New York: HarperCollins, 2002), 39; David Popenoe and Barbara Dafoe Whitehead, *Cohabitation, Marriage, and Child Well-Being: A Cross-National Perspective* (Piscataway, NJ: The National Marriage Project, 2008), 13.

29. Waite and Gallagher, *The Case for Marriage,* 44–45, 73.

30. Waite and Gallagher, *The Case for Marriage,* 38; Casey E. Copen, Kimberly Daniels, and William D. Mosher, "First Premarital Cohabitation in the United States," *National Health Statistics Reports* 64 (April 2013): 1–16, 1, 5; Popenoe and Whitehead, *Should We Live Together?,* 6–7; Georgina Binstock and Arland Thornton, "Separations, Reconciliations, and Living Apart in Cohabiting and Marital Unions," *Journal of Marriage and Family* 65, no. 2 (May 2003): 432–43, 436.

31. Wendy D. Manning, "Cohabitation and Child Wellbeing," *The Future of Children* 25, no. 2 (Fall 2015): 51–66. Manning notes that for adolescents only, those in married stepfamilies do no better than those in cohabiting stepfamilies. But neither produce on average nearly as positive outcomes as those living with biological married parents.

32. Manning, "Cohabitation and Child Wellbeing," 59 (emphasis added). The reader should notice that Manning only says that children in these more ideal cohabiting relationships have *many* of the same benefits as those in married households. She does not say that they have *all* of the same benefits.

33. Isabel V. Sawhill, "Twenty Years Later, It Turns Out Dan Quayle Was Right About Murphy Brown and Unmarried Moms," *The Brookings Institute,* May 25, 2012, https://www.brookings.edu/opinions/twenty-years-later-it-turns-out-dan-quayle-was-right-about-murphy-brown-and-unmarried-moms. See also Cherlin, *Public and Private Families,* 342.

34. Laurie DeRose, Mark Lyons-Amos, W. Bradford Wilcox, and Gloria Huarcaya, "The Cohabitation Go-Round: Cohabitation and Family Instability across the Globe," in *World Family Map 2017: Mapping Family Change and Child*

Well-Being Outcomes (New York: Social Trends Institute, 2017), 6–7. See the later reflection on and expansion of this as expressed in an interview with one of the authors in Gene Veith, "Exploding Myths about Cohabitation," *Patheos*, April 5, 2017, http://www.patheos.com/blogs/geneveith/2017/04/exploding-myths-about-cohabitation-draft/?utm_source=facebook.

35. Manning, "Cohabitation and Child Wellbeing," 54.

36. This paragraph combines information from two sources: Sydney Briggs, Emily Cantrell, and Elizabeth Karberg, "Family Instability and Children's Social Development," *Child Trends,* August 2019, https://www.childtrends.org/wp-content/uploads/2019/08/r03brief_ChildTrends_Aug2019.pdf; Anna Sutherland, "The Varying Effects of Family Instability," *Institute for Family Studies*, August 21, 2015, https://ifstudies.org/blog/the-varying-effects-of-family-instability.

37. Heather Sandstrom and Sandra Huerta, *The Negative Effect of Family Instability on Child Development: A Research Synthesis* (Washington D.C.: The Urban Institute, 2013), 24.

38. Sutherland, "The Varying Effects of Family Instability," 1.

39. ElHage, Alysse, "For Kids, Parental Cohabitation and Marriage Are Not Interchangeable," *Institute for Family Studies*, May 7, 2015, https://ifstudies.org/blog/for-kids-parental-cohabitation-and-marriage-are-not-interchangeable.

40. ElHage, Alysse, "For Kids, Parental Cohabitation and Marriage Are Not Interchangeable."

41. Data from 2019 census obtained from "Table C3. Living Arrangements of Children Under 18 Years and Marital Status of Parents, by Age, Sex, Race, and Hispanic Origin and Selected Characteristics of the Child for All Children: 2019"; "Table UC3. Opposite-Sex Unmarried Couples by Presence of Biological Children Under 18, and Age, Earnings, Education, and Race and Hispanic Origin of Both Partners: 2019"; "Table FG3. Opposite-Sex Married Couple Family Groups, by Presence of Own Children Under 18, and Age, Earnings, Education, and Race and Hispanic Origin3 of Both Spouses: 2019," https://www.census.gov/data/tables/2019/demo/families/cps-2019.html.

42. Manning, "Cohabitation and Child Wellbeing," 53.

43. The terms sexually transmitted *infections* (STIs) and sexually transmitted *diseases* are often interchangeable. Technically, STDs are when the infection produces the disease—showing symptoms beyond just the infection. I used the term "STD" in *Christian Marriage*, but I switched to STI for this book as it becomes the norm among medical professionals. Otherwise, the distinction need not concern us here.

44. I am focusing on *male* condoms, typically made of latex. There are also *female* condoms, which are rarely used. A full description and discussion of each form of contraception is outside the scope of this chapter, as my goal here is not to provide birth control instruction.

45. Centers for Disease Control and Prevention, "Fact Sheet for Public Health Personnel," https://www.cdc.gov/condomeffectiveness/latex.html.

46. Centers for Disease Control and Prevention, "Fact Sheet for Public Health Personnel."

47. Planned Parenthood, "How Effective Are Condoms?," https://www.plannedparenthood.org/learn/birth-control/condom/how-effective-are-condoms.

48. For example, Regnerus, *Forbidden Fruit*, 30, 180.

49. Howard LeWine, "HPV Transmission during Oral Sex a Growing Cause of Mouth and Throat Cancer," *Harvard Health Publishing*, November 29, 2016, http://www.health.harvard.edu/blog/hpv-transmission-during-oral-sex-a-growing-cause-of-mouth-and-throat-cancer-201306046346.

50. Centers for Disease Control and Prevention, "STD Risk and Oral Sex—CDC Fact Sheet," https://www.cdc.gov/std/healthcomm/stdfact-stdriskandoralsex.htm. Whether the sexual activity is homosexual or heterosexual, fellatio is oral sex performed upon a male, and cunnilingus is oral sex performed upon a woman.

51. Anna Elizabeth, "Nobody Uses Dental Dams," *The Atlantic*, April 21, 2019, https://www.theatlantic.com/health/archive/2019/04/dental-dams-are-more-symbolic-practical/587539/.

52. Ayers, *Christian Marriage*, 188.

53. Centers for Disease Control and Prevention, "STD Risk and Oral Sex."

54. Centers for Disease Control and Prevention, "HIV Risk and Prevention: Anal Sex," https://www.cdc.gov/hiv/risk/analsex.html#:~:text=In%20addition%20to%20HIV%2C%20a,(like%20syphilis%20or%20herpes); Isadora Baum, "4 Places You Can Get an STI—Besides Your Vagina," *Health.com*, May 29, 2018, https://www.health.com/condition/sexual-health/std-anal-sex.

55. Rachel Nall, "What Are the Risks of Anal Sex?" *Medical News Today*, March 6, 2019, https://www.medicalnewstoday.com/articles/324637.

56. Centers for Disease Control and Prevention, "HIV Risk and Prevention."

57. Sara E. Forhan, Sami L. Gottlieb, Maya R. Sternberg, Fujie Xu, S. Deblina Datta, Geraldine M. McQuillan, Stuart M. Berman, and Lauri E. Markowitz, "Prevalence of Sexually Transmitted Infections Among Female Adolescents Aged 14 to 19 in the United States," *Pediatrics* 124, no. 6 (December 2009): 1505–12.

58. For example, according to the YRBS, use of a condom at last sexual intercourse among high school students was only 54 percent in 2019, down from 63 percent in 2003 and 2005.

59. Those in cohabiting relationships are a bit less likely to use condoms, presumably because they view themselves in a monogamous relationship that will last, they think they know their partner's sexual history, and they perhaps are more willing to risk pregnancy. So, if I had included cohabiters, it would have *decreased* the condom use percentages even more. Note also that there were small numbers for fifteen-to-seventeen-year-old teens having anal sex (only seven males and six females), meaning interpret that percentage with caution. Also, numbers using condoms with oral sex were small, so the absolute numbers in those cells were small. But this was because using condoms with oral sex, though advised, is relatively uncommon across the board.

60. Susan Krauss Whitbourne, "How Casual Sex Can Affect Our Mental Health," *Psychology Today*, March 9, 2013, https://www.psychologytoday.com/us/blog/fulfillment-any-age/201303/how-casual-sex-can-affect-our-mental-health.

61. Justin Garcia, Chris Reiber, Sean G. Massey, and Ann M. Merriwether, "Sexual Hookup Culture: A Review," *Review of General Psychology* 16, no. 2 (June 2012): 168–71.

62. Garcia et al., "Sexual Hookup Culture," 169.

63. This included being pressured into unwanted sex acts and worse.

64. Sandhya Ramrakha, Charlotte Paul, Melanie L. Bell, Nigel Dickson, Terrie E. Moffitt and Avshalom Caspi, "The Relationship between Multiple Sex Partners and Anxiety, Depression, and Substance Dependence Disorders: A Cohort Study," *Archives of Sexual Behavior* 42, no. 5 (July 2013): 863–72.

65. Kirk Johnson, Lauren Noyes, and Robert Rector, "Sexually Active Teens Are More Likely to Be Depressed and to Attempt Suicide," *The Heritage Foundation*, June 2, 2003, https://www.heritage.org/education/report/sexually-active-teenagers-are-more-likely-be-depressed-and-attempt-suicide.

66. Jane Mendle, Joseph Ferrero, Sarah R. Moore, and Harden K. Paige, "Depression and Adolescent Sexual Activity in Romantic and Nonromantic Relational Contexts: A Genetically-Informative Sibling Comparison," *Journal of Abnormal Psychology* 122, no. 1 (February 2013): 51–63.

67. This was national level data, about 14,500 respondents every other year; here I used 2015, 2017, and 2019.

68. Exact items for the mental health outcomes are as follows: "During the past 12 months, did you ever feel so sad or hopeless almost every day for two weeks or more in a row that you stopped doing some usual activities?"; "During the past 12 months, did you ever seriously consider attempting suicide?"; "During the past 12 months, how many times did you actually attempt suicide?"

69. Chris Iliades, "Is There a Price to Pay for Promiscuity?" *Everyday Health*, July 15, 2010, https://www.everydayhealth.com/longevity/can-promiscuity-threaten-longevity.aspx.

70. Iliades, "Is There a Price to Pay for Promiscuity?"

71. Garcia et al., "Sexual Hookup Culture," 169.

72. Garcia et al., "Sexual Hookup Culture," 170.

73. These would include not just rape but things like unwanted kissing, touching, or fondling, forcing the date to watch pornography, and so on.

74. See, for example, Aimee Deliramach and Matthew J. Gray, "Changes in Women's Sexual Behavior Following Sexual Assault," *Behavior Modification* 32, no. 5 (March 2008): 611–21; Rebecca Campbell, Tracy Sefl, and Courtney E. Ahrens, "The Impact of Rape on Women's Sexual Health Risk Behavior," *Health Psychology* 23, no. 1 (January 2004): 67–74.

75. Iliades, "Is There a Price to Pay for Promiscuity?"

76. Jan Wagstaff, *Intimate Partner Violence in Adolescence* (Glendale, CA: Cinahl Information Systems, 2018).

77. Glenn Stanton, "Premarital Sex and Divorce Risk," *Focus on the Family*, August 16, 2011, https://www.focusonthefamily.com/marriage/premarital-sex-and-greater-risk-of-divorce/; Jay Teachman, "Premarital Sex,

Premarital Cohabitation, and the Risk of Subsequent Marital Dissolution Among Women," *Journal of Marriage and Family* 65, no. 2 (May 2003): 444–55; Galena K. Rhoades and Scott M. Stanley, *Before I Do: What Do Premarital Experiences Have to Do With Marital Quality Among Today's Young Adults?* (Charlottesville, VA: The National Marriage Project), 6, 8–9; Nicholas Wolfinger, "Counterintuitive Trends in the Link between Premarital Sex and Marital Stability," *Institute for Family Studies,* https://ifstudies.org/blog/counterintuitive-trends-in-the-link-between-premarital-sex-and-marital-stability.

78. Wolfinger, "Counterintuitive Trends." Ten or more had the highest divorce risk.

79. Wolfinger, "Counterintuitive Trends."

80. Wolfinger, "Counterintuitive Trends."

81. Wolfinger, "Counterintuitive Trends."

82. See, for example, Binstock and Thornton, "Separations, Reconciliations, and Living Apart," 441; Starbuck and Lundy, *Families in Context: Sociological Perspectives,* 246; Casey E. Copen, Kimberly Daniels, Jonathan Vespa, and William D. Mosher, "First Marriages in the United States: Data from the 2006–2010 National Survey of Family Growth," *National Health Statistics Reports* 49 (March 2012), 2, 8; Stanley et al., "Sliding Versus Deciding," 499.

83. Copen et al., "First Marriages in the United States," 2; see also Wendy D. Manning and Jessica A. Cohen, "Premarital Cohabitation and Marital Dissolution: An Examination of Recent Marriages," *Journal of Marriage and Family* 74, no. 2 (April 2012): 377–87; Arielle Kuperberg, "Age at Coresidence, Premarital Cohabitation, and Marriage Dissolution: 1985–2009," *Journal of Marriage and Family* 76, no. 2 (April 2014): 352–69; Steffen Reinhold, "Reassessing the Link between Premarital Cohabitation and Marital Instability," *Demography* 47, no. 3 (August 2010): 719–33.

84. Michael J. Rosenfeld and Katharina Roesler, "Cohabitation Experience and Cohabitation's Association with Marital Dissolution," *Journal of Marriage and Family* 81, no. 1 (September 2018): 56.

85. See Manning and Cohen, "Premarital Cohabitation and Marital Dissolution," 384.

86. Starbuck and Lundy, *Families in Context,* 247; Eva Bernhardt, "Cohabitation and Marriage Among Young Adults in Sweden: Attitudes, Expectations and Plans," *Scandinavian Population Studies* 13 (2002): 157–70.

87. Ruth Weston, Lixia Qu, and David de Vaus, "Premarital Cohabitation and Marital Stability" (paper presented at the HILDA Conference, Melbourne, Australia, 2003), 10.

88. Copen et al., "First Marriages in the United States," 2, 8–9.

89. Stanley et al., "Sliding Versus Deciding," 499.

90. Rosenfeld and Roesler, "Cohabitation Experience and Cohabitation's Association with Marital Dissolution." There is a great overview of this study and its implications by Scott Stanley and Galena Rhoades, "Premarital Cohabitation Is Still Associated With Greater Odds of Divorce," *Institute for Family Studies,* October 17, 2018, https://ifstudies.org/blog/premarital-cohabitation-is-still-associated-with-greater-odds-of-divorce. See also Reinhold, "Reassessing the Link," 719–33.

91. See Galena H. Kline, Scott M. Stanley, Howard J. Markman, P. Antonio Olmos-Gallo, Michelle St. Peters, Sarah W. Whitton, and Lydia M. Prado, "Timing Is Everything: Pre-Engagement Cohabitation and Increased Risk for Poor Marital Outcomes," *Journal of Family Psychology* 18, no. 2 (July 2004): 311, 315–16; Galena K. Rhoades, Scott M. Stanley, and Howard J. Markman, "The Pre-Engagement Cohabitation Effect: A Replication and Extension of Previous Findings," *Journal of Family Psychology* 23, no. 1 (February 2009): 107, 109–10; Starbuck and Lundy, *Families in Context,* 246; Manning and Cohen, "Premarital Cohabitation and Marital Dissolution," 382, 384.

92. See also Ayers, *Christian Marriage,* 224–25.

93. See my discussion of this overall in Ayers, *Christian Marriage,* 230–31. Not all research supports the thesis that those who are engaged or planning marriage when they move in together are no more likely to get divorced than those who do not cohabit at all. Copen et al. found that the divorce risk was higher for those who cohabit first, even for those who are engaged first—see Copen et al., "First Marriages in the United States," 8–9.

94. Peter J. Larson and David H. Olson, "Cohabitation and Relationship in Dating and Engaged Couples," *Life Innovations,* 2010, https://app.pre-pare-enrich.com/pe/pdf/research/cohab_relat_qual.pdf.

95. Stanley and Rhoades, "Testing a Relationship Is Probably the Worst Reason to Cohabit"; Manning and Cohen, "Premarital Cohabitation and Marital Dissolution," 384.

96. See the cogent explanation by Stanley and Rhoades, "Premarital Cohabitation Is Still Associated with Greater Risk of Divorce," of the complex statistical findings by Rosenfeld and Roesler in "Cohabitation Experience and Cohabitation's Association with Marital Dissolution."

97. For those who were ever divorced or widowed, some of these would have been after their first marriages and even after subsequent marriages.

98. Again, keep in mind that by limiting this to ages thirty to forty-four due to the design of the NSFG, we cannot see more long-term results, with little time for marriages and divorces to have happened at the time the respondents, some of whom were only thirty-two or thirty-three, were surveyed.

CHAPTER 9. A FRAMEWORK AND PRINCIPLES
FOR CHURCHES TO PROMOTE SEXUAL PURITY

1. C. S. Lewis, "The Weight of Glory," *Theology* 43.257 (November 1941): 263–74, 263.

2. Tim Geiger, "Why a Sexually Faithful Church?," in *Becoming a Sexually Faithful Church,* ed. Nicholas Black (Harvest USA, 2019), 2. I am taking the term "sexually faithful church" and many helpful insights and practical recommendations from this booklet. I recommend it strongly to every church serious about doing a better job dealing with sexual sin of all kinds.

3. Jim Weidenaar, "Characteristics of a Sexually Faithful Church," in *Becoming a Sexually Faithful Church,* 7.

4. Black, ed., *Becoming a Sexually Faithful Church,* 5.

5. Summit Ministries puts out some great material as well as hosting worldview seminars. For example, Jeffrey Myers and David O. Noebel,

Understanding the Times: A Survey of Competing Worldviews, vol. 2 (Colorado Springs: David C. Cook, 2015); David O. Noebel and Chuck Edwards, *Thinking Like a Christian* (Nashville: B&H Publishing, 2016); and the Lightbearers Christian Worldview Curriculum package complete with DVDs, online links, books and manuals (Manitou Springs, CO: Summit Ministries, 2016). Another great source for curriculum is Focus on the Family's Truth Project, which includes *The Truth Project Study Guide* published in 2012, and *The Truth Project Small Group Curriculum* DVD set issued in 2014 (Colorado Springs, CO). Bob Jones University Press offers the excellent *Biblical Worldview: Creation, Fall, Redemption* (Greensville, SC: Bob Jones University Press, 2017), including separate editions for instructors and students, tests and answer keys, and an activities manual. One curriculum package that tackles philosophy, literature, and film very directly, and is designed explicitly for high school students, is Kevin Swanson's *Worldviews in Conflict,* 2 vols. (Green Forest, AR: Master Books, 2015). A teacher's guide is also available for the Swanson set.

6. David S. Dockery and Trevin K. Wax, *Christian Worldview Handbook* (Nashville: B&H Publishing, 2019).

7. Herman Bavinck, *Christian Worldview,* trans. Nathaniel Gray Sutanto, James Eglinton, and Cory C. Brock (1904; repr., Wheaton, IL: Crossway Books, 2019).

8. Geiger, "Why a Sexually Faithful Church?," in *Becoming a Sexually Faithful Church,* 4.

9. Geiger, "Why a Sexually Faithful Church?," in *Becoming a Sexually Faithful Church,* 4.

10. O. Palmer Robertson, *The Genesis of Sex: Sexual Relationships in the First Book of the Bible* (Phillipsburg, NJ: P&R Publishing, 2002).

11. John Piper and Justin Taylor, eds., *Sex and the Supremacy of Christ* (Wheaton, IL: Crossway, 2005).

12. Beth Felker Jones, *Faithful: A Theology of Sex* (Grand Rapids: Zondervan, 2015).

13. Lewis B. Smedes, *Sex for Christians: The Limits and Liabilities of Sexual Living,* rev. ed. (Grand Rapids: Eerdmans, 1994).

14. Luke Gilkerson, *The Talk: 7 Lessons to Introduce Your Children to Biblical Sexuality* (CreateSpace Independent Publishing Platform, 2014). This is quite short and is for parents to use with children about ages six to ten.

15. Luke Gilkerson, *Relationships: 11 Lessons to Give Kids a Better Understanding of Biblical Sexuality* (CreateSpace Independent Publishing Platform, 2016). This is also short and is for parents to use with children about ages eleven to fourteen.

16. Dennis Rainey and Barbara Rainey, *Passport2Purity,* 4th ed. (Little Rock, AR: Family Life, 2019). These include journals, workbooks, and CDs. The latter are designed for parents to listen to and then discuss with their children to prepare them for adolescence and the sexual struggles and challenges of it. I did these with my sons while my wife did them with our daughters, which is what Family Life suggests. We found that our children were ready at different ages, so we started when we thought best.

17. The *Sexual Integrity Initiative* home page is https://sexualintegrityini-tiative.com. The *Digital Kids Initiative* home page is https://digitalkidsinitiative.com.

18. Barna Group, *Faith Leadership in a Divided Culture* (Plano, TX: Barna Group, 2018), 78–83.

19. Daniel Hyde, "Marks of a True Church: Exercise of Church Discipline," *Ligonier Ministries*, February 6, 2013, https://www.ligonier.org/blog/marks-true-church-exercise-church-discipline/.

20. The lack of church discipline or its inept or harsh implementation is a major problem in the church's response to sexual sin. I cannot go into detail on it here, though it should be a key element in the training of all ordained leaders in evangelical churches. Here are a few helpful resources: Jay Adams, *Handbook of Church Discipline: A Right and Privilege of Every Church Member* (Grand Rapids: Zondervan, 1986); Jonathan Leeman, *Church Discipline: How the Church Protects the Name of Jesus* (Wheaton, IL: Crossway, 2012); J. Carl Laney, *A Guide to Church Discipline: God's Loving Plan for Restoring Believers to Fellowship with Himself and with the Body of Christ* (Bethany House, 1985; repr., Eugene, OR: Wipf and Stock, 2010).

21. Weidenaar, "Characteristics of a Sexually Faithful Church," 8–9.

22. Ruth Graham, "The Rise and Fall of Carl Lentz, the Celebrity Pastor of Hillsong Church," *New York Times*, December 5, 2020, https://www.nytimes.com/2020/12/05/us/carl-lentz-hillsong-pastor.html.

23. Daniel Silliman, "RZIM Confirms Ravi Zacharias's Sexual Misconduct," *Christianity Today*, December 23, 2020, https://www.christianitytoday.com/news/2020/december/rzim-evidence-confirms-ravi-zacharias-sexual-mis-conduct.html.

24. Kirk Johnson, "Haggard's Church Discloses More on Sex Scandal," *New York Times*, January 26, 2009, https://www.nytimes.com/2009/01/27/us/27haggard.html; Wayne King, "Swaggart Says He Has Sinned, Will Step Down," *New York Times*, February 22, 1988, https://www.nytimes.com/1988/02/22/us/swaggart-says-he-has-sinned-will-step-down.html; Wayne King, "Bakker, Evangelist, Resigns His Ministry Over Sexual Incident," *New York Times*, March 21, 1987, https://www.nytimes.com/1987/03/21/us/bakker-evangelist-resigns-his-minstry-over-sexual-incident.html; Morgan Lee, "Tullian Tchividjian Confesses Second Affair Concealed by Two Coral Ridge Elders," *Christianity Today*, March 21, 2016, https://www.christianityto-day.com/news/2016/march/tullian-tchividjian-confesses-second-affair-cor-al-ridge.html.

25. Barna Group, *The Porn Phenomenon*, 80–81.

26. Barna Group, *The Porn Phenomenon*, 82–83.

27. The Editors, "How Common Is Pastoral Indiscretion?," *Leadership: A Practical Journal for Church Leaders* 9, no. 1 (Winter 1988): 12–13.

28. John W. Thoburn and Jack O. Balswick, "Demographic Data on Extra-Marital Sexual Behavior in the Ministry," *Pastoral Psychology* 46, no. 6 (July 1998): 451–52.

29. For example, the percentages of ever-married males and females who admit to having committed adultery in the GSS have remained fairly constant since that time period—some limited rising and falling but no obvious trends

up or down. Between 1991 and 2018: a low of 20 percent and high of 25 percent for men, and a low of 11 percent and a high of 18 percent for women. 1991 and 2018 numbers are very close: 21 percent versus 23 percent for men, and 11 percent versus 12 percent for women.

30. Here are some excellent resources addressing pastoral accountability: Mark Denison, "Pastors and Porn: Why We Struggle and the Help We Need," *Covenant Eyes*, November 25, 2019, https://www.covenanteyes.com/2019/11/25/pastors-struggle-porn/; Philip R. Gons, Matthew C. Hoskinson, and Andrew David Naselli, "Accountability," *Andy Naselli*, February 12, 2008, https://andynaselli.com/accountability; Joe Tyrpak, "Fighting Lust, Inviting Accountability, Using Covenant Eyes," *Andy Naselli*, June 18, 2012, https://andynaselli.com/covenant-eyes; Randy Alcorn, "Regular Accountability in the Battle for Purity," *Eternal Perspective Ministries*, January 23, 2014, https://www.epm.org/blog/2014/Jan/23/accountability-purity.

31. For example, the classic article by R. Kent Hughes and John H. Armstrong, "Why Adulterous Pastors Should Not Be Restored," *Christianity Today* 39, no. 4 (April 1995): 33–36.

32. Denison, "Pastors and Porn."

33. Once again, a comprehensive list of resources would be extensive. Here are some suggestions: Marshall Segal, *Not Yet Married: The Pursuit of Joy in Singleness & Dating* (Wheaton, IL: Crossway, 2017); Ben Stuart, *Single, Dating, Engaged, Married: Navigating Life and Love in the Modern Age* (Nashville: Thomas Nelson, 2017); Myles Munroe, *Waiting and Dating: A Sensible Guide to a Fulfilling Love Relationship* (Shippensburg, PA: Destiny Image, 2005); Henry Cloud and John Townsend, *Boundaries in Dating: Making Dating Work* (Grand Rapids: Zondervan, 2001) (this book has accompanying resources for separate purchase, including a leader's guide, participant guide, and workbook). I would be remiss if I failed to mention the classic book by Elisabeth Elliot, *Passion and Purity: How to Bring Your Love Life Under Christ's Control* (1984; repr., Grand Rapids: Revell, 2013). Finally, a promising book was released as I was completing this chapter: Sean McDowell, *Chasing Love: Sex, Love, and Relationships in a Confused Culture* (Nashville: B&H Books, 2020). This book is comprehensive, dealing with a broad range of issues related to sex, relationships, and marriage. However, it has four chapters on singleness and is a great resource.

34. "The Covenant Card," *Barbara Kohl Ministries*, 2018, http://barbarakohl.com/wp-content/uploads/2018/01/HO-TLW-COVENANT-CARD-Word.pdf.

35. Factors include family and parental commitment; personality differences between pledgers and non-pledgers, such as propensity to take risks; their levels of self-control; church attendance and other religious commitments; beliefs about the Bible; race; family structure; exposure to opportunities for sex through dating; drinking behavior; earlier marriage; living within more generally religious communities; fear of pregnancy and STIs; exposure to guilt, shame, and loss of status within tight-knit religious families and churches; and many more. See Jeremy E. Uecker, "Religion, Pledging and the Premarital Sexual Behavior of Married Young Adults," *Journal of Marriage and Family*, 70, no. 3 (July 2008): 731–32.

36. Uecker, "Religion, Pledging and the Premarital Sexual Behavior," 739, 741.

37. Anthony Paik, Kenneth J. Sanchagrin, and Karen Heimer, "Broken Promises: Abstinence Pledging and Sexual and Reproductive Health," *Journal of Marriage and Family* 78, no. 2 (April 2016): 554–59. The higher rates of pregnancy were probably because they used contraception less. The authors also found HPV infections were higher for pledgers but *only* if they also had high numbers of sex partners, which does not characterize most pledgers.

38. Nicole J. Murphy, *Virginity Pledges as a Preventative Measure for Preventing Unwanted Sexual, Behavioral, and Biological Outcomes: A Systematic Review of Adolescents and Young Adults in the U.S.* (master of science thesis, College of Public Health, Ohio State University, 2018), 41.

39. Murphy, *Virginity Pledges*, 40.

40. Paik et al., "Broken Promises," 557–58.

41. See Ecclesiastes 5:4–6 for the context of this passage, which is sobering.

42. See Ayers, *Christian Marriage*, chapter 9 for a thorough discussion of this critical subject.

43. That book was Tim and Beverly LaHaye, *The Act of Marriage: The Beauty of Sexual Love* (Grand Rapids: Zondervan, 1998). This book has sold about two and a half million copies. For older couples, there is now Tim and Beverly LaHaye, *The Act of Marriage After 40* (Grand Rapids: Zondervan, 2000). Another practical, solid resource is Ed and Gaye Wheat, *Intended for Pleasure: Sex Technique and Sexual Fulfillment in Christian Marriage*, 4th ed. (1977; repr., Grand Rapids: Zondervan, 2010).

44. As quoted in John L. Thompson, ed., *Genesis 1–11: The Reformation Commentary on Scripture* (Downers Grove, IL: IVP Academic, 2012), 13.

45. Pew Research Center, *Marriage and Cohabitation in the U.S.*, 10.

46. Here are some resources of many fine books and articles: Barry Danylak, *Redeeming Singleness: How the Storyline of Scripture Affirms the Single Life* (Wheaton, IL: Crossway, 2010); Owen Strachan, ed., *Whole in Christ: A Biblical Approach to Singleness* (Lancaster, PA: Veritas Press, 2016); Sam Allberry, *7 Myths About Singleness* (Wheaton, IL: Crossway, 2019); Mark Ballenger, *The Ultimate Guide to Christian Singleness: Loved, Secured, Guided* (Phoenix: CreateSpace, 2017, this resource includes study questions and is amenable to group study).

METHODOLOGY APPENDIX

1. See GSS FAQs at http://gss.norc.org/lists/gssfaqs/allitems.aspx.

2. See "About the National Survey of Family Growth," https://www.cdc.gov/nchs/nsfg/about_nsfg.htm.

3. In this combined file, there are 3,799 evangelicals, 1,702 of whom have never married. That provides a large sample to work with in comparing subgroups.

4. For more detail, see Michael J. Underwood et al., "Overview and Methods for the Youth Risk Behavior Surveillance System—United States, 2019," *Morbidity and Mortality Weekly Report* 69, no. 1, August 21, 2020, https://www.cdc.gov/mmwr/volumes/69/su/pdfs/su6901a1-H.pdf.

5. Just because a disparity is statistically "significant" does not mean it is objectively large, or that it shows that one group is doing a lot better or worse than another. We have to judge that separately, using practical discretion and judgment. This is because when you have very large samples, even tiny differences can be statistically significant because of how statistical significance is calculated, which puts a lot of weight on the number of cases that are included. This is not usually an issue, but when it is, I point that out.

SUBJECT AND MAJOR
NAMES INDEX

A

abortion, 1, 5, 55, 140, 205, 217, 220–23, 231, 275, 311, 312
  beliefs about, 161, 167
abstinence, 24, 27, 28, 32, 73, 107, 130, 149, 179, 197, 227
  and mental health, 233
  pledges, (see virginity, pledges)
abuse
  sexual, 2
  substance (drug and alcohol), 187, 188, 211, 232–35
accountability, spiritual, 142, 251, 254, 266, 275, 276
  groups, 263, 268, 272
  pornography and, 123
  software, 268
addiction
  porn, 123
  sexual, 263
adolescence, 186

adolescent(s) (see also teens, teenagers)
  abortion and, 220
  consequences of sexual activity for, 233–36
  influences upon sexual behavior and attitudes, 184–85, 188, 196, 198–200
  sexual attitudes, 200
  spirituality, 150, 185
adoption, 220, 275
adoptive parents, 187, 190, 192
adultery, 2, 18, 19, 21–23, 28, 30, 55, 58, 62, 72, 155, 181, 265, 269, 277, 295, 319
  spiritual unfaithfulness and disobedience as, 18, 31, 290
affiliation, religious (or, denominational) (see also Evangelical Protestant, Black Protestant, Mainline Protestant, Catholic, No

Religious Affiliation [None], Practicing Christian, Charismatic, Pentecostal, Fundamentalist, African Methodist Episcopal, National Baptist Conference), 75–76, 103, 112, 284, 285, 286, 299, 300

differences between in cohabitation beliefs, 88–91

differences between in cohabitation practices, 116–20

differences between in sexual beliefs, 78, 89–92

differences between in sexual practices, 108–11, 113–18, 300

African American (see also *Black*, and *Black Protestant*), 217, 221

African Methodist Episcopal Church, 75

age
  abortion by, 220–21
  at first marriage, 58–59, 200–208, 215, 272–73, 295
  at first marriage, and divorce risk, 207
  at first marriage, and sexual activity before marriage, 203–4, 272, 299, 300
  differences between in sexual beliefs, 63, 79–81, 92–94, 99
  differences between in sexual practices, 65–66, 108–09, 113–18, 121, 128, 130–32, 189–90, 231

of first sexual experience (or, "sexual onset"), 59, 106–10, 112, 131–32, 189–90, 194–95, 233–36

pregnancy by, 217–19

rates, 66

sexually transmitted infections (STI's) by, 229

alcohol (see *abuse, substance*)

American Psychiatric Association (APA), 50

American Worldview Inventory (AWVI), 140, 145, 159–69, 170, 173

anal sex (see *sex, anal*)

Anglican *Book of Common Prayer*, 15, 17, 290

anti-culture (see *worldviews, anti-culture*)

antinomianism, 145–47

Apostles' Creed, 19

Asian-Americans, 216, 217, 311

assault, sexual, 235

association, significant, definition of, 287, 306

assumptions, worldview (see *worldview, assumptions*)

attendance, church, 76–77, 81–82, 85, 98, 125, 243, 253, 264–65, 284, 286–87, 300, 303
  degree of, 82, 94, 298
    cohabitation beliefs, association with (see *evangelicals, cohabitation beliefs and, by church attendance*)
    cohabitation marital plans, association with (see

evangelicals, marital plans
and, by church attendance)
cohabitation practices,
association with (see
*evangelicals, cohabitation
practices and, by church
attendance*)
family structure, association with,
190
pornography usage,
association with (see
*evangelicals, pornography
usage of, by church
attendance*)
sexual activity, association
with (see *evangelicals,
sexual activity of, by church
attendance*)
sexual beliefs, association
with (see *evangelicals,
sexual beliefs of, by church
attendance*)
views on Bible, association with,
85
views on importance of faith to
daily life, association with,
95
attitudes, sexual (see *sex, beliefs*)
authenticity (or, "authentic self"),
33, 40–41, 155, 180
authority
biblical, 24, 75, 83, 125, 127,
144–45, 172, 185
of Christ, 85
moral, 35–37, 40–41, 45, 47,
49–53, 68, 159, 260
parental, 45, 206
auto-eroticism (see *masturbation*)
autonomy, 44, 46, 52, 55, 69, 143,
167, 206, 260

B

Baby Boom (including Boomers),
58, 68, 169, 304
Balswick, Judith and Jack, 154–57,
303, 319
Baptist, 75, 273, 302
Barbara Kohl Ministries, 320
Barna, George, 140, 144–45,
157–63, 170, 176, 303–04
Barna Research Group, 98–100,
103, 120–22, 261, 267,
299–300, 303, 318–19
Baxter, Richard, 23, 71, 290
Beggar's Daughter, 263
Bellah, Robert, 38, 40, 46, 49, 51,
68, 144, 150, 292
bestiality, 21
Bible
authority of (see *authority,
biblical*)
beliefs about, 4, 75–76, 83–84,
127, 160–61, 167, 172–73,
254, 284
association with being "born
again", 84–85
association with sexual beliefs,
82, 84–86, 298
association with sexual
activity, 174, 184–85, 301,
306, 320
modern rejection of biblical
sexual teaching, 34–35,
52–53, 62–63, 69–70,
73–74, 88, 102, 116, 138,
140–73, 178, 180, 197, 207
sexual teachings, biblical, 4–5,
7–33, 52, 57, 69, 73–74,
77–78, 83, 86, 100, 125, 167,

177, 180–82, 193, 201, 244,
246–47, 250, 252
teaching a biblical sexual ethic,
258–62, 270, 280, 291
biblical anthropology, 256
biblical worldview (see *worldview,
biblical*)
Bieber, Irving, 50–51
births
out-of-wedlock, 55, 205, 213–19,
226, 239
rates, 216
birth-control (see *contraception*)
black (not covered under Black
Protestant, below), 79, 81,
134, 137, 216, 221, 301
Black Protestant, 75–76, 284, 286,
297, 30
anal sex and, 113–15
cohabitation beliefs and, 88–91
cohabitation practices and, 117–18
cohabiter marital plans and, 118
cohabitation outcomes and, 120
early age at first sex and, 110
oral sex and, 113–15
pornography usage and, 123–24
sexual beliefs of, 78, 83, 87
sexual activity of, 108–15, 123
body
husband and wife as one, 15–17
of Christ, 15, 17, 138
theology of the, 11, 15, 19–21, 149,
164, 167–68, 177, 213, 244,
256, 259–60, 303
Bonhoeffer, Dietrich, 144, 146–47,
154, 176, 302
born-again, 87, 140, 145, 153, 160
sexual activity and, 184, 299, 301,
306
sexual beliefs and, 77, 84–86

bride, of Christ, church as, 12, 18,
31, 281–82
Bridges, Jerry, 148, 154, 302
Brooks, David, 179, 208, 310

C

Calvin, John, 15, 126, 278, 290
capstone, marriage as a, 207–08
Catechism of the Catholic Church,
291
Catechism, Westminster, 7
Catholics, Roman, 75, 152, 154, 273,
284, 286, 290
abortion and, 221, 312
anal sex and, 113–15
cohabitation beliefs and, 89, 91
cohabitation practices and, 117–18
cohabiter marital plans and, 118
cohabitation outcomes and, 120
early age at first sex and, 110
oral sex and, 113–15
pornography usage and, 123–24
sexual activity of, 104, 108–115
sexual beliefs of, 14, 24–26, 78, 83,
87, 291, 300
celibacy, 11, 24–26
Center for Parent/Youth
Understanding (CPYU),
261
charismatic, 153, 160, 211
chastity, 6–8, 11, 20, 24–28, 32,
72–73, 76, 116, 125, 127, 138,
150, 179, 193, 197, 202, 216,
227, 250–51, 253–55, 260,
268, 270, 276, 281, 291
cheap grace, 145–50, 156, 165, 249
Cherlin, Andrew, 40, 44, 207, 215,
292, 293, 295, 306, 307, 310,
311, 313

church attendance (see *attendance, church*)

churches, characteristics of sexual faithful congregations,
    biblical teaching on sex (see *Bible, sexual teachings, biblical*)
    commitment, encouraging, 264–65
    facts, handling honestly, 278–80
    ministry for sexual strugglers, 263–64
    pastoral support, 261–62
    overall, 250–55
    parents, supporting and equipping, 272
    prayer, 281
    premarital education and counseling, 275–78
    sound leadership, cultivating, 265–70
    vision, positive, 280–81
    worldview education (see *worldview, education*)

cohabitation, 3, 4, 10, 36, 87, 100, 103–04, 124, 128, 133, 189–90, 203–08, 211–12, 230–31, 262, 265, 276, 278, 300, 301, 315
    beliefs about, by age, 90, 92–93
    beliefs about, by religious affiliation, 77, 87–91
    beliefs about, differences among subgroups of evangelicals, 91–97, 156–57, 298
    children raised within cohabiting households, 223–26, 313
    divorce risk and, 119–20, 187–90, 240–44, 279, 317
    households, compared to married, 187–88, 223–26, 306
    practice of, differences among subgroups of evangelicals, 134–36, 203, 303
    increases in, 10, 55, 57, 63–65, 66–67, 205, 226
    marital intentions of cohabiters, 118–19
    outcomes of, 119–20, 300
    overall acceptance of, 66–67, 149, 208
    overall extent of, 65–66, 68
    practice of, by religious affiliation, 116–20
    practice of, differences among subgroups of evangelicals, 134–36, 138

concubines, 22

condoms, 319, 212
    anal sex and, 228–29
    effectiveness, pregnancy prevention, 228
    effectiveness, preventing sexually transmitted infections, 227–31, 279
    oral sex and, 228
    usage, degree of, 230–31, 315

confession, 123, 146, 251, 264, 266
    Westminster, 289

consent, ethic of, 36, 53–56, 103, 140, 176–77

consummation, marital, 14, 289

contraception, 49, 55, 72, 217, 227, 252, 277, 314, 320
    condoms (see *condoms*)

created (see *created order*)

created order, 10–12, 16–17, 19–21, 26, 28, 32, 35, 53, 150, 151, 157–58, 165, 168–69, 177, 209, 212–13, 255–56, 258, 279 creation (see *created order*)

Creator, God as (see *created order*)

creedal, 47

Cultural Research Institute (CRI),
159–60

cunnilingus (see *sex, oral*)

D

dating
anti-dating, 27, 291
dating and sexual activity, general,
308, 320
early dating and sexual activity,
193–95
intense dating and sexual activity,
193–95
limits, setting, 252, 272, 320
recreational, 28
serial dating and sexual activity,
193–95
sex in, divorce risk, 237
violence in, 235–36

Deism, Moralistic Therapeutic
(see *Moralistic Therapeutic
Deism*)

denomination (see *affiliation,
religious*)

dental dam, 228

Denton, Melinda Lundquist, 150,
302

designed, by God, sex as, 4, 6,
11–12, 15, 48, 246, 254,
258–59

diaphragm, 227

differential association, 183, 305

discipline, church, 146, 262, 266,
319

disease, sexually transmitted
(see *infection, sexually
transmitted*)

divorce, 297
children, association with sexual
activity of, 186–90
cohabitation and risk of (see
*cohabitation, divorce risk
and*)
early marriage and risks of, 207
ethic of consent and, 55–56, 294
expressive, 39–40
sexual permissiveness and, 80,
100
sexual promiscuity increases risk
of, 214–15, 218, 236–39,
275, 316

drug abuse (see *abuse, substance*)

E

education
cohabitation beliefs, association
with level of (see
*evangelicals, cohabitation
beliefs and, by level of
education*)
cohabitation marital plans,
association with level of
(see *evangelicals, cohabitor
marital plans and, by level of
education*)
cohabitation practices,
association with level
of (see *evangelicals,
cohabitation practices and,
by level of education*)
moral, 182
parental, 225, 272
sex, 250, 255, 263

sexual activity, association with
  level of (see *evangelicals,
  sexual activity of, by level of
  education*)
sexual beliefs, association with
  level of (see *evangelicals,
  sexual beliefs of, by level of
  education*)
worldview (see *worldview,
  education*)
ethic, biblical sexual (see *Bible,
  sexual teachings, biblical*)
ethnicity, race and (see *race and
  ethnicity*)
evangelicals, 284–86
  abortion and, 161, 167–69, 171,
    220–23, 312
  alternative worldviews and (see
    worldviews, alternative)
  anal sex and, 113–16, 129, 131–32,
    189, 231
    means to maintain "technical
      virginity" among, 114
  Bible, beliefs about (see *Bible,
    beliefs about*)
  biblical worldview and (see
    worldview, biblical)
  cheap grace and (see *cheap grace*)
  children, having them within
    cohabiting unions and, 226
  character, national, analyses of,
    44–47
  church attendance levels and (see
    attendance, church)
  cohabitation beliefs and, 100, 103
    by age, 92–93
    by church attendance, 94–96
    by family structure, 189–90
    by gender, 91, 92, 94–96
    by income, 93–94

  by level of education, 93
  by race and ethnicity, 93
  by self-identified importance
    of religion, 94–96
  compared to other religious
    affiliations, 88–91
cohabiter marital plans and,
  by church attendance, 135
  by gender, 118–19
  by income, 134
  by level of education, 134
  by race and ethnicity, 134
  by self-identified importance
    of religion, 136
  compared to other religious
    affiliations, 118–19
cohabitation outcomes and,
  by gender, 119–20
  compared to other religious
    affiliations, 119–20
cohabitation practices and, 103,
  242–43, 300
  by age, 92–93, 116–17
  by church attendance, 94–96,
    134–37
  by gender, 92, 94–96, 116–18
  by income, 93–94, 134
  by level of education, 93, 134
  by race and ethnicity, 93, 134
  by self-identified importance
    of religion, 94–96, 135–37
  compared to other religious
    affiliations, 116–18, 120
  delaying marriage
    unnecessarily and, 203–04
  undermining marital stability
    among, 243
condom usage and, 230–31
definition of, 74–77, 303
early age at first sex, 109–10

ethic of consent and, 56

family beliefs and, 171

God, beliefs about and, 162–63, 169, 171–72

human nature, beliefs about and, 165–66, 171

importance of faith to, level of, 169, 300, 94–95

moral decision making, beliefs about and, 167

Moralistic Therapeutic Deism and (see *worldview, Moralistic Therapeutic Deism*)

purpose in life, beliefs about and, 163–64, 169

out-of-wedlock pregnancy and, 218–19

oral sex and, 113–16, 129, 131–32, 189, 231

 means to maintain "technical virginity" among, 114

pornography usage of,

 by church attendance, 137

 by gender, 123, 137

 by pastors, 267–68

 by race and ethnicity, 137

 compared to other religious affiliations, 123

prayer, proportion practicing regularly, 297

salvation, beliefs about and, 164–65, 304

 cohabitation beliefs and, 88–91

 cohabitation practices and, 117–18

 cohabiter marital plans and, 118

cohabitation outcomes and, 120

early age at first sex and, 110

oral sex and, 113–16

pornography usage and, 123–24

sexual activity of, 108–15, 123, 209, 212, 300

 balancing truth and grace in addressing, 247–50

 by acceptance of biblical beliefs about sex outside of marriage, 174–76

 by age, 108–10, 113–16,

 by Bible views, 306

 by born again status, 184, 306

 by church attendance, 130–33, 137–38, 184, 306

 by gender, 108–11, 113–15, 129–30

 by level of education, 129

 by income, 129

 by family structure, 189–91

 by race and ethnicity, 129

 by self-identified importance of religion, 130–33, 137–38, 184

 conversion, sexually active before or after, 111–13

 compared to other religious affiliations, 108–11, 113–16, 194, 301

 dating behavior and, 194

 delaying marriage unnecessarily and, 200–08, 272–73, 299

 media influence and, 200

 peer influence and, 271

premarital, undermining marital stability among, 237–39

sexual beliefs of, 8, 70–73, 78, 83, 87, 160, 172, 298, 301

by age, 79–80

by born-again status, 84–86

by church attendance, 82–83, 86

by gender, 78–79, 81

by income, 81

by level of education, 81

by marital status, 79–81

by race and ethnicity, 81

by views on the Bible, 83–84, 86

compared to other religious affiliations, 78, 87

sexual activity, associations with, 173–76

sin, beliefs about and, 164–65, 169, 304

truth, beliefs about and, 167, 169, 171

expressive individualism, 40, 143, 176, 292

extramarital (see *adultery*)

F

faith, importance of (see *importance of faith to daily life, views on*)

family, 172, 212, 256, 273

life, 26, 251–53, 185, 266

instability, 224–25

structure, relationship to sexual activity and beliefs, 186–91, 197, 306, 308

ties, 186, 197, 216, 271, 320

fellatio (see *sex, oral*)

fertility rates (see *births, rates*)

fondling (see *sex, manual stimulation*)

forgiveness, 30, 32, 71, 75, 102, 145–48, 165, 250–51, 258, 276

fornication, 15, 21–24, 28, 31, 36, 56, 68, 72–74, 76, 77, 80–87, 97, 100, 104, 124, 128, 142, 152, 157, 159, 162, 164, 167, 173, 174, 176, 180, 193, 201, 202, 204–6, 208, 212, 248–51, 255, 259, 272, 278, 279, 290, 301, 303

fundamentalist, 1, 2, 10, 112, 153, 300

G

Gallup Poll, 66–67, 97–98

gay (see also *homosexuality*), 156–57

Geiger, Tim, 255–58, 317

gender

church attendance, association with, 94–95

cohabitation beliefs, association with, 91, 92, 94–96

cohabitation marital plans, association with, 118–19

cohabitation outcomes, association with, 119–20

cohabitation practices, association with, 92, 94–96, 116–18

identity, 50, 56 (see also *transgender*)

inequality, 44, 293

pornography beliefs, association with, 99

pornography usage, association with, 123, 137

sexual activity, association with, 108–11, 113–15, 129–30

sexual beliefs, association with, 78–79, 81

views on importance of faith to daily life, association with, 95–96

weighting by, 284, 286

gnostic, 154, 302–03

grace, 28, 30–32, 42, 73, 75, 125–27, 145–48, 151, 156–57, 164–65, 202, 209, 216, 244, 248–49, 275–76

cheap (see *cheap grace*)

Grenz, Stanley, 54–55, 290, 294

General Social Survey (GSS), overview of, 283–84

H

Harris, Joshua, 3, 27–29, 291

health, impact of sexual activity upon

mental, 223, 232–33

physical, 227–31, 233–34

sexual, 188–89

sexually transmitted disease (see *infection, sexually transmitted*)

sexually transmitted infection (see *infection, sexually transmitted*)

heart, 7, 13, 22, 69–70, 139, 165, 166, 181, 210

Henry, Matthew, 139

Hispanic, 79, 81, 93, 129, 134, 137, 190, 216, 217, 221, 238, 243, 306, 311, 312

Hodge, A.A., 26, 291

holiness, 3, 4, 6, 21, 30, 33, 74, 75, 124, 125, 142, 146–48, 150, 249, 251, 255, 256, 262, 277, 282

Hollinger, Dennis, 34–35, 43, 103, 105, 180, 260, 292

holy, 17, 19, 26, 48, 146, 153, 154, 156, 209, 251, 254, 256

Holy Spirit, 16, 20–21, 30–31, 148, 161–63, 183, 251, 257–58

homosexuality (homosexuals) (see also *gay, lesbian*), 3, 22, 44, 50–51, 77, 124, 149, 157, 213, 263

hookup (hooking up), 43–44, 129, 179, 232, 293

humanism (humanist, humanistic), 47, 170, 256

Hunter, James Davison, 47, 144, 29

I

identity, gender (see *gender, identity* and *transgender*)

illegitimacy (see *births, out-of-wedlock*)

immorality, sexual, 11, 15, 17–23, 69–70, 72–74, 76, 91, 101, 102, 137, 155, 164, 178, 181, 182, 184, 201, 213, 246, 247, 259, 263, 268, 271, 282, 306

importance of faith to daily life, views on

degree of, 94–95

church attendance, association with, 95

cohabitation beliefs, association with (see *evangelicals, cohabitation beliefs and, by self-identified importance of religion*)

cohabitation marital plans, association with (see *evangelicals, marital plans and, by self-identified importance of religion*)

cohabitation practices, association with (see *evangelicals, cohabitation practices and, by self-identified importance of religion*)

sexual activity, association with (see *evangelicals, sexual activity of, by self-identified importance of religion*)

impregnate, 198, 218, 219

incest, 56, 200

income

cohabitation beliefs, association with level of (see *evangelicals, cohabitation beliefs and, by income*)

cohabitation marital plans, association with level of (see *evangelicals, marital plans and, by income*)

cohabitation practices, association with level of (see *evangelicals, cohabitation practices and, by income*)

sexual activity, association with level of (see *evangelicals, sexual activity of, by income*)

sexual beliefs, association with level of (see *evangelicals, sexual beliefs of, by income*)

individualism, 37

expressive (see *expressive individualism*)

radical, 240

inerrant Bible, 1, 4, 160, 172

infection, sexually-transmitted, 191, 198, 227–31, 314, 320

intercourse, sexual (see sex, intercourse)

infidelity, 56, 269

Inglehart, Ronald, 46, 144, 293

inner-directed (see worldviews, inner-directed)

intergenerational, 214, 215, 236

J

Jews, 152, 257

Jones, Beth Felker, 261, 318

Jones, Peter, 19–20, 290

Josh McDowell Ministry, 98, 120, 267, 299

K

know, referring to sex, 13–14, 258

Kuehne, Dale, 54–55, 294

L

Lasch, Christopher, 46, 49, 68, 293

Laumann, Edward, 58, 59, 64, 65, 295

law

moral, 5, 9, 31, 167, 177, 184, 248

Mosaic, 13–14, 22

lawlessness, 74

lesbian, 156

Lewis, C. S., 20, 29, 122, 179, 255, 290, 292, 300, 317

Lewis, Michael, 38, 292

liberalism
  sexual, 143, 145, 154, 159, 173, 198, 305
  theological, 9, 261

licentiousness, 124, 177, 212, 305

Luther, Martin, 7, 14

Luker, Kristin, 35, 47–49, 56, 68, 293

M

Mainline (sometimes "Non-Evangelical") Protestants, 75, 76, 284, 286
  abortions and, 221, 312
  anal sex and, 113–15
  cohabitation beliefs and, 89–91
  cohabitation practices and, 117–18
  cohabiter marital plans and, 118
  cohabitation outcomes and, 120
  early age at first sex and, 110
  oral sex and, 113–15
  pornography usage and, 123–24
  sexual beliefs of, 78, 83, 87
  sexual activity of, 108–15, 123

marital status, 109
  sexual beliefs, association with (see *evangelicals, sexual beliefs of, by marital status*)

Markman, Howard, 241, 300, 317

marriage
  age at first (see *age, at first marriage*)
  as one-flesh, 9, 11–17, 32
  Christ and the Church, of, 17–19
  covenantal understanding of, 54–55, 69
  delaying (see *age, at first marriage*)
  goodness of sex within, 12, 15, 17, 25–27, 31, 202
  individualistic, 40
  "open," 56
  premarital counseling and, 275–78
  same-sex, 87, 124, 156–57
  sex tied and restricted to, by God, 4, 7, 9, 11–18, 21–24, 28, 32, 41, 48, 73, 105, 167, 177, 179, 201, 213–14
  therapeutic orientation to, 38–41, 54
  Trinitarian understanding of, 11, 16, 163

Marxism (see *worldviews, alternative, designated by Barna as not "Biblical," Marxism*)

masturbation, 54, 104

McCleneghan, Bromleigh, 56, 294

media influence, 26, 45, 52, 141, 183, 197–200, 271

mental health (see *health, impact of sexual activity upon, mental*)

Methodist, 152, 302

millennials, 66, 105, 168–69, 304

monogamous (monogamy), 32, 73, 237, 238, 290, 305, 315

Moralistic Therapeutic Deism (MTD) (see *worldviews, Moralistic Therapeutic Deism*)

Mormons, 152, 153

Mueller, Walt, 261

N

narcissism, culture of, 46, 69
National Academies of Science, Engineering, and Medicine, 312
National Baptist Conference, 75
National Longitudinal Survey of Adolescent Health, 233
National Study of Youth and Religion, 195
National Survey of Family Growth (NSFG), overview of, 284–86
natural order, 11, 17, 48
Nehemiah Institute, 145, 170
neutralization techniques, 141
New Spirituality (see *worldviews, alternative, designated by Barna as not "Biblical," New Spirituality*)
No Religious Affiliation (or "none," or "nones"), 103, 284, 286, 300
  abortions and, 312
  anal sex and, 113–15
  cohabitation beliefs and, 88–89, 91
  cohabitation practices and, 117
  cohabiter marital plans and, 300
  cohabitation outcomes and, 120
  early age at first sex and, 110
  oral sex and, 113–15
  pornography usage and, 123–24
  sexual beliefs of, 78
  sexual activity of, 108–15, 123

O

one-flesh (see *marriage, as one flesh*)

out-of-wedlock births (see *births, out of wedlock*)
oral sex (see sex, oral)
Orwell, George, 34
other-directed (see *worldviews, other-directed*)

P

parent (or "parental," "parenting") authority, 45
  cohabiting (see *cohabitation, children raised within cohabiting households,* and *cohabitation, households, compared to married*)
  influence, 8, 44–46, 52, 133, 154, 170, 182–83, 185–93, 197, 199, 202, 206, 223, 245, 251–53, 257, 259, 271–73, 305, 320
  single, 186–93, 214–16, 306, 307
pastors (or "pastoral," or "pastoring"), 2, 7, 8, 13, 29, 40, 41, 52, 56, 73, 76, 93, 97, 98, 115, 127, 138, 145, 202, 206, 212, 221, 251, 252, 254, 261, 262, 263, 265, 265–70, 272, 275, 276, 277, 289, 291, 292
peer influence, 195–97, 199–200, 202, 223, 271, 308
PEERS Worldview Inventory, 145, 170–73, 257, 304
Pentecostals, 160–65, 167, 303
philosophical, 5, 138, 143, 174
Platt, David, 246
polyamory, 56
polygamy, 22
porneia, 21

pornography, 4, 36, 43, 55, 57,
   68–69, 205, 273, 278
  beliefs about, 77, 97–100, 298
  Internet, 199–200
  overcoming addiction to, 263
  pastors using, 267
  premarital counseling, addressing
     in, 275–77
  usage of, 103, 120–24, 128, 137
postabortion, 222, 223, 312
Postmodernism (see *worldview,
     alternative, designated
     by George Barna as not
     "Biblical," Postmodernism*)
Practicing Christians (as defined by
     George Barna), 96, 98–100,
     121–23, 159, 300
prayer, 6, 26, 92, 125, 158, 168, 202,
     209, 251, 257, 264, 280, 281,
     290, 297, 298
pregnancy, 43, 48, 72, 149, 167, 188,
     198, 220–21, 231–32, 277,
     311, 315, 320,
  centers, pro-life, 5, 312
  out-of-wedlock (see also *births,
     out-of-wedlock*), 191, 211,
     213–19, 223, 227, 228, 231,
     232, 277
  preventing, 227–78
  teenage, 214–15
  rates, 216–20
premarital
  cohabitation (see *cohabitation*)
  counseling (see *churches,
     premarital education and
     counseling* and *pornography,
     premarital counseling,
     addressing in*)
  sex (see *sex, premarital*)
Presbyterian, 302

procreation, 9, 11, 12, 16, 25, 32, 38,
     48, 55, 213, 291
promiscuity (or, "promiscuous"), 18,
     28, 57–60, 72, 109, 116, 130,
     174, 175, 187, 188, 211, 232,
     234–39, 249
puberty, decreasing age at, 179, 203
purity culture, 3, 27–29, 245, 249,
     273–74, 291

R

race and ethnicity
  cohabitation beliefs, association
     with level of (see
     *evangelicals, cohabitation
     beliefs and, by race and
     ethnicity*)
  cohabitation marital plans,
     association with level of
     (see *evangelicals, marital
     plans and, by race and
     ethnicity*)
  cohabitation practices,
     association with level
     of (see *evangelicals,
     cohabitation practices and,
     by race and ethnicity*)
  pornography usage, association
     with level of (see
     *evangelicals, pornography
     usage, by race and ethnicity*)
  sexual activity, association with
     level of (see *evangelicals,
     sexual activity of, by race
     and ethnicity*)
  sexual beliefs, association with
     level of (see *evangelicals,
     sexual beliefs of, by race and
     ethnicity*)

Regnerus, Mark, 180, 184–86, 195, 202, 206, 297, 305, 309, 314

relativism, 37, 42, 52, 53, 69, 141, 143, 151, 152, 159, 176

repentance, 28, 29, 31, 32, 70, 73, 75, 82, 84, 125, 141, 145, 146, 149, 151, 153, 166, 174, 177, 184, 211, 212, 223, 227, 236, 240, 244, 248, 249, 250, 251, 256, 257, 264, 266, 270, 275, 276

Rhoades, Galena, 241, 296, 300, 316, 317

Rieff, Philip, 35, 37–39, 44, 49–51, 68, 144, 150, 151, 176, 292

Riesman, David, 35, 44–46, 49, 144, 176, 293

robots, sex, 56, 68, 260

S

sacred, 9, 41–42,
  human life as, 144, 161, 167–69, 304
  marriage as, 48, 167, 202
  sex as, 17, 31–32, 48, 167, 254, 256, 258, 277

salvation, 1, 17, 75, 77, 82, 113, 126, 144, 147, 157, 161, 164–66, 177, 178, 248, 257, 302, 304

same-sex attraction, 26, 294

sanctification, 21, 28, 29, 31, 73, 139, 144, 147, 153, 163, 264

Schaeffer, Francis, 18, 290

Secularism (see worldview, alternative, *designated by George Barna as not "Biblical," Secularism*)

self, modern views of, 33, 37–41, 44, 46, 48–52, 68–69, 143–44, 146, 148, 154–56, 176, 180, 206, 277, 280

self-control, 25, 46, 74, 153, 156, 183, 201, 270, 277, 281

sensate culture, 41–43, 44, 54, 143, 146, 148, 150, 176, 293

sex, as "knowing" (see *know, referring to sex*)

sex
  anal, 104–6, 113–15, 129, 131–32, 189–90, 198, 228–31, 299, 300, 307, 315
  attitudes (see *sexual attitudes*)
  intercourse, 2, 12–17, 21, 24, 25, 55, 60–61, 104–11, 114, 115, 128–33, 149, 189–90, 192, 194, 196–99, 213, 230–31, 233–36, 267–68, 300, 314, 315
  manual stimulation (or, "fondling"), 104, 105, 106, 114, 299, 300
  oral, 104–6, 113–15, 228, 131–32, 189–90, 192, 228, 230–31, 234, 279, 299, 300, 314, 315
  partners, 56, 57–62, 108–11, 129–32, 175–76, 190, 203–4, 223, 228, 229, 231, 233, 235–39, 274, 300, 301, 306, 307, 320
  premarital, 2, 29, 52, 55, 57, 59, 62, 81, 83, 84, 87, 104, 105, 107, 108–15, 123, 133, 149, 155, 172–76, 192, 209, 212, 231, 236, 237, 241–43, 249, 275–78, 305
  teenage, 106–7, 109, 184, 191–92, 204, 236, 315

sex, virgins' reasons for not having, 149–50

sexual attitudes (see *sexual beliefs*)

sexual beliefs, 8, 14, 24–26, 27, 32, 42, 55, 62, 70–73, 78–81, 83–87, 89–92, 120, 160, 172, 174, 176, 186, 192, 199, 200, 291, 298, 299, 301, 305, 306

   purity (see also *purity culture*), 21, 23, 24, 70, 74, 164, 200, 245, 248–50, 256–57, 266, 269, 273, 275, 281–82

sexually transmitted disease (see *infection, sexually transmitted*)

sexually transmitted infection (see *infection, sexually transmitted*)

Sexual Revolution, the, 43–44, 57–59, 292–93

significance, statistical, overview of, 286–87

Silver Ring Thing, 273

sliding or deciding, 119

Smalley, Greg, 13–14, 289

Smith, Christian, 144, 150–51, 153, 170, 176, 302

Sorokin, Pitirim, 35, 41–43, 68, 69, 144, 148, 150, 176, 292–93, 301

Spitzer, Robert, 50

Sproul, R. C., 24–25, 162, 291, 304

Stanley, Scott, 241, 296, 300, 316, 317

Summit Ministries, 157, 318

T

teenage pregnancy (see *pregnancy, teenage*)

teenage sex (see *sex, teenage*)

theological, 5, 9, 35, 138, 139, 141, 143, 145, 147, 149, 151, 153–55, 157, 159, 161, 163, 165, 167, 169, 171, 173–75, 177, 178, 259, 260

theology, 4, 19, 28, 33, 41, 56, 171, 172, 177, 209, 254, 259, 261, 276, 278, 279

therapeutic orientation, 37–41, 44, 50, 54, 143, 146, 151, 155, 176, 292

transgender (see also *gender, identity*), 3, 46, 50, 149, 293

True Love Waits, 273

Trueman, Carl, 51, 292, 294

U

Uecker, Jeremy, 202, 274, 309, 320

United States Conference of Catholic Bishops, 291

utilitarianism, 42, 143

V

virgins, 2, 18, 22, 31, 62, 114, 149, 236, 300, 302

virginity, 29, 71, 104, 291

   pledges, 273–74

   technical, 114

W

Wade, Lisa, 43–44, 293

Weaver, Richard, 57, 295

Weidenaar, Jim, 264, 317

Westminster Confession (see *confession, Westminster*)

White, David, 16, 102, 105, 260, 290

Whitehead, Barbara Dafoe, 40–41, 292, 312

Wolfinger, Nicholas, 236–38, 316

worldviews, 4, 35–36, 57, 138,
        143–44, 159, 176, 178, 180
    alternative, designated by George
        Barna as not "Biblical", 157,
        158–59
        Marxism, 159, 303
        New Spirituality, 158–59
        Postmodernism, 158–59
        Secularism, 158–59
    anti-culture, 36, 49–54, 68
    assumptions, 35, 37, 143, 177–78,
        260
    Biblical, nature of and adherence
        to, 140, 142, 157–74, 304
        generational differences
            in embracing Biblical
            worldview, 168–70

    contemporary, summarized, 53,
        69
    education, 255–59, 318
    inner-directed, 45
    Moralistic Therapeutic Deism
            (MTD), 150–57, 159, 160,
            302
    other-directed, 45–46
    pro-life versus pro-choice, 47–49
    transformations in, 6–37, 70, 205

Y

yada (see *know, referring to sex*)
Youth Risk Behavior Survey
        (YRBS), overview of,
        286–87

ALSO AVAILABLE
FROM DAVID J. AYERS

Christian Marriage: A Comprehensive Introduction

**To learn more and order,
visit lexhampress.com**